PLANTS THAT MERIT ATTENTION

PLANTS THAT MERIT ATTENTION

Volume I - TREES

The Garden Club of America

Janet Meakin Poor—Editor
Nancy P. Brewster—Photographic Editor
Jan Offutt Pratt
Ramsay L. Raymond—Editorial Assistance
Eleanor Muir Johnson
Sally J. MacBride
Louise G. Smith
and
The Horticulture Committee of The Garden Club of America

TIMBER PRESS
Portland, Oregon
1984

ISBN 0-917304-75-6

TIMBER PRESS
P.O. Box 1631
Beaverton, Oregon 97075

To each of you,
whose love for trees,
whose gift of time
and
generous sharing of expertise
has made this book possible.

CONTENTS

Eucommia ulmoides HARDY RUBBER TREE
Evodia danielii KOREAN EVODIA, BEBE TREE
Fagus sylvatica 'Asplenifolia' FERN-LEAVED BEECH
Firmiana simplex CHINESE PARASOL TREE
Franklinia alatamaha FRANKLIN TREE
Fraxinus oxycarpa 'Raywood' RAYWOOD ASH
Fraxinus quadrangulata BLUE ASH
Fraxinus texensis TEXAS ASH
Geijera parviflora AUSTRALIAN WILLOW, DESERT WILLOW
Gordonia lasianthus LOBLOLLY BAY
Guaiacum officinale LIGNUM VITAE, GUM GUAIACUM
Gymnocladus dioicus KENTUCKY COFFEE TREE
Halesia monticola 'Rosea' MOUNTAIN SILVER BELL
Hoheria populnea LACEBARK
Hovenia dulcis JAPANESE RAISIN TREE
Idesia polycarpa IIGIRI TREE
Ilex x altaclerensis 'James G. Esson' ESSON HOLLY
Ilex x aquipernyi 'San Jose' SAN JOSE HOLLY
Ilex opaca 'Miss Helen' MISS HELEN HOLLY
Ilex pedunculosa LONG-STALK HOLLY
Kalopanax pictus CASTOR-ARALIA
Koelreuteria bipinnata CHINESE FLAME TREE
Koelreuteria paniculata GOLDEN RAIN TREE
Laburnum x watereri 'Vossii' GOLDEN-CHAIN TREE
Lagerstroemia indica 'Alba' WHITE CRAPE MYRTLE
Larix decidua EUROPEAN LARCH
Larix kaempferi JAPANESE LARCH
Luma apiculata
Maackia amurensis AMUR MAACKIA
Magnolia acuminata CUCUMBER TREE, INDIAN BITTER
Magnolia heptapeta YULAN MAGNOLIA
Magnolia x loebneri 'Merrill'
Magnolia virginiana SWEET BAY MAGNOLIA, SWAMP BAY MAGNOLIA
Malus 'Adams' ADAMS CRAB APPLE
Malus 'Donald Wyman' DONALD WYMAN CRAB APPLE
Malus hupehensis TEA CRAB APPLE
Malus 'Mary Potter' MARY POTTER CRAB APPLE
Malus 'Professor Sprenger' PROFESSOR SPRENGER CRAB APPLE
Metasequoia glyptostroboides DAWN REDWOOD
Metrosideros excelsus NEW ZEALAND CHRISTMAS TREE
Michelia doltsopa
Nothofagus antarctica NIRRE
Nyssa sylvatica TUPELO, PEPPERIDGE, SOUR GUM, BLACK GUM
Olmediella betschleriana COSTA RICA HOLLY
                          GUATEMALAN HOLLY, MANZANOLE
Ostrya virginiana AMERICAN HOP HORNBEAM, IRONWOOD
Oxydendrum arboreum SOURWOOD, SORREL TREE
Parkinsonia aculeata JERUSALEM THORN, MEXICAN PALO VERDE
Parrotia persica PERSIAN PARROTIA
Phellodendron amurense AMUR or CHINESE CORK TREE
Picea omorika SERBIAN SPRUCE

Picea orientalis ORIENTAL SPRUCE
Pinus bungeana LACEBARK PINE
Pinus cembra SWISS STONE PINE, AROLLA PINE
Pinus flexilis LIMBER PINE
Pinus koraiensis KOREAN PINE
Pinus parviflora 'Glauca' JAPANESE WHITE PINE
Pinus wallichiana HIMALAYAN PINE, BHUTAN PINE
Pithecellobium flexicaule TEXAS EBONY
Prunus maacki AMUR CHOKECHERRY
Prunus 'Okame' OKAME CHERRY
Prunus sargentii SARGENT CHERRY
Prunus subhirtella 'Autumnalis' DOUBLE-FLOWERED HIGAN CHERRY
Pseudolarix kaempferi GOLDEN LARCH
Ptelea trifoliata HOP TREE, WAFER ASH, WATER ASH
Pterostyrax hispida EPAULETTE TREE
Pyrus ussuriensis USSURIAN PEAR
Quercus acutissima SAWTOOTH OAK
Quercus bicolor SWAMP WHITE OAK
Quercus imbricaria SHINGLE OAK
Quercus macrocarpa BUR OAK, MOSSYCUP OAK
Quercus robur 'Fastigiata' ENGLISH OAK
Quercus shumardii SHUMARD OAK
Roystonea regia ROYAL PALM
Sapindus drummondii WESTERN SOAPBERRY, CHINA-BERRY
Sapium sebiferum CHINESE TALLOW TREE
Sciadopitys verticillata JAPANESE UMBRELLA PINE
Sophora japonica 'Regent' JAPANESE PAGODA TREE
       JAPANESE SCHOLAR TREE
Sophora secundiflora TEXAS MOUNTAIN-LAUREL, MESCAL BEAN,
     MESCAL-BEAN SOPHORA, FRIJOLITO
Sorbus alnifolia KOREAN MOUNTAIN ASH
Stewartia koreana KOREAN STEWARTIA
Stewartia monadelpha TALL STEWARTIA
Stewartia pseudocamellia JAPANESE STEWARTIA
Styrax japonica JAPANESE SNOWBELL
Styrax obassia FRAGRANT SNOWBELL
Symplocos paniculata SAPPHIREBERRY
Syringa reticulata JAPANESE TREE LILAC
Tabebuia chrysotricha GOLDEN TRUMPET TREE
Tamarindus indica TAMARIND TREE
Taxodium distichum BALD CYPRESS
Thuja plicata GIANT ARBORVITAE, WESTERN RED CEDAR
Tilia tomentosa SILVER LINDEN
Torreya nucifera JAPANESE TORREYA, KAYA
Trochodendron aralioides WHEEL TREE
Ulmus japonica JAPANESE ELM
Ulmus parvifolia CHINESE ELM, LACE-BARK ELM
Xanthoceras sorbifolium YELLOWHORN
Zelkova serrata 'Village Green' JAPANESE ZELKOVA

"Were I to await for perfection, my book would never be finished."

Tai T'ung
13th century

ACKNOWLEDGEMENTS

The authorship of this book is unique. Hundreds of "authors" have contributed to this publication. In addition to the participation of Garden Club of America members, others who have played an important role in the initial selection process and contributed invaluable information and photographs include horticulturists, botanists, taxonomists, dendrologists, nurserymen and landscape architects. These interested and supportive individuals are dedicated to preserving diversity in the horticultural world.

The person who gave me the initial courage to tackle the Plants That Merit Attention project is Charles A. Lewis, Collections Group Administrator and Horticulturist, the Morton Arboretum. For his encouragement, patience and invaluable suggestions, I am greatly indebted.

Mrs. Richardson Pratt, Vice Chairman of the Garden Club of America Horticulture Committee, has been a conscientious and dedicated right hand. Her contributions to this volume have been immeasurable.

Mrs. Andre W. Brewster, Vice Chairman of the Garden Club of America Horticulture Committee, accomplished the difficult task of obtaining and assembling the 450 high-quality photographs that add a further dimension to this publication. Her dedication, tenacity, and countless hours of work are greatly appreciated.

The majority of excellent photographs are credited to Dr. Michael A. Dirr, Professor of Horticulture, University of Georgia, and Director of the University of Georgia Botanical Garden; Dr. Edward R. Hasselkus, Professor of Horticulture, University of Wisconsin-Madison; Mr. Albert W. Bussewitz, naturalist, teacher and photographer at the Arnold Arboretum; the staff of the Morton Arboretum, and Mrs. Andre W. Brewster. These dedicated photographer-horticulturists have given generously of their time and talent. Numerous other color plates are credited to many photographers across the United States and abroad, and I am most appreciative of the efforts of those who have graciously submitted their slides for consideration.

Our immediate committee was composed of Garden Club of America members representing different regions of the United States. In order to collect and coordinate materials, each member worked with professionals from botanical gardens, arboreta, nurseries and universities in her specific area. These workers were responsible for obtaining research information, many of the color photographs, and for assuring a representative collection from each geographical region. This committee has been working diligently for almost three years. A deep and grateful thank-you to: Mrs. Andre W. Brewster, Mrs. Collister Johnson, Mrs. Robert MacBride, Mrs. Richardson Pratt, Jr. and Mrs. Lindsay Smith.

Mrs. Macpherson Raymond was not only an expert in helping to edit this text, but also an invaluable consultant to me.

I am most appreciative of the always willing and helpful cooperation of our Garden Club of America Horticulture Committee Secretary, Mrs. Monica Freeman.

Hortus Third is the general reference authority for nomenclature in this volume. However, we have chosen to use the lower case initial letter for all species, following the International Code of Botanical Nomenclature (Leningrad Edition, 1978) Article 73, Recommendation 73 F.1. Dr. Theodore R. Dudley, Research Botanist and Taxonomist at the National Arboretum, and Floyd A. Swink, Taxonomist at the Morton Arboretum, have served as advisors for specific botanical questions. My most sincere gratitude to these knowledgeable gentlemen who have so ably served our project.

The botanical nomenclature in this publication is skillfully illustrated by the beautiful line drawings of artist-horticulturist Mrs. Austin Zimmerman. In order to further clarify the text, Mrs. Zimmerman and Dr. Ross Clark, Curator of Education at the Morton Arboretum, collaborated to write the Botanical Glossary. A sincere thank-you to these dedicated contributors.

One of the most unusual aspects of this book is that so many interested individuals have generously shared their knowledge. There are no direct quotations; rather, the text is a compilation of the information gleaned from these willing participants. A most grateful thank-you to these generous individuals who have spent countless hours answering questions, evaluating specific genera, and obtaining photographs:

William Adams, Horticulturist, Extension Service, Texas A & M

Thomas M. Antonio, Ph.D., Taxonomist, Chicago Botanic Garden

Mrs. David Arbegast, Berkeley, CA, Member at Large, GCA

George S. Avery, Jr., Ph.D., Director Emeritus, Brooklyn Botanic Garden, Member at Large, GCA

John P. Baumgardt, Ph.D., Botanist, Cassville, MO

Benjamin Blackburn, Ph.D., Professor of Botany Emeritus, Willowwood Arboretum

Mrs. Edward A. Blackburn, Jr., Houston, TX, GCA

Mrs. Benjamin P. Bole, Cleveland, OH, GCA

Peter Bristol, Horticulturist, Holden Arboretum

Mrs. George B. Cammann, Darien, CT, GCA

Ross Clark, Ph.D., Curator of Education, Morton Arboretum

Barrie D. Coate, Horticultural Consultant, Los Gatos, CA

Alan D. Cook, Senior Horticulturist, Dawes Arboretum

Mrs. Erastus Corning, II, Albany, NY, GCA

Ann L. Crammond, Executive Director, Atlanta Botanic Garden

Thomas J. Delendick, Ph.D., Taxonomist, Brooklyn Botanic Garden

Samuel J. de Turo, Jr., Arborist, President, Woodwinds Associates, Inc.

Francis de Vos, Ph.D., Director, University of Minnesota Landscape Arboretum

Michael A. Dirr, Ph.D., Professor of Horticulture, University of Georgia, and Director, University of Georgia Botanical Garden

George Dobbins, American River College

Emmett Dodd, Horticulturist, Lowrey Nurseries

Tom Dodd, President, Tom Dodd Nurseries, Inc.

Theodore R. Dudley, Ph.D., Research Botanist, National Arboretum, Member at Large, GCA

Gene Eisenbeiss, Research Horticulturist, National Arboretum

Jake Figg, Horticulturist, Strybing Arboretum

William Flemer, III, President, Princeton Nurseries

Will Fleming, Horticulturist, Lowrey Nurseries

Harrison L. Flint, Ph.D., Professor of Horticulture, Purdue University

John A. Floyd, Jr., Senior Horticulturist, Southern Living Magazine

Mrs. Kathleen Freeland, Propagator, Chicago Botanic Garden

Mrs. Peter R. Gallagher, Atherton, CA, GCA

Fred C. Galle, Retired Director of Horticulture, Callaway Gardens

Mrs. S. Hughes Garvin, Basking Ridge, NJ, GCA

Henry D. Gerhold, Ph.D., Professor of Forest Genetics, Pennsylvania State University

Mrs. William Goodan, Pasadena, CA, GCA
Mrs. Nicholas Gotten, Memphis, TN, GCA
Thomas Green, Ph.D., Plant Pathologist, Morton Arboretum
Mrs. J. Waller Harrison, Richmond, VA, GCA
Edward R. Hasselkus, Ph.D., Professor of Horticulture, University of Wisconsin-Madison
Robert S. Hebb, Horticulturist, Cary Arboretum
Dale E. Herman, Ph.D., Professor, Department of Forestry, North Dakota State University
Mrs. Marshall Hieronimus, Portland, OR, GCA
Mrs. Julian W. Hill, Wilmington, DE, GCA
Duncan Himmelman, Instructor Horticulture Programmes, Olds College, Alberta, Canada
Mrs. William G. Houskeeper, Newton, NJ, GCA
Kris Jarantowski, Assistant Director, Chicago Botanic Garden
Mrs. William Jennings, Greenwich, CT, GCA
Gordon E. Jones, Director, Planting Fields Arboretum
George Kackley, Washington, D.C.
Paul S. Kingsley, Horticulturist, Dixon Gallery and Gardens
Charles Klehm, Charles Klehm and Son Nursery
Joann S. Knapp, Staff Member, Planting Fields Arboretum
Gary L. Koller, Managing Horticulturist, Arnold Arboretum
John Koros, Director, Mercer Arboretum
Mrs. William F. Kraft, Islip, NY, GCA
Larry J. Kuhns, Department of Horticulture, Pennsylvania State University
Anne Kuhry, Milwaukee, WI, Horticultural Consultant
Mrs. Warren Lammert, St. Louis, MO, GCA
Fred Lape, Director, George Landis Arboretum
Robert F. Lederer, Vice President, American Association of Nurserymen Inc.
Andrew Leiser, Ph.D., Professor, Department of Environmental Horticulture, University of California-Davis
Charles A. Lewis, Collections Group Administrator and Horticulturist, Morton Arboretum
Clarence E. Lewis, Ph.D., East Lansing, MI
Ted Lockwood, Director, Bartlett Arboretum
Mrs. W.Z. Lotowycz, Former Curator of Herbarium, Planting Fields Arboretum
Mrs. Albert Ludecke, Jr., Morrisville, PA, GCA
Mildred E. Mathias, Ph.D., Professor Emeritus of Botany, University of California, Los Angeles
Robert B. McCartney, Horticulturist, Woodlanders Nursery, Inc.
Mrs. Armin S. McGregor, Milwaukee, WI, GCA
Roy A. Mecklenburg, Ph.D., Director, Chicago Botanic Garden
Paul W. Meyer, Assistant Director of Horticulture, Morris Arboretum
Edmund V. Mezitt, President, Weston Nurseries, Inc.
Mrs. Pendleton Miller, Seattle, WA, GCA
Gary Moll, Urban Forestry Coordinator, Maryland Forest Service
Donald E. Moore, President, Brooklyn Botanic Garden
Merle Moore, Director, Denver Botanic Garden
Mrs. J. Raymond Moore, Jr., Baltimore, MD, GCA
Mrs. Richard M. Moore, Des Moines, IA, GCA
Edmund O. Moulin, Director of Horticulture, Brooklyn Botanic Garden

Brian Mulligan, Former Director, University of Washington Arboretum
Mrs. Patrick Neligan, Ridgefield, CT, GCA
William R. Nelson, Extension Specialist, Landscape Architecture, University of Illinois
R. Henry Norweb, Jr., Former Executive Director, Holden Arboretum
Mrs. George R. Numrich, Kingston, NY, GCA
Marvin Olinsky, Director, Cox Arboretum
Hadley Osborn, Executive Director, Filoli Center
Thomas F. Patterson, President, Panfield Nursery
Mrs. Edward G. Pearson, Houston, TX, GCA
J. Liddon Pennock, Jr., Meadowbrook Farm, Meadowbrook, PA, Member at Large, GCA
John W.S. Platt, Portland, OR
Mrs. John W.S. Platt, Portland, OR, GCA
Mrs. Theodore Purtell, Milwaukee, WI, GCA
J.C. Raulston, Ph.D., Professor, Department of Horticultural Science, North Carolina
    State University Arboretum
Mrs. J. Pancoast Reath, Philadelphia, PA, GCA
Mrs. Edward H. Richardson, Jr., Baltimore, MD, GCA
Mrs. Sheldon Riley, Santa Barbara, CA, GCA
Frank S. Santamour, Jr., Ph.D., Research Geneticist, National Arboretum
Elizabeth Scholtz, Ph.D., Vice President, Brooklyn Botanic Garden
Ray Schulenberg, Curator of Plant Collections, Morton Arboretum
Robert K. Siebenthaler, President, Siebenthaler Nursery
Mrs. Robert K. Siebenthaler, Dayton, OH, GCA
Larry Simpson, Superintendent, Sedgwick Garden, Long Hill Reservation, Beverly,
    MA
Ruth H. Smiley, Director, Mohonk Garden, New Paltz, NY
Mr. and Mrs. Don Smith, Watnong Nursery
Stephen A. Spongberg, Ph.D., Curatorial Taxonomist, Arnold Arboretum
Mrs. Charles F. Squire, Houston, TX, GCA
Augie Stark, President, Evergreen Nursery
Mrs. John P. Swan, West Chester, PA, GCA
Ron Tauen, Horticulturist, University of Missouri
Mrs. Wesley Thomas, Kanoehe, HI, GCA
William Thomas, Department of Education, Longwood Gardens
Mrs. Michael G. T. Thompson, Santa Barbara, CA, GCA
Mrs. Stephen E. Thompson, Portland, OR, GCA
Robert G. Titus, Former Assistant Director, Planting Fields Arboretum
Robert S. Tomson, Vice President Operations, Brooklyn Botanic Garden
Carl A. Totemeier, Jr., Director, Old Westbury Gardens, Inc.
Plato Touliatos, President, Trees by Touliatos, Memphis, TN
Harold B. Tukey, Jr., Ph.D., Director of Arboreta, Center for Urban Horticulture,
    University of Washington
Walden Valen, Director, Strybing Arboretum
J.D. Vertrees, President, Maplewood Nursery
Mrs. Ganahl Walker, Houston, TX, GCA
George H. Ware, Ph.D., Dendrologist, Morton Arboretum
Mrs. Nelson Weller, Piedmont, CA, GCA
Mrs. Wellington Wells, Marlborough, NH, GCA
Donald B. Williams, Ph.D., Department of Ornamental Horticulture and Landscape
    Design, University of Tennessee

Douglas Williams, Botanist, Houston Arboretum and Botanical Society
Joseph A. Witt, Ph.D., Curator, Washington Park Arboretum, University of Washington
Mrs. Myron Wright, New York, NY, GCA
Mrs. John N. Wrinkle, Birmingham, AL, GCA

My conscientious secretary, Joanne Freeman, typed the manuscript, but as the book slowly evolved, also became a most helpful editor, critic and supporter.

I am most grateful for the help, and enduring patience of my family, Edward King Poor III, Thomas Meakin Poor, Hope Stevens Poor and Edward King Poor IV.

Having an understanding, enthusiastic publisher is essential to any publication. No one could have been more encouraging and supportive than Mr. Richard Abel, president of Timber Press. It has been a privilege to work with Mr. Abel these past three years.

The interest and cooperation of the Horticulture Committee and the hundreds of Garden Club of America participants cannot be measured in words. And without the dedication and support of our former president Mrs. Samuel M. Beattie, our current president Mrs. Niels W. Johnsen, and the Executive Committee of the Garden Club of America, this book would not have become a reality. I am deeply grateful.

Janet Meakin Poor

INTRODUCTION:
PLANTS THAT MERIT ATTENTION—
VOLUME I, TREES

There is no perfect tree. However, there are many little known trees with superior characteristics that merit attention.

This publication is the result of a nationwide search for such trees. A tree that is seldom seen and not readily available in one area of the country may be commonly known and plentiful in another; the trees selected for this book are unusual and not readily available in at least one major region of the country, even though that region's climate is favorable. These trees have been selected by nurseries, botanical gardens, arboreta, universities, landscape architects, gardeners and members of The Garden Club of America from among the trees whose cultivation they know.

To qualify as a "Plant That Merits Attention," each plant must be one seldom seen in the general landscape. It may be a traditional old favorite that has been neglected and is in danger of disappearing from nurseries, or perhaps a species or new cultivar that has not received adequate recognition. In addition to being unusual, it must exhibit other desirable characteristics. It should be an attractive addition to gardens, parks, and cityscapes, with seasonal interest such as distinctive blossoms, fruit, foliage color, or bark pattern. If it shows tolerance to one or more environmental factors (such as drought, pollution, insects, diseases, etc.), it is more likely to have been selected. These qualities identify plants which deserve recognition and should be available for planting in gardens and civic areas.

It is hoped that this selective compilation of trees, which includes their sources, will turn the attention of nurserymen, landscape architects and homeowners to a wider diversity of plants for city and suburb than is now available, and will ultimately enhance the environmental quality of the places in which people work, play, and live.

LEAVES

The illustrations of *simple* and *compound* leaves are self-explanatory. Not all leaves are subtended by leaf-like *stipules*. In many plants stipules are present only in the early stages of a season's growth, drying up and falling off as the season advances.

Early in the season the *bud* containing next year's leaf begins to develop where the base of the leaf stalk, *petiole*, joins the twig. It reaches its full development in late summer and then remains as a bud until the following spring triggers the development of a new leaf.

LEAVES OF CONIFERS

A number of conifers have *scale-like* leaves which are very small, often not more than ⅛ inch wide or long, and closely adpressed to the twig in pairs of opposite leaves or in whorls of three or four leaves. The mighty Sequoia, the Big Tree of California, has these tiny leaves.

Some conifers with scale-like leaves also have *awl-shaped*, or *subulate*, leaves, especially on young growth. Certain Junipers and a few other conifers display these very sharp leaves on new twigs.

Pines: *Pinus* species, have *needle-like* leaves in bundles of two to five leaves which are enclosed at the base in a papery sheath.

Spruces: *Picea* species, have leaves borne singly on the twigs, each leaf arising from a small peg-like structure which remains on the twig after the leaf falls, so that the part of the twig which has lost its leaves is rough. The leaves are square in cross section and more or less sharply pointed.

Firs: *Abies* species, have leaves attached directly to the twig. When these leaves fall off only a small, flat scar remains, so that the twig is smooth to the touch. The leaves of firs are flat, flexible and not sharply pointed.

LEAF SHAPES and LEAF TIPS-EDGES-BASES

The illustrations are self-explanatory.

FLOWERS

The illustration, *Flower Parts*, is purely diagramatic; there is no typical flower. Flower parts vary in shape, size, and number from species to species. In many flowers some of these parts are absent. The *essential parts* of a flower are the *pistils*, one or more (female), and the *stamens* (male). Either the pistils or stamens may be absent or small and infertile in some flowers. Such flowers are said to be *unisexual*.

Petals, Sepals, and *Receptacles* are *accessory parts.*

Petals are often brightly colored. The petals as a whole are called the *corolla.*

Sepals are usually green but may be colored like petals. The sepals as a whole are called the *calyx.*

Calyx and corolla together constitute the *perianth.*

Pistil: The female reproductive organ is the pistil. It has a stigma, a style, and an ovary within which are the ovules, one or more. The ovules mature into seeds.

Stamen: The male reproductive organ is the stamen, consisting of a pollen-bearing anther carried on a filament.

In wind-pollinated trees the entire perianth may be missing and the reproductive organs contained either in bracts or in cup-like structures.

MONOECIOUS and DIOECIOUS TREES

When flowers are unisexual both male (staminate) and female (pistillate) flowers are found on a single plant; such a plant is described as being *monoecious* (meaning 'one household'). When staminate flowers occur on one plant and pistillate flowers occur on another plant that species is said to be *dioecious* (meaning 'two households'). When dioecious species such as *Ilex* are planted, a staminate tree should be planted in fairly close proximity to pistillate trees to ensure pollination and hence ample production of the desired fruit.

OVARY POSITION

It is sometimes necessary to know the position of the ovary to identify plants correctly and to understand the structure of fruits.

Hypogynous flowers: In these flowers all flower parts are seated on the receptacle beneath the pistil. The pistil is said to be *superior.*

Perigynous flowers: In these flowers the receptacle has developed into a cup, open at the top. Bases of the sepals, petals, and stamens are fused with the tissues of the enlarged receptacle. The resulting structure is called an *hypanthium.* The one or more pistils are free-standing within the hypanthium. The ovary is still said to be *superior.*

Epigynous flowers: In epigynous flowers the hypanthium is closed at the top, enclosing the ovary of the pistil completely. The tissues of the ovary wall are fused with those of the enclosing hypanthium. The ovary is now said to be *inferior,* since it is beneath the other flower parts which apparently arise from a position above it in the flower.

INFLORESCENCES

Catkins (Aments)

Catkins are spike-like inflorescences found on a number of tree species. Flowers of catkins are very small, inconspicuous, and unisexual. *Staminate catkins* are usually flexible and dangling. The small staminate flowers are borne beneath the scales of the catkin. Pistillate flowers may be borne on shorter, more or less erect *pistillate catkins* as in *Betula* (Birch), the example illustrated; or they may be solitary or clustered in a scaly cup-like structure on the twig as in oaks.

Solitary: Magnolia and Fawpaw are examples of trees with solitary flowers.

Spike: The flowers are *sessile* (without stalks) on a central stem (rachis). The lowest flower opens first.

Raceme: A raceme is like a spike except that the flowers have stalks (*pedicels*). Again the lowest flower opens first.

Corymb: A corymb is a flat-topped development of a raceme in which the outside flowers on elongated pedicels open first.

Umbel: In an umbel all the flowers arise from a single point at the top of the flowering shoot.

Cyme: A cyme is a complex inflorescence in which the center flower at the top of the shoot opens first. Side branches develop beneath this flower and these may branch again, the center flower always opening first. Some species of *Cornus* (Dogwood) have cymose inflorescences.

Panicle: A panicle is a much-branched development of a raceme.

FRUITS

A fruit always involves a ripened ovary or group of ovaries. It may include other floral parts. A seed is a ripened ovule.

Dry, Indehiscent Fruits do not break open at maturity until weathering softens the hard coat or an animal breaks it open.

Achenes: An achene is a hard, dry, one-celled fruit developed from an ovary that has one cell, *locule;* the seed is fastened to the ovary wall at only one point. The achenes illustrated are those of sycamore, sunflower (not a tree, but producing achenes everyone knows), and the plumed achene of a small western tree, *Cercocarpus.* The plume is the persistent style of the pistil.

Samaras: These are the winged dry fruits of maples, elms, ashes, and a number of other trees.

Nuts: A nut is a relatively large one-seeded fruit with a hard ovary wall. They are often held in a cup as in oaks, or surrounded by a husk as in hickories.

Nutlet: A nutlet is a diminutive nut. Achenes are sometimes called nutlets.

Dry, Dehiscent Fruits break open (*dehisce*) naturally at maturity to release their seeds.

Follicle: A follicle is a one-celled fruit that splits on only one side. Milkweed pods are a familiar example.

Legume: Legumes are like follicles except that they split open on two sides. Pea pods and beans are examples.

Capsule: Capsules develop from ovaries having several locules. They dehisce along the tissues dividing the locules or at the back of each locule.

Fleshy Fruits

Drupe: Drupes are fleshy fruits that contain in their centers one or more hard seed-like structures, each of which contains a seed. Familiar drupes are the "stone fruits"—cherries, peaches, and plums.

Berry: In a berry the entire ovary enlarges to become fleshy, with the seeds embedded in the flesh. Examples are pawpaw, grapes and tomatoes.

Pome: Pomes are the fruits of apples, hawthorns and their relatives. They develop from epigynous flowers in which the hypanthium enlarges to become the fleshy part of the fruit. The membrane at the outer boundary of the core is the ovary wall. The core is the ripened ovary which contains within its locules the ripened ovules, the seeds.

Conifers: Conifers belong to the sub-division of the seed-bearing plants known as *Gymnosperms* which means 'naked seeds'. Such seeds develop from ovules not enclosed in an ovary.

Conifers are monoecious (rarely dioecious) producing inconspicuous staminate flowers on small scaly aments and conspicuous pistillate seed cones. The naked seeds are borne beneath the scales of the cone.

Cones are of various forms as illustrated.

Juniperus: The junipers. The cone scales become fleshy and coalesce. They are called "juniper berries", but they are true cones, not berries.

Some Gymnosperms bear their hard-coated seeds singly and more or less enclosed in a fleshy *aril. Taxus,* Yew, is a familiar example. *Torreya,* a rare gymnosperm, is another example.

LEAVES

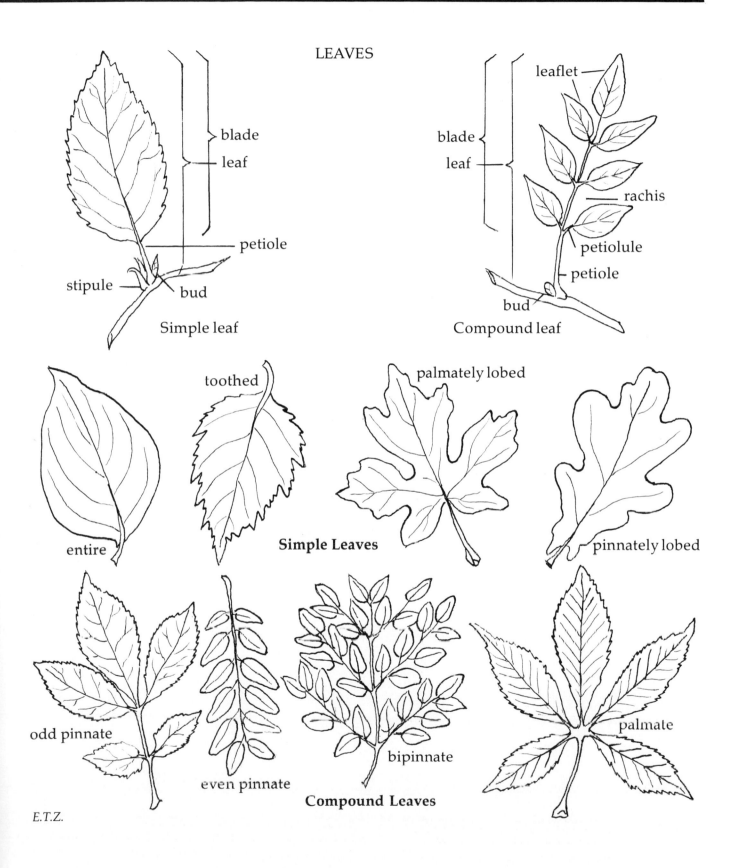

blade

leaf

petiole

stipule

bud

Simple leaf

leaflet

blade

leaf

rachis

petiolule

petiole

bud

Compound leaf

entire

toothed

Simple Leaves

palmately lobed

pinnately lobed

odd pinnate

even pinnate

bipinnate

Compound Leaves

palmate

E.T.Z.

LEAVES OF CONIFERS

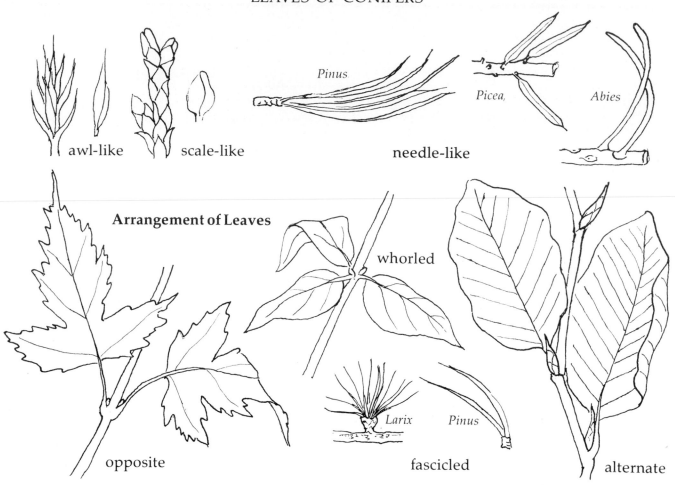

awl-like   scale-like

Pinus

Picea,   *Abies*

needle-like

Arrangement of Leaves

whorled

Larix   *Pinus*

opposite   fascicled   alternate

Venation of Leaves

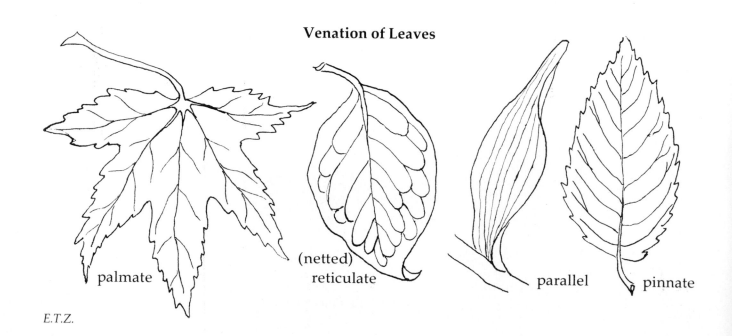

palmate   (netted) reticulate   parallel   pinnate

E.T.Z.

LEAF SHAPES

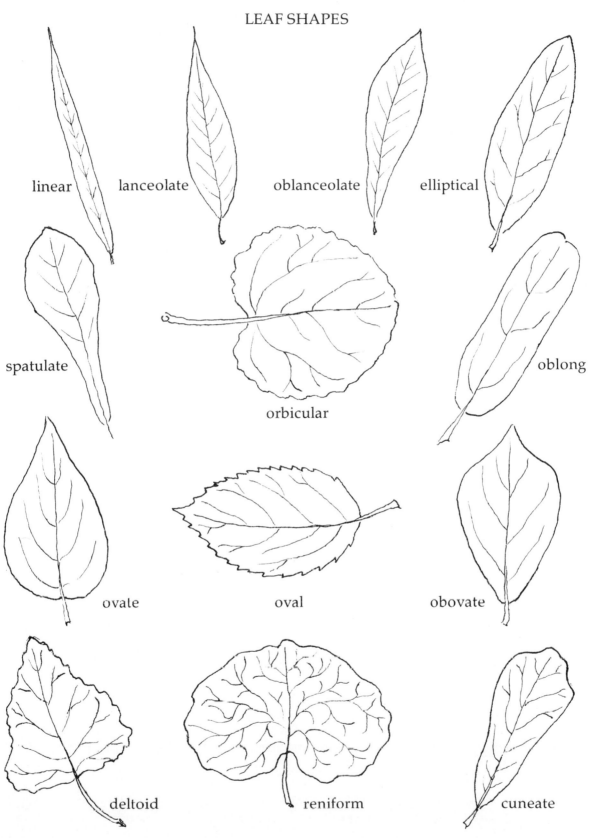

linear

lanceolate

oblanceolate

elliptical

spatulate

orbicular

oblong

ovate

oval

obovate

deltoid

reniform

cuneate

E.T.Z.

LEAF TIPS—EDGES—BASES

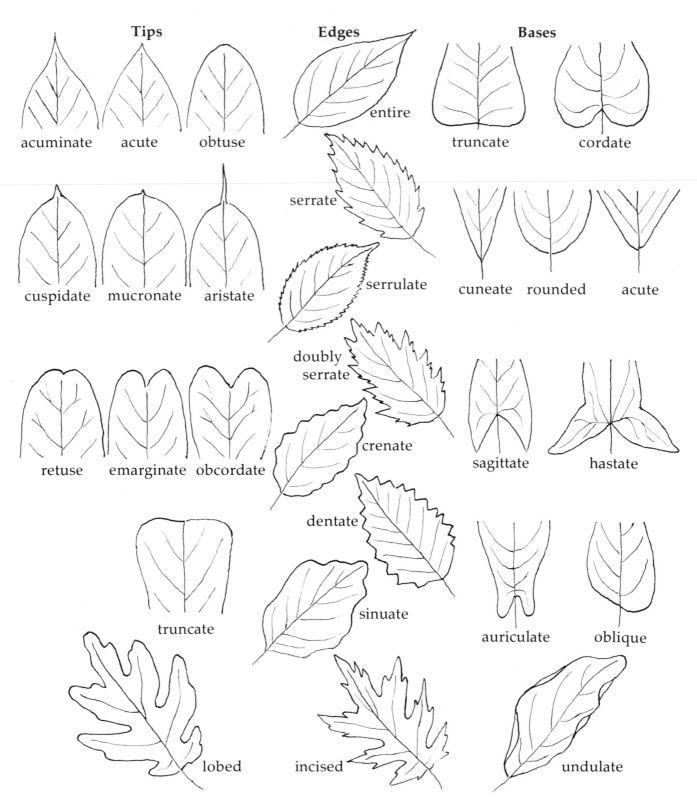

Tips **Edges** **Bases**

acuminate acute obtuse

entire

truncate cordate

serrate

cuspidate mucronate aristate

serrulate

cuneate rounded acute

doubly serrate

retuse emarginate obcordate

crenate

sagittate hastate

dentate

truncate

sinuate

auriculate oblique

lobed incised undulate

E.T.Z.

FLOWERS

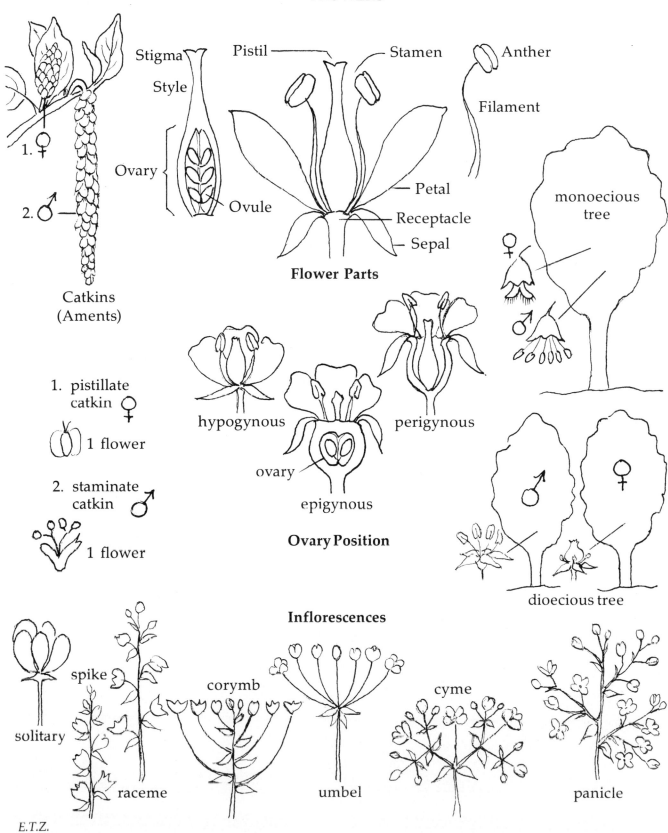

Stigma

Style

Pistil — Stamen

Anther

Filament

Ovary

Ovule

Petal

Receptacle

Sepal

Flower Parts

1. ♀

2. ♂

Catkins
(Aments)

1. pistillate
   catkin ♀

   1 flower

2. staminate
   catkin ♂

   1 flower

hypogynous

perigynous

ovary

epigynous

Ovary Position

monoecious
tree

♀

♂

dioecious tree

♂   ♀

Inflorescences

solitary

spike

raceme

corymb

umbel

cyme

panicle

E.T.Z.

FRUITS

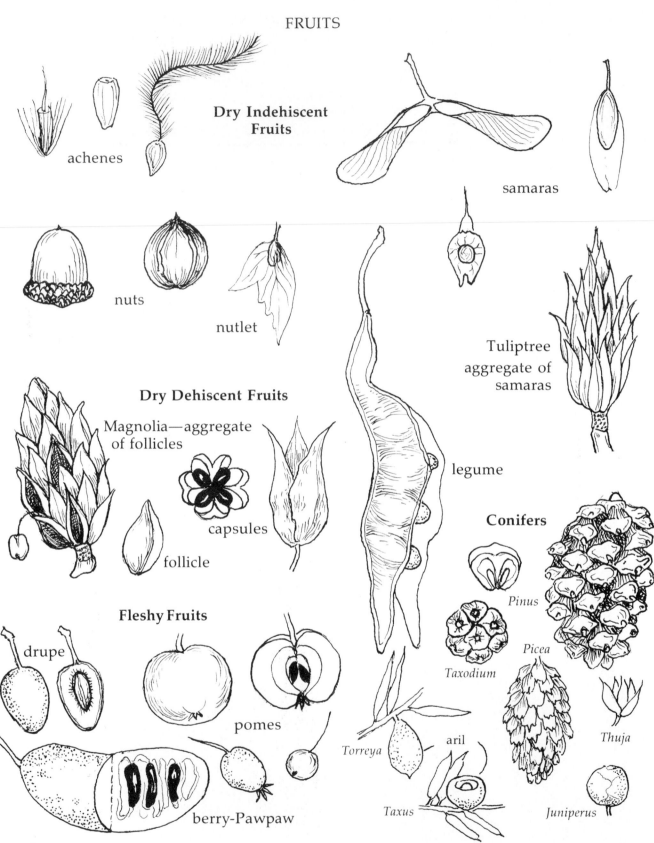

Dry Indehiscent Fruits

achenes

samaras

nuts

nutlet

Tuliptree aggregate of samaras

Dry Dehiscent Fruits

Magnolia—aggregate of follicles

capsules

follicle

legume

Conifers

Pinus

Taxodium

Picea

Thuja

Fleshy Fruits

drupe

pomes

Torreya

aril

berry-Pawpaw

Taxus

Juniperus

E.T.Z.

U.S.D.A. HARDINESS ZONES OF NORTH AMERICA

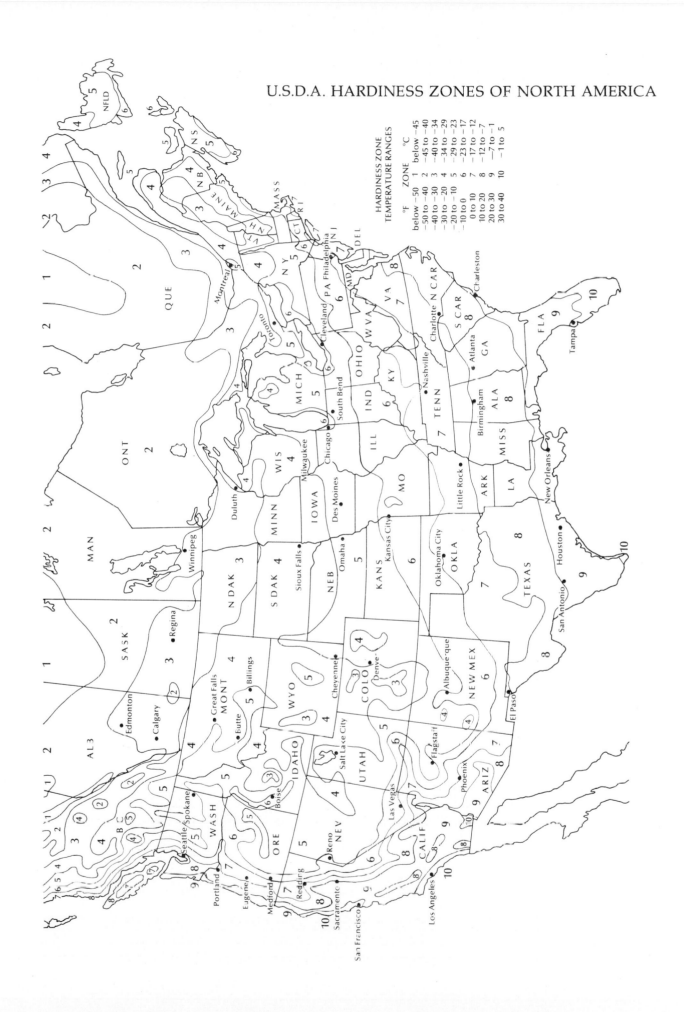

HARDINESS ZONE TEMPERATURE RANGES		
°F	ZONE	°C
below −50	1	below −45
−50 to −40	2	−45 to −40
−40 to −30	3	−40 to −34
−30 to −20	4	−34 to −29
−20 to −10	5	−29 to −23
−10 to 0	6	−23 to −17
0 to 10	7	−17 to −12
10 to 20	8	−12 to −7
20 to 30	9	−7 to −1
30 to 40	10	−1 to 5

PLANTS THAT MERIT ATTENTION

Abies concolor (Gordon) Lindley ex Hildebrandt. COLORADO or WHITE FIR. *Pinaceae.* USDA Zones 3–7. U.S. Rocky Mountains, Colorado to California and New Mexico. Introduced 1872.

DESCRIPTION *Evergreen conifer,* narrow-pyramidal in form. Generally grows 1½' per year to a mature height of 30–50' and spread of 15–30', though has been known to reach a height of 120'. Casts dense shade.

Leaves: Needles to 2" long, rounded or acute at apex, blue-green above, pale blue bands beneath. When crushed they produce a strong lemon scent.

Flowers: Inconspicuous, monoecious. Male flowers are round and yellow; female are yellow-green, about 1" long.

Fruit: Cones cylindrical to 5" long, pale green when young, often with a purplish bloom. Female cones erect, two seeds to a scale, winged, maturing in one year.

Winter aspect: Bark smooth on young stems, ash gray and furrowed on old trunks. Branching habit horizontal with drooping lower branches.

CULTURE Prefers full sun and rich, moist, well drained sandy loam for fullest development. Will tolerate light shade, and will grow well in hot, dry situations when established. Dislikes heavy clay soils and industrial pollution.

Disease and insect problems: Not serious.

Transplanting: Best done while tree is young, balled and burlapped.

Propagation: By seed, which should be stratified, or by cuttings taken late in the season (some recommend cuttings taken in March and treated with 100 ppm IBA for 24 hours).

LANDSCAPE VALUE This conifer has wide adaptability and withstands heat and drought better than most firs. It can be planted farther north than most, and is hardy in the Boston area. It tolerates city conditions better, and can adapt to both wet and dry situations. Its growth habit forms a softer-looking tree than the spruces, and provides an interesting blue-green color contrast with other evergreens.

A. concolor is grown in botanic collections and gardens but is rare in the trade. There are many cultivars, such as 'Lowiana', common name Low's Fir, or Pacific Mountain Fir, which is generally taller than the species; it can be seen at Bayard Cutting Arboretum. 'Conica' is more dwarf and pyramidal.

Plant may be observed at: *Arboreta*—Arnold, Bayard Cutting, Bernheim Forest, Holden, Minnesota Landscape, Morton, Planting Fields, Spring Grove, U. of Washington, U. of Wisconsin-Madison; *Botanical Gardens*— Brooklyn, Chicago, Denver, Munich, Palmgarten, Royal/Kew, Royal/Ontario; *Gardens*—Longwood, Winterthur.

E. HASSELKUS

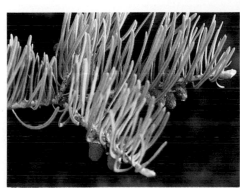

A. BUSSEWITZ

E. HASSELKUS

Abies koreana E. H. Wilson. KOREAN FIR. *Pinaceae.* USDA Zone 5. South Korea. Introduced in France in 1908 by Father Urbain Faurie, though plants in U.S. derive from E. H. Wilson's collection in 1917 and possibly from later expeditions.

DESCRIPTION

Evergreen conifer, conical in shape, growing 8″ to 1½′ per year to a height of 60′ at maturity. Casts dense shade.

Leaves: ½-¾″ long, broadly needle-shaped, widest toward apex, usually notched; gray-green above and white beneath.

Fruit: Blue to violet-purple cones, cylindric, 2–3½″ long, 1‴ thick; showy in autumn and winter.

Winter aspect: Bark finally rough, dark and fissured. Branching habit horizontal, excurrent from central axis. Fruits persistent in winter.

CULTURE

Grows in full sun and well drained acid loam. Tolerant of wind and possibly of salt spray, but not of road salt, air pollution or soil compaction.

Disease and insect problems: None noted, but red spider must be a possibility.

Transplanting: Easy; root system shallow.

Propagation: Preferably by seed; grafted plants often unreliable. Cuttings may be taken in late winter.

LANDSCAPE VALUE

Excellent as an accent or specimen tree; a very beautiful and distinctive conifer, especially when young. Heavily waxed buds, blue cones, and distinctive leaves make it outstanding. Particularly fine below a house or terrace, as on a sloping bank from which one can look into the tops of the conical firs and see the bluish cones. Good for small gardens, since it grows more slowly than other firs. Unfavorable situations produce scragginess and dying lower branches; however, this condition may be wrongly diagnosed as it is not mentioned in European texts.

Plant may be observed at: *Arboreta*—Bayard Cutting, Holden, Morton, Minnesota Landscape, National, Planting Fields, Spring Grove, U. of Washington; *Botanical Gardens*—Brooklyn, Chicago, Munich, Royal/Kew; *Gardens*—Longwood.

N. BREWSTER

A. BUSSEWITZ

R. HEBB

Abies nordmanniana (Steven) Spach. CAUCASIAN FIR, NORDMANN FIR. *Pinaceae.*
USDA Zones 4–7. Greece, Caucasus Mountains, Asia Minor. Introduced
in 1848 by Edouard Spach.

DESCRIPTION
Evergreen conifer of narrowly pyramidal form. Grows moderately fast
while young, then more slowly, to mature height of 100–200′. Casts dense
shade; branches to the ground.

Leaves: Needles 1½ x ⅛″, densely set; dark, shining green, silver lines on
undersides. A characteristic feature is their scent of orange peel when
crushed.

Fruit: 6″ cylindrical cones on tops of branches, pinkish brown with blue
grape-like bloom in summer, rich brown in fall. Splendid effect. Cones
shatter in winter.

Winter aspect: Bark blistery silver-gray, brown with age. Branches in
dense whorls, very graceful.

CULTURE
Grows in full sun, in loam with pH range of 5.8–7.0. Moderately tolerant
of wind. Tolerates wet weather but not wet ground or drought. Not too
tolerant of environmental stresses, but does beautifully in reasonably
sheltered Middle West gardens where climate is stressful in itself.

Disease and insect problems: None noted; generally disease resistant.

Transplanting: Fairly easy, especially as bare root seedling. Root system
moderately deep.

Propagation: By seed.

LANDSCAPE
VALUE
A fine lawn specimen as well as excellent background or screening plant
when set fairly close on 12–15′ centers. It is easy to grow, and an
exceptionally beautiful tree whose tiered branches sweeping downwards
have year-round ornamental value. The best fir for the central Midwest,
where firs ordinarily do not thrive and may sunburn during a hot, dry,
windy summer; this one does handsomely.

Plant may be observed at: *Arboreta*—Bayard Cutting, Morton, Planting
Fields, U. of Washington; *Botanical Gardens*—New York, Munich,
Palmgarten, Royal/Kew; *Gardens*—Longwood, Winterthur.

E. HASSELKUS

PLANTING FIELDS

W. THOMAS

Acer buergerianum Miquel. TRIDENT MAPLE. *Aceraceae.* USDA Zones 5 to 8–9. China, Korea, Japan. Cult. 1890. Introduced into England 1896.

DESCRIPTION   *Deciduous* tree, upright, round-headed, of bushy habit, growing 2' per year and reaching 35–45' at maturity; 25–30' spread.

Leaves: Opposite, with three shallow, forward-pointing lobes, 2¼–4" long and 1½–3" wide; distinctly three-nerved, deep green above, glaucous beneath. Fall color orange and red tones. Colors later than many maples. Casts medium shade.

Flowers: Inconspicuous, greenish-yellow, small, in panicles.

Fruit: Samaras ¾–1" long.

Winter aspect: Bark orange-brown, exfoliating.

CULTURE   Grows in full sun in clay, loam or sand in pH range of 6–7.5. Moderately tolerant of wet conditions, very tolerant of wind and drought; accepts salt, air pollution and soil compaction.

Disease and insect problems: Tolerant.

Transplanting: Easy because of shallow root system. Best moved in spring.

Propagation: By seed, cultivars by grafting.

LANDSCAPE VALUE   Attractive, medium-sized patio and street tree; could be used more extensively as an urban tree. Strikingly brilliant fall color and exfoliating bark year-round are distinctive features. Several worthy named cultivars are available: dwarf forms, corky bark, variegated leaves and unusual leaf shapes. This tree is widely grown and dwarfed by bonsai enthusiasts.

Cultivars of interest:
   A. buergerianum 'Akebono'
   A. buergerianum 'Goshiki Kaede'
   A. buergerianum integrifolium 'Maruba'
   A. buergerianum 'Mino Yatsubusa'

Additional information: *Japanese Maples,* J.D. Vertrees, Timber Press.

Plant may be observed at: *Arboreta*—Bernheim Forest, Dawes, Los Angeles, Morton, Planting Fields, Strybing, U. of Washington; *Botanical Gardens*—Birmingham, Brooklyn, Missouri, New York, Palmgarten, Royal/Kew; *Parks*—Golden Gate.

N. BREWSTER

P. KINGSLEY

M. DIRR

Acer campestre L. HEDGE MAPLE, FIELD MAPLE. *Aceraceae.* USDA Zones 5–9.
Europe, Near East, North Africa. Introduced in Colonial times.

DESCRIPTION   *Deciduous*, round-headed, dense tree, often branched to ground. Grows
slowly to 35' in height and spread; a few specimens have reached 70'.
Casts dense shade.

Leaves: Opposite, palmate, with 3–5 rounded lobes, 2–4" across and as
long, deep green. Fall color yellowish-green or clear yellow; one of the
latest trees to color.

Flowers: Inconspicuous, greenish, in upright corymbs, in May.

Fruit: Samaras 2" long, ⅓–½" wide, wings spreading horizontally.

Winter aspect: Bark gray-black and furrowed.

CULTURE   Grows in full sun or light shade in clay or loam in pH range of 6.0–7.5;
also does well at pH of 5.5 and over. Tolerates wind, dry soils, slight wet
conditions, soil compaction, and air pollution.

Disease and insect problems: Slight; relatively resistant to both.

Transplanting: Easy, root system shallow.

Propagation: By seed for the species, by grafting for named cultivars.

LANDSCAPE
VALUE   Probably the best maple for dry alkaline soils. A good, hardy, non-
invasive round-headed tree which is not competitive with flowering
shrubs. Can be pruned and shaped into smaller landscaping. It also
responds well to shearing and makes an excellent hedge, as in Europe
where it is used in this way extensively. Some of the hedges near Vienna
form walls 35' high. Potential street tree.

There are several named cultivars including the dwarf 'Compactum', a
golden-leaved 'Postelense', and the variegated 'Pulveratum'.

Plant may be observed at: *Arboreta*—Bernheim Forest, Cary, Dawes,
Holden, Morton, Minnesota Landscape, National, Planting Fields, U. of
Washington, U. of Wisconsin-Madison; *Botanical Gardens*—Brooklyn,
Chicago, Denver, Missouri, Munich, Palmgarten, Royal/Kew,
Royal/Ontario; *Gardens*—Longwood.

M. DIRR

K. KOHOUT

A. BUSSEWITZ

Acer davidii Franchet. STRIPED-BARK MAPLE or CHINESE STRIPED-BARK MAPLE.
Aceraceae. USDA Zones 5–7. China. Introduced by Veitch 1879.

DESCRIPTION *Deciduous,* upright, slightly spreading tree, growing 2–3' a year to 30–50' at maturity. Casts medium shade.

Leaves: Glossy, green, slightly heart-shaped, unevenly toothed, 3–7" long, 1½–4" wide. Golden fall color with some orange.

Flowers: Inconspicuous, yellowish, on slender, pendent racemes 1½–2½" long.

Fruit: Glabrous; samaras 1¼" long, wings ¼" wide, almost horizontal spread.

Winter aspect: Beautiful striped bark year around.

CULTURE Grows in sun in clay, loam or sand in normal pH range; somewhat tolerant of wind, wet conditions, drought.

Disease and insect problems: Few.

Transplanting: Easy; root system shallow.

Propagation: By seed.

LANDSCAPE VALUE Widely known for its handsome striped bark. Bark on young growth is purplish-red to green, striped with white. Lovely fall yellow to purple foliage. Species easy to identify as leaves are unlobed. This tree should be on every list. It is not only beautiful but available, and becoming more so.

Other species closely resembling *A. davidii* are: *A. capillipes, A. grosseri, A. tegmentosum, A. forrestii,* all becoming available commercially. *A. pensylvanicum* is one of 'Snakebark' group, cv. 'George Forrest' recommended.

Plant may be observed at: *Arboreta*—Los Angeles, National, Strybing, U. of Washington; *Botanical Gardens*—British Columbia, Brooklyn, Huntington, New York, Palmgarten, Royal/Kew, Van Dusen; *Parks*—Golden Gate.

N. BREWSTER

N. BREWSTER

N. BREWSTER

Acer ginnala Maximowicz [*A. tataricum* var. *aidzuense* Franchet]. AMUR MAPLE.
Aceraceae. USDA Zones 3–8. China, Japan. Introduced 1860.

DESCRIPTION
Deciduous tree growing slowly to 15–20′ with equal spread; multi-stemmed, with rounded head. Casts dense shade.

Leaves: Opposite, simple, 1½–3″ long; 3-lobed, lobes ovate with middle the longest; doubly serrate; dark green above, light green below; excellent brilliant scarlet in fall.

Flowers: Panicles of very fragrant white-yellow flowers in spring.

Fruit: Samara, 1″ long; in some trees these samaras are red during the summer.

Winter aspect: Gray-brown bark; dense branching habit.

CULTURE
Needs sun for best fall color, but tolerates light shade. Adaptable to wide range of soils and pH ranges; however, performs best in moist, well-drained soil. Tolerates wind and drought.

Disease and insect problems: Relatively problem-free.

Transplanting: Easy.

Propagation: By seed, stratified at 70° for 1–2 months, followed by 41° for 4–5 months; by softwood cuttings in June in peat and perlite with mist.

LANDSCAPE VALUE
Lovely small specimen tree, good for patio or for mass plantings. Withstands heavy pruning and also can be used for screening as a hedge. Can be grown successfully as a container plant. Needs minimum maintenance. One of the few maples with fragrant flowers and one that will tolerate some shade. Moderately tolerant of urban stress, but its multi-stemmed character limits its use as a street tree.

Plant may be observed at: *Arboreta*—Arnold, Bernheim Forest, Cary, Minnesota Landscape, Morton, National, Planting Fields, U. of Washington, U. of Wisconsin; *Botanical Gardens*—Brooklyn, British Columbia, Chicago, Huntington, Missouri, Munich, Palmgarten, Royal/Kew, U. of Georgia, Van Dusen; *Parks*—Golden Gate.

M. DIRR

M. DIRR

N. BREWSTER

Acer griseum (Franchet) Pax. PAPERBARK MAPLE. *Aceraceae.* USDA Zones 5–7. Western China. Introduced 1901 by Arnold Arboretum.

DESCRIPTION **Deciduous**, rounded, spreading tree, growing slowly to 20–40' with 15–25' spread at maturity. Casts light shade.

Leaves: Trifoliate, soft green above, silvery beneath; terminal leaflet ovate-lanceolate, 1½–3″ long. Fall color bright red and orange.

Flowers: Inconspicuous; red flowers in drooping cymes developing into showy samaras with wings spreading at acute to right angles.

Fruit: Samara, pubescent, woody.

Winter aspect: Old bark on trunk and primary branches purple-brown; exfoliates in thin flakes to reveal cinnamon-orange bark beneath. Bark against the snow spectacular sight.

CULTURE Tolerates sun, shade and wind but not drought. Needs well-drained loam with pH range of 5.0–7.0. Not tolerant of environmental stresses.

Disease and insect problems: None serious.

Transplanting: Must be balled and burlapped; root system of medium depth.

Propagation: By seed, difficult since seeds are mostly sterile and germination is less than 5%. Cuttings may be rooted with a high concentration of indolebutyric acid.

LANDSCAPE VALUE Exquisite bark creates interest throughout the year. This is one of the most beautiful of small trees and one that "stays put." Vibrant fall color; the last of the trifoliate maples to color. Should be used as a focal point, especially in winter landscape. A good patio-sized tree, not messy, and maintenance free. Its only unfavorable aspects are its slow growth (an asset in small areas), and the difficulty in propagating it. A very unusual species of maple that merits wide use if it could be more easily obtained.

Plant may be observed at: *Arboreta*—Arnold, Bernheim Forest, Cary, Dawes, Morton, National, Planting Fields, U. of Washington, U. of Wisconsin-Madison; *Botanical Gardens*—Berry, British Columbia, Brooklyn, Chicago, New York, Missouri, Palmgarten, Royal/Kew, Van Dusen; *Gardens*—Callaway, Dixon, Longwood; *Parks*—Forest Parks-Ibaraki, Japan.

E. HASSELKUS

P. KINGSLEY

P. KINGSLEY

Acer miyabei Maximowicz [*A. shibatai* T. Nakai]. MIYABE MAPLE. *Aceraceae.* USDA Zones 5–7. Hokkaido, Japan. Introduced 1892 by C.S. Sargent.

DESCRIPTION
Deciduous tree growing moderately rapidly to 40–50'; round to loosely conical habit. Casts dense shade.

Leaves: 5-lobed, 4–6″ diam., lobes tapering to points that are blunt at tips; medium green to dark green, hairy on undersides; remain green into fall then rapidly develop golden yellow color that lasts for short time.

Flowers: Greenish-yellow, downy, in 10–15 flowered pyramidal clusters, each 2–3″ long; in spring.

Fruit: Samaras borne in pairs; slightly hairy; produced in great abundance. Fruit remains green until it falls.

Winter aspect: Dark gray bark with vertical scales; tendency to branch freely and fully; lower branches persist.

CULTURE
Grows in sun and shade; prefers moist, well-drained loamy soils with pH range of 6.0–7.4. May be stunted by soil compaction and may be sensitive to ozone. Moderately tolerant of drought.

Disease and insect problems: No significant problems.

Transplanting: Moderately easy; root system shallow.

Propagation: By seed, grafting, budding.

LANDSCAPE VALUE
Durable, long-lived, medium-sized tree with dense crown and exquisite foliage. More elegant than Norway Maple. Related to *A. campestre* but seems to be more showy and versatile. The many specimens at the Morton Arboretum show a variety of leaf shapes and growth forms. Selections for vigor and form should be made. Needs selective thinning of crown periodically to remove small limbs in center of crown. Discovery of this rare tree occurred accidentally when Professor C. S. Sargent of the Arnold Arboretum was waiting for a train in Yezo, Japan. He strolled into a small grove of trees on the border of a stream; there he found *A. miyabei* covered with fruit. Professor Sargent later obtained from these trees a supply of seeds for America and Europe.

Plant may be observed at: *Arboreta*—Arnold, Dawes, Minnesota Landscape, Morton, Spring Grove, U. of Washington, U. of Wisconsin-Madison; *Botanical Gardens*—British Columbia, Chicago, Royal/Kew; *Parks*—Forest Parks-Ibaraki, Japan.

E. HASSELKUS

M. DIRR

V. KOHOUT

Acer nikoense Miquel [*A. maximowiczianum* Miquel ex Koidzumi]. NIKKO MAPLE. *Aceraceae.* USDA Zones 5–7. Japan, Central China. Introduced 1881 by Veitch.

DESCRIPTION *Deciduous,* vase-shaped, round-headed tree; grows slowly to 20–30' (40–50' in wild); trunk 12–18" in diam.

Leaves: Opposite leaves 2–5", compound; three leaflets ovate-elliptic, oblong, hairy on hairy stalks. Bronze as emerging, green in summer; brilliant scarlet-red, yellow-red or purple in fall.

Flowers: Yellow, ½" diam., three together on drooping pedicels in May; appear before leaves.

Fruit: Samaras 1½–2" long, felted.

Winter aspect: Smooth, gray-brown bark.

CULTURE Grows in sun in loam or sand; prefers well-drained, slightly acid soil.

Disease and insect problems: Seemingly disease and pest-free.

Transplanting: Moderately easy.

Propagation: By seed; seed not always produced, takes two years for germination.

LANDSCAPE VALUE One of the very few maples with interesting vase shape; picturesque most seasons of the year. Extremely attractive, rich autumn color when leaves turn vivid red or yellow. A slow-growing tree, excellent choice for small property.

Plant may be observed at: *Arboreta*—Bernheim Forest, Dawes, Minnesota Landscape, Morton, National, U. of Washington, U. of Wisconsin-Madison; *Botanical Gardens*—British Columbia, Brooklyn, Missouri, Munich, Palmgarten, Royal/Kew; *Parks*—Forest Parks-Ibaraki, Japan.

N. BREWSTER

N. BREWSTER

P. KINGSLEY

Acer triflorum Komarov. THREE-FLOWER MAPLE. *Aceraceae.* USDA Zones 5–8. North China, Korea. Introduced 1923.

DESCRIPTION **Deciduous** tree with slow to moderate growth rate to 24′ high; rounded to oval dense crown. Casts moderate to dense shade.

Leaves: 1½–3½″ long, ½–1¼″ wide; leaves compound, trifoliate leaflets oblong-ovate, sometimes with coarse teeth; slightly covered with pale hairs, especially when young. Attractive orange to carmine fall color.

Flowers: Three flowers in a cluster, greenish-yellow, hairy; in spring.

Fruit: Large, thick, hairy samaras in pairs; wings 1–1¼″ long, ⅜–⅝″ wide.

Winter aspect: Bark is cinnamon-red, with finely patterned exfoliation, vertically peeling scales; somewhat thickly branched; scattered fruits persist.

CULTURE Grows in sun and shade; prefers loam and sand with pH range of 6.0 to 7.2. Intolerant of soil compaction and excessive wetness.

Disease and insect problems: None serious.

Transplanting: Moderately easy; root system shallow.

Propagation: Seed; cuttings; grafting is probably possible.

LANDSCAPE VALUE Valuable as a small tree that displays lovely oval form, very attractive bark and splendidly enduring fall color. At home in the shelter of larger trees.

Plant may be observed at: *Arboreta*—Cary, Dawes, Holden, Minnesota Landscape, Morton, U. of Washington, U. of Wisconsin-Madison; *Botanical Gardens*—British Columbia, Chicago, Missouri.

P. KINGSLEY

A. BUSSEWITZ

P. KINGSLEY

Aesculus x carnea Hayne 'Briotii' [*A. x rubicunda* Loiseleur-Deslongchamps] (*A. hippocastanum* L. × *A. pavia* L.). RED HORSECHESTNUT. *Hippocastanaceae.* USDA Zones 5–8. Parent: Greece, Albania. Introduced from seed grown at Trianon, France, 1858.

DESCRIPTION   *Deciduous* tree growing at medium rate to 30–50′, sometimes to 60–80′; pyramidal when young, becoming round-headed. Casts dense shade.

Leaves: Palmately compound with 5 or 7 leaflets; similar to common Horsechestnut but smaller (10″ long) and darker green; no fall color.

Flowers: Large, bright scarlet, in panicles 8″ long, 3–4″ wide; spring blooms.

Fruit: Capsules 1½″ dia., globose and slightly prickly; glossy brown nuts.

Winter aspect: Gray-brown bark; winter buds slightly resinous.

CULTURE   Grows in full sun or light shade; prefers moist, well-drained soil with pH no higher than 6.5. More drought-tolerant than *A. hippocastanum;* tolerates some wind.

Disease and insect problems: Leaf-scorch, so prevalent on *A. hippocastanum,* far less serious on this tree.

Transplanting: Balled and burlapped.

Propagation: Comes true to type from seed.

LANDSCAPE VALUE   Spectacular ornamental. Valued for its dark green foliage, which remains into fall, as it is less susceptible to leaf-scorch than the common Horsechestnut. Its scarlet flowers create a brilliant display in spring. One of the most popular trees in England. This species is the most ornamental of the *Aesculus* genus.

Cultivar 'O'Neil's Red' is a rare double-flowered form, available at Weston Nurseries, Hopkinton, Mass.

Plant may be observed at: *Arboreta*—Arnold, Bernheim Forest, Holden, National, Planting Fields, U. of Washington; *Botanical Gardens*—Chicago, Missouri, New York, Palmgarten; *Gardens*—Winterthur; *Parks*—Golden Gate.

M. DIRR

M. DIRR

E. HASSELKUS

Aesculus flava Aiton (*A. octandra* H. Marshall). YELLOW BUCKEYE, SWEET
BUCKEYE. *Hippocastanaceae.* USDA Zones 4–8. Pennsylvania to Tennessee
and northern Georgia, west to Ohio and Illinois and Texas. Introduced
1764.

DESCRIPTION   *Deciduous* tree growing to 60–75 feet; may grow to over 100'; upright
habit; oval to slightly spreading crown. Casts dense shade.

Leaves: Palmately compound, 5 leaflets 8–9" long, obovate-oblong to
elliptic-oblong, finely toothed; downy on veins above, completely downy
beneath; clear yellow in fall.

Flowers: Yellow, borne on erect panicles 5–7" long, 2–3" wide, each
flower with a bell-shaped calyx and 4 petals; early spring blooms.

Fruit: Smooth, leathery capsule, 2–2½" long, round-oblique; contains 1
or 2 shiny brown seeds.

Winter aspect: Gray-brown bark with plates and scales on older trees;
straight, thick trunk, hanging branches.

CULTURE   Grows in sun but tolerant of shade from other large trees; prefers moist,
well-drained, deep humus. The best growth occurs along stream banks.

Disease and insect problems: Not as troubled by foliar disease as many
Aesculus.

Transplanting: Balled and burlapped.

Propagation: By seed, collected as soon as capsules show sign of
dehiscence.

LANDSCAPE
VALUE   An attractive specimen valued for many landscape sites. Its habit, foliage
and beautiful flowers, which open when the leaves are half grown, create
a handsome ornamental shade tree. Seedlings develop rapidly, and the
tree is moderately long-lived, reaching maturity in 60–80 years.

Plant may be observed at: *Arboreta*—Dawes, Holden, National, Spring
Grove, U. of Washington, U. of Wisconsin-Madison; *Botanical Gardens*—
Brooklyn, Royal/Kew, U. of Georgia.

E. HASSELKUS

E. HASSELKUS

M. DIRR

Alectryon excelsus J. Gaertner. TITOKI. *Sapindaceae.* USDA Zone 10. New Zealand, Australia, Pacific Islands and Hawaii. Known in San Francisco Bay area since Panama-Pacific Exhibition, 1915.

DESCRIPTION *Evergreen* tree growing at slow to moderate rate to 20–40', with upright habit. Casts dense shade.

Leaves: Alternate, pinnate, 8–10″ long, 4–6 pairs of glossy leaflets each 2–4″ long, ovate-lanceolate to ovate-oblong, medium green.

Flowers: Inconspicuous blooms in May-June on terminal panicles.

Fruit: Brilliant red fruits enclosed in splitting capsule covered with reddish hairs.

Winter aspect: Nearly black bark.

CULTURE Grows in sun and shade in loam and sand. Tolerates acid soils and wind, including salt-laden wind. Can withstand some drought.

Disease and insect problems: None.

Transplanting: Balled and burlapped.

Propagation: By seed and cuttings.

LANDSCAPE VALUE An attractive tree with excellent adaptation to coastal climates and soils. May be used as a specimen or in mass plantings. Potential street tree for coastal cities. Wood used for cabinetry.

Plant may be observed at: *Arboreta*—Strybing; *Parks*—Golden Gate.

P.K. THOMPSON

P.K. THOMPSON

P.K. THOMPSON

Alnus glutinosa (L.) J. Gaertner [*A. Communis* Mirbel; *A. rotundifolia* P. Miller; *A. vulgaris* Persoon]. BLACK ALDER, EUROPEAN ALDER. *Betulaceae.* USDA Zones 4–7. Introduced 1700s.

DESCRIPTION   *Deciduous* tree growing at a fast rate to 40–70′ with 20–40′ spread; can grow to 100′; young trees have pyramidal habit, often developing a rounded crown later.

Leaves: Alternate, 2–4½″ long, 1–3″ wide, with coarse teeth along margin; dark green, glabrous above, paler and finely hairy beneath; elliptic or nearly orbicular.

Flowers: Monoecious; male flowers red-brown, 2–4″ long catkins; female flowers egg-shaped strobile with purple cast; early spring blooms.

Fruit: Egg-shaped, ⅓–⅔″ long, clustered and brown in fall and winter.

Winter aspect: Gray-green-brown bark when young, maturing to lightly furrowed, dark brown bark; often multi-stemmed; persistent fruit and catkins.

CULTURE   Grows in sun and partial shade; prefers moist soils but will grow in dry and poor soils with a wide pH range. Species growing in submerged conditions have been documented.

Disease and insect problems: Powdery mildew rarely serious; cankers, leaf miner, tent caterpillars can be a problem.

Transplanting: Easy.

Propagation: By seed, with stratification; however, there is some indication that fresh seed will germinate without treatment. Cultivars usually grafted onto the species.

LANDSCAPE VALUE   Alders have an unusual tolerance of wet conditions and the ability to fix atmospheric nitrogen with the help of nitrogen-fixing bacteria. Consequently this tree is readily adaptable; it grows rapidly in poorly-drained, dry and infertile soils, and thus is an excellent candidate for urban conditions. The catkins are fascinating and attractive and add to the tree's winter interest, especially when the male catkins open in late winter and early spring. In England the timber has been used in the manufacture of clogs, commonly used in Lancashire mill towns.

Cultivars include:
   'Aurea'—Golden yellow leaves; introduced 1865
   'Imperialis'—Deeply and pinnately lobed
   'Laciniata'—Similar to 'Imperialis' but leaves not so deeply lobed, and lobes not toothed; vigorous grower, 50–70′ high. It is thought that all plants of the Cut-leaf Alder descend from one grown in a garden near St. Germain.

Plant may be observed at: *Arboreta*—Cary, Dawes, Morton, National, U. of Washington, U. of Wisconsin-Madison; *Botanical Gardens*—Brooklyn, Munich, Royal/Kew, Van Dusen.

N. BREWSTER

N. BREWSTER

E.R. HASSELKUS

Amelanchier x grandiflora Redher [*A. arborea* (Michaux f.) Fernald x *A. laevis* Wiegand] APPLE SERVICEBERRY. *Rosaceae.* USDA Zones 4–7. U.S.A. Introduced 1870.

DESCRIPTION **Deciduous** tree, usually multi-trunked; grows at medium rate to 25′ high. Casts light shade.

Leaves: Simple; young leaves bronze or purple with silky hairs; orange to red in fall.

Flowers: Large, white, borne in drooping clusters, pink in bud; late April to early May in Midwest.

Fruit: June-July fruiting; edible, large berries, red to purple.

Winter aspect: Smooth gray bark with vertical striations; horizontal branching habit.

CULTURE Grows in sun and partial shade; adaptable to wide variety of soils in pH range from 4.0–8.0. Tolerates drought but not wind; branches brittle.

Disease and insect problems: Fire blight under unusual conditions (high nitrogen or excessive pruning).

Transplanting: Slow to respond following transplant.

Propagation: By cuttings, grafting or micropropagation.

LANDSCAPE VALUE Fine specimen with year-round interest. Lovely, large white flowers in spring before foliage. Edible fruit attractive to birds. Beautiful fall color, handsome gray bark. Best of the *Amelanchiers* as tree form; more wide-spreading than other serviceberries and usually less suckering.

Cultivars currently being introduced include 'Robin Hill', pink in bud, and 'Rubescens', with purplish-pink buds and flowers tinged with pink.

Plant may be observed at: *Arboreta*—Minnesota Landscape, Morton, U. of Wisconsin; *Botanical Gardens*—Chicago, U. of Georgia; *Gardens*—Callaway, Longwood, Winterthur.

E. HASSELKUS

E. HASSELKUS

W. THOMAS

Arbutus unedo L. STRAWBERRY TREE. *Ericaceae.* USDA Zones 8–9. Southern Europe, Ireland. Introduced 1789.

DESCRIPTION

Broadleaved evergreen growing at moderate rate to 15–30', occasionally to 40'. Bushy, widespread habit. Casts dense shade.

Leaves: Alternate, 2–4" long, ¾" wide, oval to obovate, serrate, shining; dark green and leathery.

Flowers: White to pink opalescent, small, bell-shaped flowers in panicles 2" long.

Fruit: Globose, ¾" red fruit with rough surface; strawberry-like; appears at same time as blossoms in autumn.

Winter aspect: Rich red-brown, fibrous, shaggy bark; shrubby habit; persistent fruit and leaves.

CULTURE

Withstands sun and shade. Grows well in limestone soils; also flourishes in peaty rhododendron soil. Will withstand some drought.

Disease and insect problems: Few.

Transplanting: Difficult except when young.

Propagation: By seed or layering.

LANDSCAPE VALUE

Handsome, adaptable evergreen with beautiful flowers and colorful fruit at a welcome time of year. Fruit is attractive to birds. Trunk has striking color at maturity. May be planted as a specimen tree or effective as a hedge. Susceptible to cold damage below 15°F. Needs cross fertilization to fruit.

Plant may be observed at: *Arboreta*—Los Angeles, Planting Fields, Strybing, U. of Washington; *Botanical Gardens*—Brooklyn, Huntington, Munich, Palmgarten, Royal/Kew; *Gardens*—Filoli; *Parks*—Golden Gate.

A. MacBRIDE

NORFOLK BOTANIC GARDEN

J.C. RAULSTON

Asimina triloba (L.) Dunal. PAWPAW. *Annonaceae.* USDA Zones 3–8. U.S.A.: New York to Florida, west to Nebraska and Texas. Introduced 1736 by Peter Collinson.

DESCRIPTION
Deciduous tree has moderate growth rate to 15–30' high, occasionally to 40'; spreading, upright branches form dense pyramidal shape. Casts light to dense shade.

Leaves: Alternate, 6–12" narrowly obovate leaves; medium green in summer, yellow in fall; abscissing quickly.

Flowers: 2" solitary, nodding, thick-petaled, purple flowers produced singly on wood of previous year; blooms before leaves.

Fruit: 1–3" ellipsoid, yellowish, edible fruit in late summer.

Winter aspect: Bark dark brown, rough with age; dense habit in sun, open in shade.

CULTURE
Performs well in full sun or heavy shade. Prefers fertile, moist, slightly acid soil; tolerant of soggy soil.

Disease and insect problems: None serious.

Transplanting: Difficult because of wide root system; should be moved balled and burlapped as small tree (under 6').

Propagation: By seed, root cutting, layering.

LANDSCAPE
VALUE
Neglected American native tree good for naturalizing in shaded and damp areas. Recent nutritional evaluation indicates that the delicious PawPaw fruit, unusually low in moisture content, is higher in unsaturated fats, proteins and carbohydrates than apples, peaches and grapes; it also contains high levels of amino acids, Vitamin A and C, potassium, phosphorus, magnesium, sulfur and iron. In addition to its value as a fruit tree, the PawPaw is an attractive tree exhibiting handsome foliage, interesting flowers. It is almost pest and disease free and is adaptable to a wide range of growing conditions. Its landscape value is enhanced when used in a massed planting; also a perfect tree for planting on a raised elevation.

Plant may be observed at: *Arboreta*—Bernheim Forest, Dawes, Holden, Morton, National; *Botanical Gardens*—Birmingham, Chicago, Houston, Missouri, Munich, Palmgarten, San Antonio.

E.R. HASSELKUS

E.R. HASSELKUS

A. BUSSEWITZ

Bauhinia forficata Link [*B. candicans* Bentham]. WHITE ORCHID. *Leguminosae.* USDA
Zones 9–10. Peru, Argentina, Brazil. Introduced into the Glasgow Botanic
Garden 1837.

DESCRIPTION
Evergreen to deciduous tree with erect habit, growing to 20–30' at
maturity.

Leaves: Alternate, deep green above, glaucous beneath; to 4" long, 2½–3"
wide; distinctive character, each divided into two kidney-shaped lobes by
a cleft in center; lobes pointed.

Flowers: Creamy white flowers to 3" wide with narrow petals. Blooming
period spring and through summer.

Fruit: Dark brown flat pod.

Winter aspect: Twisting trunk with picturesque, angled branches, pendent
with spines; sharp thorns at branch joints.

CULTURE
Needs sun, warmth and moderate water; tolerates some shade and
drought.

Disease and insect problems: No known problems.

Transplanting: Balled and burlapped.

Propagation: By seed, suckers, layering, cuttings with bottom heat.

LANDSCAPE
VALUE
The hardiest of the *Bauhinias.* A handsome and flamboyant tree, good for
canopy patio specimen. The twisted, leaning trunk and angled branches
create picturesque and architectural interest at all seasons. The name
commemorates two famous botanists of the 16th century, John and
Casper Bauhin. They worked together so closely that the tree's distinctive
characteristic of twin leaflets was thought to symbolize their work.

Plant may be observed at: *Arboreta*—Los Angeles; *Botanical Gardens*—
Houston, Huntington, San Antonio.

D. KENT

D. KENT

P.K. THOMPSON

Betula nigra L. [*B. rubra* F. Michaux]. RIVER BIRCH. *Betulaceae.* USDA Zones 5–9. Eastern and Central U.S. Introduced by Peter Collinson in 1736.

DESCRIPTION

Deciduous tree growing rapidly to 90', pyramidal when young, oval at maturity. Slender branches in old age form a narrow irregular picturesque crown. Trunk sometimes 5' in diameter, or often divided 15–20' above ground into two or three slightly diverging limbs. Casts light shade.

Leaves: Simple, alternate, oval to diamond-shaped, 1½–3" long, 1–2" wide, glossy dark green above, glaucous beneath. Fall color yellow.

Flowers: Inconspicuous female catkins; male catkins 2–3" long.

Fruit: ripening in May or June into 1½" long cylindrical catkins, ½" thick.

Winter aspect: Bark on young stems and large branches thin, lustrous, light reddish brown or silvery gray, exfoliating into persistent thin papery scales which expose tan tints of inner layers, becoming at base of old trunks dark red-brown, deeply furrowed and scaled.

CULTURE

Grows in sun; prefers most sandy soil in pH range of 6.5–7.0, but tolerates well-drained loam. Tolerance of environmental stress undetermined.

Disease and insect problems: Subject to birch leaf miner but has shown resistance to bronze birch borer. It is subject to iron necrosis in heavy alkaline soils and is a short-lived tree under stressful conditions.

Transplanting: Reasonably easy; shallow root system.

Propagation: By both seeds and cuttings.

LANDSCAPE VALUE

Can be trained as single- or multi-stemmed tree. A graceful tree, remarkable for its colorful and ragged bark, it is the only semiaquatic species of *Betulaceae,* the only species ripening its seeds in early summer and the only birch of the warm regions of Florida, Louisiana, and Texas. Grows on banks of streams, ponds and swamps in deep rich soil often inundated for weeks at a time. Used for erosion control. It is one of the finest trees for planting in damp ground. An excellent selection.

Plant may be observed at: *Arboreta*—Arnold, Dawes, Bernheim Forest, Holden, Los Angeles, Minnesota Landscape, Morton, National, U. of Washington; *Botanical Gardens*—Atlanta, Birmingham, Chicago, Missouri, Munich, New York, Palmgarten, Royal/Kew, U. of Georgia; *Gardens*—Brookgreen, Callaway, Longwood.

M. DIRR

M. DIRR   A. BUSSEWITZ

Betula platyphylla japonica Sukachev 'Whitespire' [*B. latifolia* Komarov, *B. mandshurica* (Regel) Nakai]. WHITESPIRE JAPANESE WHITE BIRCH. *Betulaceae.* USDA Zones 4–7. Japan, Yatsugatake Mountains. Introduced 1983 by Dr. E. Hasselkus, University of Wisconsin, Madison. Seedlings from U.S. Plant Introduction Station in 1957 collected by Dr. John Creech as P.I. 235128.

DESCRIPTION *Deciduous* tree with slender, pyramidal form, growing moderately fast to 40′ high with spread of 15′.

Leaves: 1½–3″, glossy green, arrowhead shape, fine-textured; clear yellow in autumn.

Flowers: Inconspicuous; catkins provide textured effect when present.

Fruit: Conelets ripen late August.

Winter aspect: Non-exfoliating, chalky white bark, marked with black triangles at bases of lateral branches.

CULTURE Tolerates sun, high temperature, some wind and drought, but not wet conditions; prefers loam and sandy soils.

Disease and insect problems: Has proven to be most borer-resistant white-barked birch under evaluation in Longenecker Horticultural Gardens of University of Wisconsin Arboretum, Madison. Three 26-year-old trees have remained free of bronze birch borer on droughty site where plants of *B. pendula, B. populifolia, B. pubescens, B. utilis* and other seed strains of *B. platyphylla japonica* have become infested with borers. Leaf miner easy to control with Disyston.

Transplanting: Easy, balled and burlapped in spring.

Propagation: By seed from isolated parent trees, or vegetatively; in future through micropropagation.

LANDSCAPE VALUE Graceful and uniform in habit; attractive foliage, distinctive white bark. A birch that will tolerate extremes of temperature (−30° to 120°F). Most importantly, a birch that has proven resistant to prevalent bronze birch borer. In 1957 Dr. John Creech collected seed from a single tree in a native stand in the Yatsugatake mountain range, Nagano Prefecture, Japan. Seed has been distributed annually to several nurseries for seven years; consequently, liners have been widely distributed throughout the country. Having been propagated from seed, there is no assurance that these seedling progeny are not hybrids; however, relative isolation of parent trees makes this unlikely. Vegetative propagation of Whitespire birch through micropropagation could assure its genetic purity.

Plant may be observed at: *Arboreta*—U. of Wisconsin-Madison; *Botanical Gardens*—Chicago, Denver, Munich.

E. HASSELKUS

E. HASSELKUS

E. HASSELKUS

Calocedrus decurrens (J. Torrey)Florin [*Heyderia decurrens* (J. Torrey) C. Koch; *Libocedrus decurrens* J. Torrey]. INCENSE CEDAR. *Cupressaceae.* USDA Zones 6–10. U.S.A.: western Oregon, California, western Nevada. Introduced 1853.

DESCRIPTION
Evergreen conifer with conical head of spreading branches; may grow slowly to 150′ in wild; most cultivated trees are cv. 'Columnaris', narrowly columnar, 30–50′ high and 8–10′ wide at maturity. Branches to the ground; shade beneath is dense, but dappled in old age.

Leaves: Tiny oblong-obovate scales pressed tightly to branches, free at apex; shiny, rich, dark green on green twigs, hold color year-round. When crushed produce an aromatic scent.

Flowers: Inconspicuous, monoecious.

Fruit: Cylindric, to 1″ long, urn-shaped, on short flattened branches.

Winter aspect: Young stems gray-green, tinged with red; old trunks cinnamon-red, deeply fissured. Cones persistent through winter. Branching habit dense, resembling Arborvitae.

CULTURE
Prefers full sun and moist, well-drained fertile loam in pH range of 6.0–7.0. Must have humidity; does not tolerate dry air, wind or smog, or wet conditions. Tolerates salt spray (not road salt), drought and heat.

Disease and insect problems: Only serious problem is heart rot caused by *Polyporus amarus;* other less serious ones are a *Gymnosporangium* rust and a leafy mistletoe.

Transplanting: Easy; root system shallow.

Propagation: By seed, also by cuttings.

LANDSCAPE VALUE
Excellent as a lawn specimen of formal habit; a fine screening and background tree, also for planting in groves in large formal areas. Tolerates shearing for hedges or topiary. While strictly a tree for good soil and humid, quiet air, this is worth growing for its good color and lacy texture. Although growth is slow, trees may live 500 to 1,000 years. Seeds are a food source for various birds. The wood is durable and lightweight and is used commercially for interiors, doors and fences.

There are seven recorded cultivars, mostly quite dwarf and beautiful: one is cv. 'Aureovariegata', a yellow variegated form, not too dwarf, with sprays of yellow leaves occurring irregularly.

Trees usually grow with pine and fir and are not often found in pure stands.

Plant may be observed at: *Arboreta*—Bernheim Forest, Los Angeles, National, Planting Fields, Strybing, U. of Washington; *Botanical Gardens*—British Columbia, Huntington, New York, Palmgarten, Royal/Kew, U. of Georgia, Van Dusen; *Gardens*—Longwood; *Parks*—Golden Gate.

M. DIRR

J. RAULSTON

W. THOMAS

Carpinus betulus L. EUROPEAN HORNBEAM. *Betulaceae.* USDA Zones 5–7. Europe and Iran. Introduced 18th century.

DESCRIPTION **Deciduous** tree growing 10' in 10 years to 40–60' high at maturity; pyramidal in youth, oval-rounded at maturity.

Leaves: 1½–3½" long, 1–2" wide, oval, simple, doubly serrate; dark green in summer, yellow in fall.

Flowers: Monoecious; male 1½" catkin, female 1½–3" with conspicuous 3-lobed bracts; in spring.

Fruit: Nut, ¼" long, borne at base of flower bract.

Winter aspect: Smooth gray, fluted bark; muscular trunk; slender branches around main leader.

CULTURE Grows best in sun but will tolerate light shade; tolerates clay and loam in wide pH range. Withstands wind and is somewhat tolerant of environmental stress.

Disease and insect problems: None serious.

Transplanting: Small trees (8–10'), balled and burlapped in spring.

Propagation: By seed stratified 28 days at 68°F, followed by 87–98 days at 41°F in sand and peat.

LANDSCAPE VALUE Handsome tree of great distinction; may be used as a single specimen tree or as a screen. Withstands shearing and heavy pruning. Thus, it is often used as a hedge or pleached allée. Nearly all of the hedges in the R.H.S. Garden at Wisley are of Hornbeam. Beautiful, clean, rich green summer foliage since leaves are highly resistant to insect and disease damage. Often described as the hardiest, heaviest and toughest of woods; wood is valued for intricate parts of the pianoforte.

Cultivars:
    'Asplenifolia'—leaves deeply cut
    'Columnaris'—densely branched, narrowly columnar with a central
                trunk; egg-shaped when mature
    'Fastigiata'—upright habit, faster growing than 'Columnaris'
    'Globosa'—rounded and globose in habit; no central trunk.

Related species *Carpinus japonica*—excellent specimen tree with large spreading head, often multi-trunked; branches loaded with many bright bracts in fall.

Plant may be observed at: *Arboreta*—Arnold, Bernheim Forest, Dawes, Minnesota Landscape, Morton, Planting Fields, U. of Washington, U. of Wisconsin-Madison; *Botanical Gardens*—Brooklyn, Munich, New York, Royal/Kew; *Gardens*—Longwood.

M. DIRR

A. BUSSEWITZ

M. DIRR

Carpinus caroliniana T. Walter [*C. americana* A. Michaux]. AMERICAN HORNBEAM. *Betulaceae*. USDA Zones 3-9. U.S.A.; east Texas to Oklahoma and Florida, north to New England and west to Illinois. Cultivated since 1812.

DESCRIPTION **Deciduous** tree; grows slowly to 35' in height, with a spreading, rounded crown and crooked growth. Casts medium shade.

Leaves: Simple, alternate, to 2–5" long and wedge-shaped, similar to elm leaves; pointed and serrated; 10–14 pairs of veins; appear in groups of 3. Deep green in summer; fall color varies considerably from bright yellow to orange and scarlet.

Flowers: Insignificant green catkins to 4" long, blooming in April-June; staminate and pistillate flowers separate but on same tree.

Fruit: August-October; ⅓" nutlet attached to 3-lobed bracts; many together to form loose cluster.

Winter aspect: Trunk fluted with irregular ridges extending vertically on bole. Bark smooth, blue-gray in color, sometimes blotched. Branching habit irregular and horizontal.

CULTURE Grows in sun or shade. Does well in heavy shade as understory tree in rich woods and on bottom lands. Tolerates wet conditions usually found along streams and on low ground, usually in shade of larger trees. Prefers rich, moist, slightly acid soil, but will adapt to clay or loam soils. Does not like compacted soils and will not tolerate grade changes or land fill.

Disease and insect problems: None serious.

Transplanting: Difficult after second year; plant balled and burlapped or in container in the spring.

Propagation: By seed, slightly green and planted in August in rich, moist, loamy soil.

LANDSCAPE VALUE Handsome specimen tree, especially in naturalized landscape. An excellent understory tree, long-lived, with spreading root system. Its interesting architectural shape is attractive feature of the winter landscape. Will tolerate periodic flooding. Known for its very hard wood, which is used for mallets, handles, golf clubs and fuel. Seed eaten by many species of birds. Also called Blue Beech, Ironwood, Musclewood, and Water Beech.

Plant may be observed at: *Arboreta*—Arnold, Bernheim Forest, Dawes, Minnesota Landscape, Planting Fields, U. of Washington, U. of Wisconsin; *Botanical Gardens*—Birmingham, British Columbia, Brooklyn, Chicago, New York, Palmgarten, Royal/Kew, Royal/Ontario, U. of Georgia; *Gardens*—Brookgreen, Callaway, Filoli, Longwood, Winterthur.

J. RAULSTON

E. HASSELKUS

HOLDEN ARB.

Carya ovata (P. Miller) K. Koch. [C. alba Nuttall] SHAGBARK HICKORY. *Juglandaceae.*
USDA Zones 4–9. Quebec to Minnesota, south to Georgia and Texas.
Cult. 1629.

DESCRIPTION *Deciduous* tree of narrow, upright, irregular habit. Rate of growth slow,
60–80' to possible 120' at maturity. Casts medium shade.

Leaves: Alternate, pinnately compound, 5 elliptical leaflets to 6" long,
deep yellow-green, all long-pointed and toothed; glabrous above, downy
beneath when young, glabrous when mature. Leaflets vary in size; young
tree terminal leaflet may be 12" long and 5" wide. Fall foliage warm
yellow and golden-brown.

Flowers: Without petals, males in pendulous catkins from leaf axils,
females in terminal spikes.

Fruit: A drupe with edible nut enclosed in thick green husk that splits into
4 valves. Nut, white and four-angled.

Winter aspect: Distinctive gray bark, flaking in loose plates, shaggy.
Branchlets rich red-brown.

CULTURE A native woodland tree; grows well in full sun. Adaptable to clay soils;
prefers rich, well-drained loam.

Disease and insect problems: Subject to hickory bark beetle, canker worm,
gall aphid, cigar casebearer, borer, leaf spot, witches broom, powdery
mildew, crown gall.

Transplanting: Difficult because of large, deep tap root; best results up to
2" caliper.

Propagation: By seed, root sprouts, or special varieties by grafting.

LANDSCAPE
VALUE Second to Pecan, Shagbark Hickory is the most popular of nut trees. Good
winter interest deriving from picturesque bark and open branching habit.
Best ornamental hickory for shade, specimen, naturalizing, or park
planting.

Plant may be observed at: *Arboreta*—Arnold, Bernheim Forest, Cary,
Holden, Minnesota Landscape, Morton, Planting Fields, U. of Wisconsin-
Madison; *Botanical Gardens*—Birmingham, Chicago, Missouri, Munich,
New York, Palmgarten, Royal/Kew, Royal/Ontario, U. of Georgia;
Gardens—Longwood, Winterthur.

E. HASSELKUS

J. POOR

E. HASSELKUS

Cedrus atlantica (Endlicher) G. Manetti ex Carrier 'Glauca' [*C. libani, subsp. atlantica* (Endlicher) Franco]. BLUE ATLAS CEDAR. *Pinaceae.* USDA Zones 6–9. Algeria, Morocco. Introduced 1840.

DESCRIPTION *Evergreen conifer* growing rapidly when young, then slowly to 60–100' with up to 40' spread. When young characterized by stiff habit and erect leader; widely pyramidal with flat-topped habit as it matures. Casts dense shade.

Leaves: Narrow, needle-like, green to silvery-blue, in spirals on terminal shoots and borne in rosettes on the numerous spur-like side growths; needles ½–1" long and curved toward their tips; young shoots downy.

Flowers: Monoecious male cones shed yellow pollen in fall; female in stout, erect cones.

Fruit: Cones 2–3" long, 1½–2" wide, barrel-shaped, erect, on upper side of branch, maturing in 2 years; winged seeds.

Winter aspect: Bark gray, smooth and shiny for first 25 years, then cracks to form scales; stiff, horizontally spreading branches.

CULTURE Grows in sun and partial shade. Prefers moist loam but will grow in dry, clay or sandy soils. Does not tolerate wind or wet conditions but tolerates drought when established. Resistant to air and exhaust pollution. Withstands smoke better than *C. deodara* or *C. libani.*

Disease and insect problems: Tip blight.

Transplanting: Difficult; move balled and burlapped.

Propagation: By seed sown when ripe; stratify 2–3 weeks for best germination. When grown from seed there is a great variation in color. By grafting.

LANDSCAPE VALUE An exceptional and stately lawn specimen, effective for its striking silver-blue leaves. If planted in fertile soil, it needs little attention. The lower branches are retained throughout its life. Timber has strong scent which repels insects. Wood is excellent for carpentry. Needs large areas for full development and should not be crowded. Similar to *C. libani,* but more open in form and young shoots always downy.

Plant may be observed at: *Arboreta*—National; *Botanical Gardens*—Royal/Kew, U. of Georgia.

N. BREWSTER

N. BREWSTER   W. THOMAS

Cedrus deodara (D. Don) G. Don. DEODAR CEDAR. *Pinaceae.* USDA Zones 7–9. Himalayas, East Afghanistan to Garwahl. Introduced 1831 by The Hon. Leslie Melville.

DESCRIPTION   *Evergreen conifer* growing at a fast rate to 50–70′ high; can grow to 250′ in wild, with spread of 150′; broadly pyramidal habit.

Leaves: Needles 1–1½″ long, clustered on short lateral spurs, sharply pointed, dark green and glaucous.

Flowers: Monoecious; male cones dense, 2–3″ long, ½″ wide; female borne in stout erect cones.

Fruit: Cones 4–5″ long, approximately 2″ wide, broadly egg-shaped with blue cast, turning red-brown.

Winter aspect: Distinctive evergreen in the winter landscape; branchlets pendulous and graceful; persistent fruit and leaves.

CULTURE   Prefers a sunny location with well-drained soil; tolerates drought but needs some protection from strong winds.

Disease and insect problems: None serious.

Transplanting: Easy, if root-pruned.

Propagation: By seed or cuttings.

LANDSCAPE VALUE   Graceful evergreen specimen with distinctive arching and drooping branches. Distinguished from other cedars because of its longer needles and graceful, pendulous habit. An important timber tree in India, where the wood is also used for incense.

Cultivars:
   C. deodara 'Kashmir'—cv. of interest because of its hardiness and its lovely silvery blue-green cast
   C. deodara 'Shalimar'—introduced by the Arnold Arboretum; exhibits excellent lustrous green foliage and is the hardiest cultivar

Plant may be observed at: *Arboreta*—Planting Fields, National, Strybing, U. of Washington; *Botanical Gardens*—British Columbia, Brooklyn, Palmgarten, Royal/Kew, U. of Georgia, Van Dusen; *Gardens*—Callaway, Filoli, Longwood; *Parks*—Golden Gate, Forest Parks-Ibaraki, Japan.

M. DIRR

M. DIRR

N. BREWSTER

Cercidiphyllum japonicum Siebold & Zuccarini ex J. Hoffman & H. Schultes.
KATSURA TREE. *Cercidiphyllaceae.* USDA Zones 5–8. Temperate East
Asia, Japan, China. Introduced 1865.

DESCRIPTION *Deciduous* tree, usually with several trunks. Spread is variable: staminate tree is more upright and pistillate is more spreading (sexes are separate). Growth is medium to fast to mature height of 60–100′. Casts medium shade.

Leaves: Orbicular to ovate, 2–4″ long and shaped like those of *Cercis* (Redbud); hence its generic name. Purple-bronze in spring when unfolding; in summer glabrous dark green above and glaucescent blue-green beneath; in fall clear yellow sometimes touched with scarlet. Foliage is open and loose, allowing free air circulation.

Flowers: Male and female on separate trees in spring before leaves emerge, in follicles about ¾″ long. Female flower has green fringed sepals and 3–5 red styles ¼″ long. Male has 15–20 red stamens ⅓″ long.

Fruit: Small dry capsules ½–¾″ are formed on pistillate trees in summer, persist through winter, and are shed in early spring.

Winter aspect: Bark smooth when young, shaggy in maturity. Fruit capsules on pistillate trees persistent.

CULTURE Grows in sun or shade; prefers rich, moist soil, slightly acid. Tolerant of wind but not of drought; needs supplemental watering during hot dry periods.

Disease and insect problems: None serious; some sun scald. Even canker worms and gypsy moth caterpillars leave it alone.

Transplanting: Balled and burlapped, or in early spring when container-grown.

Propagation: By seed, softwood cuttings, and layering.

LANDSCAPE VALUE A handsome tree of great distinction, very hardy, particularly valued for unusual multiple trunks and graceful leaves on petioles 1¼″ long. A fine specimen for large areas; parks or arboreta, and if grown as a single trunk is a possible street tree. Excellent for residential properties, golf courses, commercial areas, should be used more than it is. Its timber is straight grained and highly valued, used for general construction in Japan. Its only unfavorable characteristic is that if grown with several main trunks it can develop tremendous breadth and be subject to breaking with age.

This has been termed the largest deciduous tree of China. Var. *sinense* is the Chinese form, almost indistinguishable from the species except that it is taller and usually confined to a single trunk.

Plant may be observed at: *Arboreta*—Arnold, Bayard Cutting, Bernheim Forest, Cary, Holden, Los Angeles, Morton, National, Planting Fields, Spring Grove, U. of Wisconsin-Madison; *Botanical Gardens*—Berry, British Columbia, Brooklyn, Chicago, Huntington, Missouri, Munich, Palmgarten, Royal/Kew, U. of Georgia, Van Dusen; *Gardens*—Filoli, Longwood; *Parks*—Forest Parks-Ibaraki, Japan.

E. HASSELKUS

P. KINGSLEY

P. KINGSLEY

Cercis canadensis f. alba Rehder. WHITE REDBUD. *Leguminosae.* USDA Zones 4–9. Native U.S.A.

DESCRIPTION
Deciduous tree growing at medium rate (7–10′ in 6 years) to 20–30′ high with 25–35′ spread; spreading, rounded crown.

Leaves: Alternate, simple, 4″ across, broadly ovate to orbicular, cordate basally; lustrous green in summer; fall color yellow.

Flowers: White flowers about ½″ long, borne in clusters of 4–8 along bare shoots 1 year old or older, in spring; flowers often borne on bare trunks.

Flowers: Fall legumes 2–3″ long; persistent.

Winter aspect: Black to brownish bark; gracefully ascending habit; persistent pods.

CULTURE
Grows in sun and shade in moist loam in a wide pH range. Needs water but will not tolerate wet conditions; will not withstand drought or wind. Hardy from zones 4–9, but seed should be collected from local sources, since those grown in South will not withstand Northern cold.

Disease and insect problems: Canker, leaf spot, verticillum wilt.

Propagation: By layering; softwood cuttings in spring; seed, scarified and followed by 8 weeks cool (41°F), moist stratification.

LANDSCAPE VALUE
Hardy woodland tree, effective as a single specimen or in groupings in a shrub border. Good understory tree and nice in naturalized areas. Lovely white blooms in early spring; handsome, heart-shaped foliage. An attractive and graceful small tree.

Plant may be observed at: *Arboreta*—Arnold, Holden, Los Angeles, Morton; *Botanical Gardens*—Atlanta, Birmingham, Chicago, Missouri; *Gardens*—Brookgreen, Callaway.

E. HASSELKUS

R. HEBB

J. POOR

Chamaecyparis nootkatensis (D. Don) Spach 'Pendula'. ALASKA CEDAR,
YELLOW CYPRESS, NOOTKA CEDAR. *Cupressaceae.* USDA Zones 5–8.
North America, southeast Alaska, British Columbia, Washington, northern
Oregon. Raised by nurseryman A. Van Leeuwen in Netherlands before
1884.

DESCRIPTION *Evergreen conifer,* with narrowly pyramidal, open habit. Grows
moderately fast—about 1' per year in best site—to 65–90'. May live 500–
600 years. Casts moderate shade.

Leaves: Scale-like, in 4 ranks, closely appressed, sharply pointed, to ⅛"
long. Dark green to blue-green with no white markings; malodorous
when bruised.

Flowers: Staminate cones, yellow, inconspicuous, 3/16" long.

Fruit: Ovulate cones, glaucous blue changing to red-brown, ⅜" dia.,
ripening September-October of second year; inconspicuous.

Winter aspect: Thin, stringy, irregularly fissured bark, ash-brown to
purple-brown. Pendulous branchlets hang loosely, giving drooping
appearance to entire tree.

CULTURE Grows in sun or partial shade. Grows in clay but prefers loam and moist
sand with acidic pH and damp but not saturated conditions; optimum
growth in moist, well-drained soils in moderate climate with high
humidity and precipitation. Not tolerant of extended drought but will
tolerate wind if environment cool and moist. Protection from drought and
hot, dry winds imperative outside of native range. Tolerance to environmental stresses unknown.

Disease and insect problems: One of the most disease- and insect-free
conifers; scale can be problem on plants growing in hot, dry conditions.

Transplanting: Easy when plants less than 1' tall; otherwise use
containerized material; deep root system.

Propagation: By seed, cuttings or grafting; seed germination low.

LANDSCAPE
VALUE A striking, graceful cultivar of Alaska Cedar that exaggerates the
pendulous branchlets characteristic of the species. Horizontal branches
are draped with covering of pendulous branchlets. Because of its strong
character and intense vertical line, this extremely attractive, unusual tree is
best used as a specimen plant. Not commonly encountered outside of its
native range because of its need for cool, moist conditions, but will grow
on East Coast if such conditions are present. This species tolerates damp
soils better than *C. lawsoniana* and is resistant to late spring frosts, making
it good for frost pockets; as cold-hardy as the oriental *Chamaecyparis*
species. *C. nootkatensis* was often used in the Victorian era, then forgotten.
Its lightweight, fine-grained, hard, durable wood is used in fences, railroad
ties, boat-building, but commercial use is restricted because of availability.

Plant may be observed at: *Arboreta*—Arnold, Bayard Cutting, Cary, Dawes,
National, Planting Fields, U. of Washington; *Botanical Gardens*—British
Columbia, Chicago, Munich, Palmgarten, Royal/Kew, Van Dusen;
Gardens—Longwood.

Chamaecyparis nootkatensis 'Pendula'   ALASKA CEDAR, YELLOW CYPRESS, NOOTKA CEDAR

F. NUMRICH

N. BREWSTER

PLANTING FIELDS

Chilopsis linearis (Cavanilles) Sweet [*Bignonia linearis* Cavanilles]. DESERT WILLOW, FLOR DE MIMBRES. *Bignoniaceae.* USDA Zones 8–10. Southwestern U.S.A. and northern Mexico. Cultivation before 1800.

DESCRIPTION
Deciduous small tree with gnarled trunk, often multiple, and slender upright branches forming a rounded crown; grows 2' a year when young reaching 25' at maturity.

Leaves: Simple, alternate, linear to linear-lanceolate, 6–12" long and ¼–⅓" wide; bright green and green to yellow in fall.

Flowers: Orchid-like, to 2" long, lavendar to white in racemes or narrow panicles 3–4" long, appearing in early summer and continuing for several months.

Fruit: Narrow pods 10" long, ¼" in diameter, green maturing to brown in autumn; split longitudinally to release numerous seeds.

Winter aspect: Trunk often reclining and hollow, sometimes 1' in diameter. Bark dark brown, divided into ridges broken into small plate-like scales on surface. Branchlets light chestnut brown, glabrous or covered with dense tomentum when young, later darker and tinged with red, or sometimes ashy gray. Fruit persistent in winter.

CULTURE
Full sun promotes healthiest growth; shade reduces vigor. Grows best in dry gravelly or sandy soil, loam if well drained. Clay soil sometimes fatal to seedlings. Withstands 50 mph winds with no damage; tolerates wet conditions to a point. Tolerates drought well once established; will root deeply to use subsurface water. Tolerant of environmental stresses.

Disease and insect problems: None noted. Plants can be short-lived if constantly overwatered and heavily fertilized.

Transplanting: Easy when young.

Propagation: By seed (best germination in warm soil at 70–80°F; at 5600 seeds per ounce approximately 50% germinates, on the average), and by cuttings both soft and hardwood.

LANDSCAPE VALUE
Desert Willow is very versatile, long flowering and requires little maintenance. A recently released cultivar 'Barranco' was selected for dark flower color, but varies from dark purple to white when plants are propagated from seed; cuttings ensure flower color of parent plant. Though it produces seed prolifically it is not particularly weedy, as young seedlings are quite tender and don't survive unassisted. This tree is particularly valuable in arid gardens.

Plant may be observed at: *Botanical Gardens*—Huntington, Royal/Kew.

J. RAULSTON

J. RAULSTON

J. RAULSTON

Chionanthus retusus Lindley & Paxton. CHINESE FRINGE TREE. *Oleaceae.* USDA Zones 6–8. China. Introduced 1845 by Fortune.

DESCRIPTION
Deciduous tree with slow rate of growth; rarely over 20′ (to 40′ in wild), with equal spread; broadly rounded head, spreading habit. Casts light shade.

Leaves: Variable in shape, usually oval, sometimes obovate or almost round; 1–4″ long, ¾–2″ wide, blunt at tip, tapered at base; lustrous above, downy on midrib and beneath. Leaves smaller than those of *C. virginicus.*

Flowers: Pure white panicles, 2–4″ long, produced in profusion on current growth; blooms 2–3 weeks before *C. virginicus.*

Fruit: Damson-like ½″ blue drupe, only on female trees, in September or October.

Winter aspect: Gray-brown, furrowed bark; open habit.

CULTURE
Requires full sun for profuse flowers, but will stand partial shade; prefers moist, well-drained loam in pH range of 6.0–6.5; tolerates air pollution.

Disease and insect problems: None serious; occasional mildew and scale.

Transplanting: Balled and burlapped, in spring.

Propagation: By seed, which is difficult; double dormancy needed.

LANDSCAPE VALUE
A spectacular specimen tree. Soft, fleecy, snow-like blooms in spring, attractive fruit in fall and handsome, gray-brown bark in winter create year-round interest. May be used as a small urban tree, since it is tolerant of air pollution. Name originated from Greek *chion*—snow, and *anthos*—flower.

Plant may be observed at: *Arboreta*—Arnold, Cary, Holden, Los Angeles, National, U. of Wisconsin-Madison; *Botanical Gardens*—Brooklyn, Chicago, Missouri, New York, Palmgarten, Royal/Kew; *Gardens*—Callaway, Filoli, Winterthur; *Parks*—Forest Parks-Ibaraki, Japan.

M. DIRR

E. HASSELKUS

E. HASSELKUS

Chionanthus virginicus L. WHITE FRINGE TREE. *Oleaceae.* USDA Zones 5–9.
Southeastern and south central U.S. Introduced 1736.

DESCRIPTION *Deciduous* tree growing slowly to 12–20' in cultivation (20–30' in wild);
spreading habit, often as wide as tall. Casts light shade.

Leaves: Opposite, entire, coarsely-textured, elliptical leaves ⅜" long,
tapering at base; dark green, yellow in fall.

Flowers: White, fringe-like dioecious flowers in loose clusters 4–8" long
(largest on male plants), developed from upper parts of previous year's
shoots; spring bloom.

Fruit: Egg-shaped, blue-black drupe to ⅝" in clusters on female plants
only. Male plants needed for pollination and fruit set. Effective display in
August and September.

Winter aspect: Smooth gray bark furrowed at maturity; spreading habit.
Persistent fruit and leaves.

CULTURE Prefers deep, moist, acid, fertile soil but will tolerate a wide pH range,
some wet conditions and wind. Will not tolerate drought. Performs best in
full sun. Tolerant of air pollution.

Disease and insect problems: None serious.

Transplanting: Balled and burlapped in spring.

Propagation: By seed, which needs double dormancy; by grafting.

LANDSCAPE
VALUE One of the most beautiful and striking of North American specimen trees.
The showy, fringe-like flowers create a spectacular effect in spring.
Handsome dark blue fruits are interesting in late summer and early fall
and are extremely attractive to birds. A tree which needs little
maintenance and tolerates city conditions. No tree is comparable in flower
except its Asian relative *C. retusus.*

Plant may be observed at: *Arboreta*—Arnold, Bernheim Forest, Cary,
Dawes, Minnesota Landscape, Morton, National, Planting Fields, U. of
Washington; *Botanical Gardens*—Brooklyn, Chicago, Missouri, Munich,
New York, Palmgarten, Royal/Kew, U. of Georgia, Van Dusen; *Gardens*—
Brookgreen, Callaway, Dixon, Longwood, Winterthur.

M. DIRR

P. KINGSLEY

M. DIRR

Cladrastis lutea (Dumont de Courset) v. Rudd [*C. lutea* (Michaux f.) K. Koch].
YELLOWWOOD. *Leguminosae* (subfamily *Faboideae*). USDA Zones 4–8.
East central U.S.A., introduced 1812 by Michaux.

DESCRIPTION
Deciduous, open-arching, dome-shaped tree; growing 2–3′ per year to 50′,
rarely to 65′; spread at maturity 40–50′. Casts dense shade.

Leaves: Pinnately compound to 1′ long, with 7–11 broadly ovate leaflets to
4″ long. Foliage dark green and dense, turning clear yellow in autumn.

Flowers: White, fragrant, 1″ long in pendant panicles to 15″ long, in June.

Fruit: Flat, thin, dehiscent pods, 4″ long; inconspicuous, somewhat
persistent in winter.

Winter aspect: Dramatic framework of branches accented by smooth gray
bark.

CULTURE
Grows in sun in well-drained loam or moist sandy soil with medium acid
pH. Not tolerant of "wet feet" or environmental stress; has withstood
many periods of excessive drought.

Disease and insect problems: None of note; shunned by gypsy moth and
canker worms.

Transplanting: Easy with proper handling; root system of average depth.

Propagation: By seed in spring; does not self-seed.

LANDSCAPE
VALUE
Distinctive. Some authorities consider it the foremost American flowering
tree; Dogwood and Sweet Buckeye are not superior in terms of flower
beauty. Its roots support nitrogen-fixing bacteria and so improve the
fertility of the surrounding soil. Like many leguminous trees, it drops
peduncles in winter, and its brittle branches are somewhat susceptible to
breakage in ice storms. Balancing these minor drawbacks, the tree seems
virtually indestructible. The trunk of one specimen was gnawed through
by a dog; the tree came up from the roots and soon after had to be moved.
Twenty-two years later it is a handsome, healthy specimen 40′ tall with a
spread of 45′, and its nearly annual flowering is breathtaking. In winter the
smooth pale-gray trunk and branches have a sinewy, luminous quality.
Despite this tree's superior qualities, it is rarely used by private gardeners
and often ignored by professionals.

Plant may be observed at: *Arboreta*—Bernheim Forest, Cary, Dawes,
Holden, Los Angeles, Minnesota Landscape, National, Planting Fields, U.
of Washington, U. of Wisconsin-Madison; *Botanical Gardens*—Brooklyn,
Chicago, Missouri, Munich, New York, Palmgarten, Royal/Kew,
Royal/Ontario, U. of Georgia; *Gardens*—Callaway, Dixon, Longwood,
Winterthur.

E. HASSELKUS

A. BUSSEWITZ

K. KOHOUT

Cornus alternifolia (L.) f. [Swida alternifolia (L.f.) Small] PAGODA DOGWOOD, GREEN OSIER. *Cornaceae.* USDA Zones 3–8. North America (New Brunswick and Minnesota to Georgia and Alabama). Introduced into Europe 1760.

DESCRIPTION *Deciduous,* small tree growing moderately fast to 10–25' high; spreading, horizontal habit, with flat-topped crown. Casts dense shade.

Leaves: Alternate, simple, entire, clustered at ends of branches; oval, ovate, elliptic to 5" long. Bright pale green on upper surface; rich red and orange tints to foliage in autumn.

Flowers: Yellow-white, in flat cymes 2–3" wide. Inflorescenses not exceedingly showy, yet often so abundant that they do create an effect.

Fruit: Dark blue on red stalks in early autumn, July-September; consumed by birds and small mammals; fruits rarely yellow.

Winter aspect: Bare green branches and green twigs emphasize horizontal, tiered branching habit; no persistent fruit or leaves.

CULTURE Grows in full sun, partial or full shade in acidic soil. Tolerates wet conditions if on well-drained sites; prefers moist, rich soils along borders of streams. Will tolerate drought for short periods. Tolerance to wind and environmental stresses unknown.

Disease and insect problems: Blight will occur in some regions of U.S. Use *C. controversa* as a substitute where blight is present.

Transplanting: Does not transplant well despite shallow root system; plants from the wild will not thrive. Nursery-grown, containerized material best suited for transplanting.

Propagation: By seed, stratified for about 4 months at 40°F.

LANDSCAPE VALUE This species valuable for its distinctive habit of strong horizontal line and tiered appearance. Excellent as a multi-branched, small tree and as an ornamental plant for landscapes. Tolerance to shade makes it suitable for naturalized landscapes. Birds enjoy the fruit. Not used extensively because of its similarity to the showier eastern dogwood, *C. florida.* Yet this is a subtly beautiful plant worthy of more widespread use. It is best to buy native plants derived from seed produced in the same area as the plant will be grown.

Cv. 'Argentea' has leaves marked with white, lovely but difficult to find.

Plant may be observed at: *Arboreta*—Arnold, Bernheim Forest, Los Angeles, Minnesota Landscape, Morton, National, Planting Fields, U. of Washington, U. of Wisconsin-Madison; *Botanical Gardens*—Brooklyn, Chicago, Missouri, New York, Palmgarten, Royal/Kew; *Gardens*—Longwood, Winterthur.

M. DIRR

M. DIRR

A. BUSSEWITZ

Cornus kousa Hance. KOUSA DOGWOOD. *Cornaceae.* USDA Zones 5–8. Japan, Korea, China. Introduced 1875, Arnold Arboretum.

DESCRIPTION
Deciduous, vase-shaped tree; medium growth rate when young, slow when old. Size at maturity 20–30' high, 15–20' spread, though size varies in different parts of the country. Casts light shade.

Leaves: 2–4" long, ovate, dark green; maroon to scarlet in fall.

Flowers: True flower inconspicuous, round button-like mass ⅜" diam.; pointed white bracts are showy part of the inflorescence. Appear after leaves and 2–3 weeks later than bloom of *Cornus florida;* four taper-pointed bracts, 1–2" long, persist up to six weeks, often turn pink with age.

Fruit: Raspberry-like drupe to 1" dia. appears late August to October; very decorative, edible.

Winter aspect: Bark has patterns of gray, tan and warm brown, exfoliating in irregular patches. Handsome in winter because of strong horizontal branching pattern; arches markedly when mature.

CULTURE
Prefers acid, well-drained sandy loam with pH of 4.5–6.5; grows in sun or partial shade. Not tolerant of wet conditions or drought, but more drought-resistant than *C. florida.*

Disease and insect problems: None serious; seems immune to fungus, borer and wilt that attack *C. florida.*

Transplanting: Root system shallow; best moved, balled and burlapped, in early spring, and when young.

Propagation: By softwood cuttings in June, seed collected in fall— stratified 120 days at 40°; variable from seed.

LANDSCAPE VALUE
Perfect small tree; strikingly handsome specimen plant. Good for most landscapes; works well in shrub border or in foundation planting at corner of house. Blooms in great profusion in early summer when there is little other bloom; attractive berries in fall are enjoyed by many birds; winter tree silhouette is distinctive, and the exfoliating bark creates interest. Flower buds more cold-hardy than *Cornus florida.*

Many choice more floriferous larger-bracted varieties, as well as some variegated and weeping varieties, becoming available:
Var. *chinensis,* Chinese Dogwood, introduced from China in 1907 by E. H. Wilson, has bracts slightly longer, grows more freely.
C. kousa 'Milky Way', cultivar of var. *chinensis,* has profuse flowers.
C. kousa 'Summer Stars' is introduction from Princeton Nurseries.

Plant may be observed at: *Arboreta*—Arnold, Bernheim Forest, Cary, Holden, Morton, National, Planting Fields, U. of Washington; *Botanical Gardens*—Atlanta, Berry, Birmingham, Brooklyn, Chicago, Missouri, Munich, New York, Palmgarten, Royal/Kew, U. of Georgia, Van Dusen; *Gardens*—Callaway, Dixon, Filoli, Longwood, Old Westbury, Winterthur.

M. DIRR

P. KINGSLEY

P. KINGSLEY

Cornus nuttallii Audubon. PACIFIC DOGWOOD. *Cornaceae.* USDA Zones 6–9. Canada, western U.S.A. to southern California. Introduced 1834 by Thomas Nuttall.

DESCRIPTION   *Deciduous* tree growing to 50'; may reach 80–100' in wild; pyramidal habit.

Leaves: 3–5" long, 1½–3" wide; ovate-obovate; margins wavy-toothed; upper surface bright green, lower pubescent.

Flowers: Very small purple and green flowers gathered into a dense head, ¾" diam.; white bracts flushed with pink (4–8) surround flower head; bracts are oval or obovate, pointed, 1½-3" long, 1–2" wide. Flower head formed previous fall and is not enclosed by bracts in winter. Blooms early spring-summer and again in autumn.

Fruit: Dense, spherical heads of 30–40 red or orange, berry-like stone fruits, each ½" long.

Winter aspect: Thin brown bark tinged with red, divided into thin, close-fitting scales; horizontal branching habit.

CULTURE   Grows in shade; prefers loam in acid pH range; requires a plentiful water supply, but with exceptionally good drainage. Does not tolerate air pollution. Does not grow well on the East Coast; seems to require the moist, moderate conditions of the Pacific Coast. Plant under high trees at edge of wooded area where bark will not sunburn.

Disease and insect problems: Subject to disease in cultivation which blackens and curls leaves.

Transplanting: Move balled and burlapped as a small tree.

Propagation: By cuttings, layering, budding/grafting.

LANDSCAPE VALUE   One of the most beautiful flowering trees of its native western North America. Spectacular in flower and highly colorful in autumn with its yellow and scarlet leaves and clusters of crimson berries. Differs from the Eastern Dogwood in having the larger bracts, white and rounded out, whereas the Eastern species has a notched and green-tipped bract. *C. florida* usually has 4 bracts; *C. nuttallii* has 4–6 (commonly 5) to create a 5-pointed "star." Boiled bark was used by Indians to cure fever. The berries are the favorite food of the Band-Tailed pigeon. John James Audubon painted *C. nuttallii* when representing the Band-Tailed Pigeon in his *Ornithological Biography.* Audubon named the tree after his friend Thomas Nuttall.

Plant may be observed at: *Arboreta*—National, U. of Washington; *Botanical Gardens*—Berry, British Columbia, Munich, Royal/Kew, Van Dusen; *Gardens*—Filoli.

G. COURTRIGHT

N. BREWSTER

R. HAND

Cornus officinalis Siebold & Zuccarini. JAPANESE CORNEL DOGWOOD. *Cornaceae.*
USDA Zones 5–8. China and N. Korea. Introduced 1877.

DESCRIPTION *Deciduous* tree growing at a medium rate to 15–25′, with 10–15′ spread; multi-stemmed, low-branched, oval to round habit. Casts dense shade.

Leaves: Ovate to elliptic, to 4″ long, pointed; conspicuous tufts of hairs at axils of veins on underside of leaves; dark glossy green; purple in fall.

Flowers: Clusters of short-stalked, yellow, ¾″ flowers with drooping yellow bracts, borne on naked twigs in umbels, appearing before leaves in March-April.

Fruit: Oblong drupe, ⅝″ long and ½″ wide; bright, very shiny red, in September.

Winter aspect: Exfoliating brown, orange and gray bark; showier, with more open habit than *C. mas.*

CULTURE Grows best in sun but can tolerate shade; adaptable to all soils but prefers rich loam. Tolerates wind.

Disease and insect problems: None serious.

Transplanting: Easy when young, balled and burlapped.

Propagation: Stratified seed, 3–4 months at 70–75°, followed by 2–3 months at 40–50°.

LANDSCAPE VALUE Picturesque, early flowering tree with a wide hardiness range. Useful as a small patio specimen. Similar to *Cornus mas,* but the attractive gray, brown and orange bark and the yellow flowers on the naked branches create a more spectacular overall effect. A tree of great beauty in March-April when few others are in bloom.

Plant may be observed at: *Arboreta*—Secrest; *Gardens*—Longwood, Winterthur.

M. DIRR

M. DIRR

M. DIRR

Corylus colurna L. TURKISH HAZEL. *Betulaceae.* USDA Zones 5–7. Southeastern Europe, western Asia. Introduced 1582.

DESCRIPTION

Deciduous tree of symmetrical pyramidal habit, growing 6–8" per year to 70–80' with a spread of ½ to ⅔ its height, usually having a short trunk and pendulous lower branches. Casts dense shade.

Leaves: Simple, alternate, broadly ovate, 2½–6" long, 2–4" wide, coarsely toothed to almost lobed, heart-shaped at base; nearly smooth above, downy on veins beneath.

Flowers: Female inconspicuous; male 2–3" long catkins, in early spring.

Fruit: Nuts ½–⅝" in diameter, 1½–2" long, in clusters of 3–6, with conspicuous husk or involucre much longer than nut. Fruit is edible in October.

Winter aspect: Bark tan to gray; older bark furrowed and corky in platelets exposing orange-brown bark beneath. Branching strongly horizontal. Leaves persistent to late fall.

CULTURE

Grows in full sun in well-drained loamy soil with pH range of 6.5–7.5, though adapts to wider range. Tolerates heavy soils, wind, drought and other adverse conditions such as hot summers and cold winters.

Disease and insect problems: Not noticeable.

Transplanting: Reasonably easy; root system shallow. Needs supplemental watering for several seasons until it is established, after which it is drought tolerant.

Propagation: By seed and cuttings, but difficult. Requires specialized techniques.

LANDSCAPE VALUE

Valued for its stately pyramidal form, handsome summer foliage and interesting winter characteristics. Male catkins attractive in early spring. Fruit attracts squirrels in fall. An excellent tree for city conditions and dry situations, being perfectly hardy and holding its green vigor where maples have suffered leaf-drop and sun scorch due to lack of moisture. This tree is too little known and grown.

Plant may be observed at: *Arboreta*—Arnold, Bernheim Forest, Dawes, Holden, Los Angeles, Minnesota Landscape, Morton, U. of Washington, U. of Wisconsin-Madison; *Botanical Gardens*—Brooklyn, Chicago, Munich, New York, Palmgarten, Royal/Kew, Royal/Ontario, Van Dusen.

M. DIRR

K. KOHOUT

E. HASSELKUS

Cotinus obovatus Rafinesque [*C. americanus* Nuttall; *C. cotinoides* (Nuttall ex Chapman) Britton; *Rhus cotinoides* Nuttall ex Chapman; *R. cotinus* Torrey & A. Gray, not L.]. AMERICAN SMOKE TREE, CHITTAMWOOD. *Anacardiaceae.* USDA Zones 5–8. U.S.A., Tennessee south to Alabama and Missouri,west to Texas. Introduced 1819 by Nuttall.

DESCRIPTION
Deciduous tree growing slowly to 20–35', with round-headed habit. Casts dense shade.

Leaves: Dark blue-green, obovate to 6" long, cuneate, turning yellow, orange, red to purple in fall.

Flowers: Fuzzy, smoke-like masses of greenish flowers. In female plant, flowers are borne on large, sparse, terminal panicles, 7–12" long; male has better inflorescence.

Flowers: ⅛" long and sparse.

Winter aspect: Gray to gray-brown bark with small, scaly plates; upright and dense habit.

CULTURE
Grows in sun and semi-shade in clay and loam in pH range of 5–7; will adapt to limestone soils. Tolerates wind, drought and soil compaction.

Disease and insect problems: Fall webworm, but rare.

Transplanting: Difficult.

Propagation: By seed or softwood cuttings.

LANDSCAPE VALUE
Lovely small tree with beautiful pink-bronze spring foliage. In fall, the foliage turns various shades of scarlet, claret and orange. Valued for the intensity and consistency of autumn color, its interesting fish-like scaly bark and its adaptability to varied growing conditions. Many large trees have been cut down for the yellow to orange dye obtained from the wood, and it is feared that in the wild this tree is in danger of extinction.

Cultivar:
   'Red Leaf', especially good fall color.

Plant may be observed at: *Botanical Gardens*—Royal/Kew; Princeton University.

M. DIRR

W. THOMAS

M. DIRR

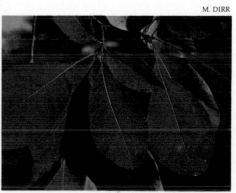

Crataegus viridis L. 'Winter King'. GREEN HAWTHORN. *Rosaceae.* USDA Zones 5–7. Maryland, Virginia, Illinois, Texas, Florida. Introduced 1955 by Simpson Orchard Co., Vincennes, Indiana.

DESCRIPTION *Deciduous,* rounded tree with sharp thorns; moderately slow growth to 30–40' and almost equal spread. Casts dense shade.

Leaves: Oblong-ovate to elliptic, toothed, ¾–2¼" long; glossy green in summer, golden yellow, scarlet to purple in fall.

Flowers: White, ¾" in dia., borne in flat clusters 2" across.

Fruit: Orange-red, ⅜" in dia., persistent and showy throughout winter. Fruit larger than species.

Winter aspect: Bark light brown; branching habit spreading and dense, almost vase-shaped.

CULTURE Grows in sun; not fussy about soil but prefers loam. Adaptable to city conditions; tolerant.

Disease and insect problems: Aphids, borers, caterpillars, leaf miners.

Transplanting: Some difficulty; best to move with ball of soil.

Propagation: By seed or grafting.

LANDSCAPE VALUE Moderate size makes it suitable for small properties and limited spaces; use as hedge, specimen, or screening. Tolerates environments unfavorable to many trees and shrubs. Thorns can be a nuisance. Excellent winter interest, with red-orange fruit against light gray branches. More trouble-free than many hawthorns.

Plant may be observed at: *Arboreta*—Dawes, Holden, Spring Grove, U. of Wisconsin-Madison; *Botanical Gardens*—Chicago, Missouri; *Gardens*—Longwood.

J. POOR

M. DIRR

M. DIRR

Crescentia cujete L. CALABASH TREE. *Bignoniaceae.* USDA Zone 10. Tropical America, Mexico. Introduced 1690 by Earl of Portland.

DESCRIPTION
Evergreen tree growing at moderate rate to 20–30' high; open, irregular crown. Casts moderate shade.

Leaves: Alternate, simple, 2–6" long, 0.8–2" wide, oblanceolate, entire, smooth, nearly sessile and clustered at nodes; bright green; no fall color.

Flowers: Cup-shaped calyx, 5 petals with wavy-edge lobes in a funnel shape, 2–2½" long; yellow-green with purple markings; year-round blooms.

Fruit: Nearly rounded, 5–12" diam. with hard shell; ripens to yellow and later turns black, enclosing a thin white pulp and dark brown seeds which may be easily and effectively polished; bears fruit year-round.

Winter aspect: Year-round interest; long, spreading branches.

CULTURE
Requires full sun; becomes straggly in shade. Grows in clay, loam and sand in a wide pH range. Tolerates wind and some moisture but not extremely wet conditions; cannot tolerate salt; pollution tolerance unknown.

Disease and insect problems: Chinese rose beetles; self-sterility sometimes a problem.

Transplanting: Easy; rather shallow root system is invasive but not aggressive.

Propagation: By seed.

LANDSCAPE VALUE
An unusual and highly ornamental tree. Flowers and fruits may be produced any month of the year. The interesting fruit resembles the gourd and is widely used for bowls, cups, utensils and musical instruments.

Plant may be observed at: *Botanical Gardens*—Pacific Tropical; *Gardens*—Fairchild Tropical.

G.C. OF HONOLULU

G.C. OF HONOLULU

G.C. OF HONOLULU

x Cupressocyparis leylandii (A.B. Jackson & Dallimore) Dallimore and A.B. Jackson
(*Chamaecyparis nootkatensis* Spach x *Cupressus macrocarpa* Hartweg).
LEYLAND CYPRESS. *Cupressaceae.* USDA Zones 6–10. Wales. Introduced
1888 in Wales.

DESCRIPTION *Evergreen conifer* with columnar to pyramidal growth habit like
Chamaecyparis nootkatensis. Grows fast when young to 60–70′ high; spread
about one-fourth of height.

Leaves: ⅛–¼″ long, pointed; dark blue-green.

Flowers: Scale-like, similar to *Chamaecyparis nootkatensis.*

Fruit: Cones ⅜–¾″ across with 8 scales.

Winter aspect: Red-brown, scaly bark; branchlets flattened, somewhat
quadrangular.

CULTURE Grows in sun; adaptable to many soils, acid to lime; withstands some salt
spray and wind.

Disease and insect problems: None serious.

Transplanting: Easy, but should be container-grown as fibrous root
system makes it difficult to ball and burlap.

Propagation: Cuttings from side growths late March or half-ripened wood
late summer.

LANDSCAPE
VALUE Magnificent and adaptable tree. Good for hedging since it withstands
heavy pruning. Also can be used as single specimen tree. Fine, feathery
foliage creates graceful appearance. One of the most important tree
introductions, x *C. leylandii* has all virtues of one parent, *Cupressus
macrocarpa,* and none of its faults. Capable of becoming attractive
specimen; 50–60′ in 25 years. First cross made on estate of Mr. Naylor in
Wales in 1888. Seedlings taken by Naylor's brother-in-law, C. J. Leyland,
and planted on his property, Haggerston Hall, Northumberland in 1892–
93. Five still exist and are parents by vegetative propagation of x *C.
leylandii.*

Some excellent cultivars:
  'Leighton Green'—branches and branchlets upturned at ends; gray-
    green leaves when young, becoming darker with age, paler beneath.
  'Haggerston Gray'—branches loose, upturned at ends; leaves sage
    green above, pale gray-green beneath.
  'Naylor's Blue'—columnar; shoots and leaves grayish-blue above, pale
    gray-green beneath.
  'Stapehill'—dense, columnar form.
  'Castlewellan'—yellow foliage; supposed to be cross between *Cupressus
    macrocarpa* 'Lutea' and *Chamaecyparis nootkatensis* 'Aurea'.

Plant may be observed at: *Arboreta*—Bayard Cutting, National, Strybing, U.
of Washington; *Botanical Gardens*—Birmingham, Brooklyn, Munich,
Palmgarten, Royal/Kew, U. of Georgia, Van Dusen; *Gardens*—Brookgreen,
Callaway, Longwood; *Parks*—Golden Gate.

W. THOMAS

N. BREWSTER

A. BELL

Cydonia sinensis Thouin [*Chaenomeles sinensis* (Thouin) Koehne]. CHINESE QUINCE. *Rosaceae.* USDA Zones 6–8. China. Introduced 1800.

DESCRIPTION
Deciduous tree with slow growth rate to 10–20' high; dense, oval to rounded habit. Casts light shade.

Leaves: Alternate, simple, ovate, 3–4" long, minutely serrate; dark green above, pale green below.

Flowers: Pink petals with white base 1½" across; fragrant; in spring.

Fruit: Pome, citron yellow, oblong-ovoid, 4–6" long; very fragrant.

Winter aspect: Flaking, gray-green to brown bark; upright branching habit.

CULTURE
Grows in sun and light shade; needs moist, acid, well-drained loam. Tolerates wind but will not withstand wet conditions or drought.

Disease and insect problems: Fire blight.

Transplanting: Easy when small.

Propagation: By seed, mound, stool or trench layering.

LANDSCAPE VALUE
Sturdy tree with fragrant fruit and flowers. Fruit used for jelly. Tree may be used as landscape specimen. It is extremely long-lived with beautiful, flaking, tri-colored bark. Attractive flowers, fruit and bark create interest at all seasons.

Plant may be observed at: *Arboreta*—Los Angeles; *Botanical Gardens*—Birmingham, Brooklyn, Chicago, Palmgarten, U. of Georgia; *Gardens*—Longwood.

N. BREWSTER

M. DIRR

N. BREWSTER

Davidia involucrata Baillon. DOVE TREE. *Nyssaceae.* USDA Zones 6–8. China. First discovered by the French missionary Armand David in 1869. Introduced by E. H. Wilson 1904.

DESCRIPTION *Deciduous* tree grows slowly to 20–40' high (40–65' in wild) with equal spread; broad pyramidal habit. Casts light shade.

Leaves: Alternate, simple, broad-ovate to 5" long, serrate; scented; bright green in summer; fall color of no consequence.

Flowers: 2 creamy white conspicuous bracts, the lower one approximately 7" long, surround yellow ball-like flower head; blooms in May for up to 2 weeks. Does not bloom until mature (10 years).

Fruit: 1½" drupe, green changing to rust and speckled with red; contains hard nut with seeds.

Winter aspect: Orange-brown, scaly bark; spreading habit.

CULTURE Prefers light shade but will tolerate sun if soil is kept moist. Prefers loam. Does not tolerate wind, wet conditions, drought or environmental stress. May not set flower buds in cold climates.

Disease and insect problems: None serious.

Transplanting: Balled and burlapped in spring in well-drained, moist soil.

Propagation: By seed, cuttings of half-ripened wood, layering.

LANDSCAPE VALUE One of the most handsome flowering trees. Should be planted as a specimen. The conspicuous, large, white, unequal bracts have been likened to handkerchiefs. Bark provides winter interest. E. H. Wilson considered it to be "the most interesting and beautiful of all trees of the north temperate flora" and likened the white bracts to "huge butterflies hovering among the trees."

Plant may be observed at: *Arboreta*—Arnold, National, Planting Fields, Strybing, U. of Washington; *Botanical Gardens*—Berry, Birmingham, Brooklyn, Canton, Munich, Palmgarten, Royal/Kew; *Gardens*—Winterthur; *Parks*—Golden Gate.

E. SCHOLTZ

M. DIRR

A. BUSSEWITZ

Diospyros virginiana L. PERSIMMON. *Ebenaceae.* USDA Zones 5–9. Connecticut to Florida, west to Kansas and Texas. Introduced 1629.

DESCRIPTION *Deciduous* tree growing slowly to 40–65′ (can grow to 100′ in wild) with 20–30′ spread; straight, graceful trunk and rounded crown. Casts dense canopy of shade.

Leaves: Alternate, simple, oval to ovate, tapering; heart-shaped at base, pointed at apex, 3–5″ long, 1–1½″ wide, leathery; dark green above, pale beneath; yellow to dark red-purple in fall.

Flowers: Mostly dioecious; female solitary, yellow-white on short recurved stalks, urn-shaped corolla, 3/5″ dia.; male, 2–3 flowered stalked clusters, ⅜″ dia.; May-June bloom.

Fruit: Light green berry, turning to yellow-orange, 1–2″ dia. with tough skin, globe-shaped and fleshy; ripens after frost and shrivels when ripe; flattened seeds, ½″ long, red-brown, edible, valued as food; astringent when unripe but delicious when ripe; best when ripened on tree before leaves fall.

Winter aspect: Thick, dark brown or dark gray bark, deeply divided into square plates exposing red-orange inner bark; horizontal and pendulous branches at maturity.

CULTURE Grows in sun and shade in moist, well-drained, sandy soils with a wide pH range. The best growth is achieved in the Mississippi River Valley in rich bottom lands. Tolerates some air pollution; performs well in city conditions.

Disease and insect problems: None serious.

Transplanting: Deep taproot; advisable to move balled and burlapped as a small tree in spring; where possible use container-grown trees.

Propagation: By seed stratified 2–3 months, and by cuttings.

LANDSCAPE VALUE An interesting and attractive tree with many attributes: excellent fruit, adaptability in low-maintenance situations, tolerates a wide range of temperatures and soil types, relative freedom from pests and a long life. Its picturesque bark, tiny, fragrant flowers and strikingly beautiful fruit make it an excellent candidate for home landscapes, parks, golf courses, naturalized areas; its tolerance permits its use as a city tree where fruit litter is not a concern. Produces a hard, close-grained wood used in golf club heads. Fruit also a valuable food source for wildlife.

Related species *D. kaki*, Oriental Persimmon, not as hardy as *D. virginiana* but excellent tree in milder climates; provides primary fruit in the diet of Chinese, Japanese, Taiwanese and Koreans. Cultivar 'Early Golden' valued for early ripening and non-astringent fruit.

Plant may be observed at: *Arboreta*—Arnold, Holden, Planting Fields, Spring Grove; *Botanical Gardens*—Brooklyn, Huntington, Munich; *Gardens*—Dixon, Filoli, Longwood, Winterthur.

N. BREWSTER

A. BUSSEWITZ

A. BUSSEWITZ

Eucommia ulmoides D. Oliver. HARDY RUBBER TREE. *Eucommiaceae.* USDA Zones 5–7. Ancient tree discovered in Central China by Henry; introduced 1896 to France from China.

DESCRIPTION **Deciduous** tree with elm-like ascending branches, rounded form; medium to vigorous growth to 40–60' with equal spread.

Leaves: Alternate, simple, ovate to oblong-ovate, 3-8" long, glossy, dark green. No fall color; leaves tend to fall early when still green.

Flowers: Unimportant, sexes separate; flowers before or with leaves.

Fruit: 1" to 1¾" flat, winged nuts.

Winter aspect: Bark an interesting gray-brown, ridged or furrowed; ascending, relatively low-branched habit.

CULTURE Grows in sun, prefers moist loam, in a wide range of pH. Very soil-tolerant and can stand some drought.

Disease and insect problems: None serious.

Transplanting: Easy.

Propagation: Softwood cuttings or stratified seed.

LANDSCAPE VALUE Excellent lawn tree, providing summer shade; adaptable, handsome, disease-free tree with glossy foliage and leaf shape resembling that of the elm, therefore *ulmoides*. It is a source of rubber, but not in commercial quantities; rubber content only about 3%, of inferior quality and difficult to extract. Only tree hardy in these zones that contains a rubber substance. For 2,000 years bark has been greatly valued by Chinese for tonic and other medicinal values. In China it is not permitted to attain full growth since it is cut down and stripped of its bark.

Plant may be observed at: *Arboreta*—Arnold, Bernheim Forest, Holden, Morton, National, Planting Fields, Spring Grove; *Botanical Gardens*—Brooklyn, Canton, Missouri, Munich, New York, Palmgarten, Royal/Kew.

MORTON ARB.

A. BUSSEWITZ

A. BUSSEWITZ

Evodia danielii J.R. & G. Forster (*Evodia danielii* Hemsley). KOREAN EVODIA, BEBE TREE. *Rutaceae.* USDA Zones 5–8. Korea, northern China. Introduced to Arnold Arboretum 1905 by E.H. Wilson.

DESCRIPTION
Deciduous tree with spreading, flat-topped habit; growth rate medium to fast, to 30–50' with equal spread; open branching, casts light shade.

Leaves: Opposite, pinnately compound leaves, 9–15" long; 7–11 leaflets ovate to oblong-ovate, 2–5" long, lustrous dark green. No special fall color; can turn yellow, although leaves often drop when green.

Flowers: Small, white, in 4–6" flat corymbs on current season's growth; blooms July-August.

Fruit: Brown-black showy seeds, fruit in capsules composed of 4–5 carpels, red to black; effective late August through November.

Winter aspect: Smooth gray bark, developing raised lenticels with age, similar to birch bark. Spreading, broad branching habit.

CULTURE
Grows in sun; prefers moist, well-drained soil; will tolerate drought and some air pollution. Relatively short-lived; subject to damage from high winds, ice and snow.

Disease and insect problems: Seems pest free.

Transplanting: Easy, although tender when young and should be well mulched; root system shallow.

Propagation: By seed.

LANDSCAPE VALUE
Good small tree for home garden. Dark lustrous green foliage, attractive all summer. Late, showy flowers borne in large quantities create a lovely small tree. Highly ornamental when few other plants are in bloom. Loved by bees. An adaptable and attractive tree little.used in the landscape.

Brooklyn Botanic grows *E. hupehensis*, Hupeh Evodia, native to central China, introduced 1907. Stalked leaflets larger and beak of fruit longer than *E. danielii*. Nice tree with no problems.

Plant may be observed at: *Arboreta*—Arnold, Bernheim Forest, National, Planting Fields, Spring Grove; *Botanical Gardens*—Birmingham, Missouri, Munich, Palmgarten, Royal/Kew, U. of Georgia; *Gardens*—Winterthur.

M. DIRR

N. BREWSTER

A. BUSSEWITZ

Fagus sylvatica L. 'Asplenifolia'. FERN-LEAVED BEECH. *Fagaceae.* USDA Zones 5–7. Central and southern Europe. Introduced 1840.

DESCRIPTION ***Deciduous*** tree growing at slow to medium rate to 80′ with 35–45′ spread; densely pyramidal. Casts dense shade.

Leaves: Alternate, 2–4″ long, gracefully cut with a fern-like appearance; lustrous dark green; warm golden-brown in fall.

Flowers: Monoecious; male and female separate on same tree; spring blooms.

Fruit: Solitary or 2–3 nuts partly or wholly enclosed by a prickly involucre.

Winter aspect: Smooth, light-gray bark; trunk and branches muscular; branching close to ground.

CULTURE Grows in full sun; prefers moist, well-drained, acid soil in pH range of 5.0–6.5; will not grow in wet, compacted soils but has been known to tolerate limestone soil. Will not tolerate change of grade or soil cultivation when established; does not grow well in extreme heat.

Disease and insect problems: Some scale, mildew, beech bark disease and, in recent years, two-line chestnut borer.

Transplanting: Easy when young, balled and burlapped in spring; root system shallow and extensive.

Propagation: By seed, stratified 3–5 months, or by grafting.

LANDSCAPE VALUE A large, graceful and majestic ornamental tree, excellent for parks and other public areas. Valued for the fresh green of its early spring growth, its brilliant fall color and spectacular skeletal structure in winter. Its leaves more deeply serrate than those of 'Laciniata', hence more graceful. Its dense shade and shallow roots deter grass growth beneath. It is tolerant of a wider range of growing conditions than *F. grandifolia,* American Beech. Its wood is widely used for timber; beechnuts are used for stock food in Europe; oil can be extracted from the nuts (as was done in Germany on a large scale during both World Wars). The oil was made into a substance similar to margarine.

Other cultivars:

'Fastigiata'—Columnar Beech; narrow columnar form similar to that of Lombardy Poplar. Planting Fields Arboretum

'Pendula'—Weeping Beech, with pendulous branches. Hunnewell Estates, Wellesley, Mass.

'Laciniata'—Leaves ovate-lanceolate with 7–9 deep and regular serrations on each side. Variation of degree of serration occurs on each tree, thus there exists a rather confusing group of serrated-leaf beeches. Tree has been known since 1792.

'Rohanii'—Cut-leaf Purple Beech; leaves similar in shape to 'Laciniata'. Vigorous grower, thought to be a cross between a Purple Beech and 'Quercifolia' in 1894.

'Tricolor'

'Rotundifolia'

Plant may be observed at: *Arboreta*—Arnold, Bayard Cutting, Bernheim Forest, Planting Fields, U. of Wisconsin-Madison; *Botanical Gardens*—Brooklyn, Chicago, Missouri, Royal/Kew, Van Dusen; *Gardens*—Old Westbury.

E. HASSELKUS

PLANTING FIELDS

A. COOK

Firmiana simplex (L.) W.F. Wight [*F. platanifolia* (L.f.) Marsili; *Sterculia platanifolia.* L.f.].
CHINESE PARASOL TREE. *Sterculiaceae.* USDA Zones 7–9. China, Japan.
Introduced 1757 from Japan.

DESCRIPTION *Deciduous* tree growing at fast rate to 60' at maturity; upright, round-headed habit. Casts extremely dense shade.

Leaves: Alternate, simple, large, maple-like, palmately 3- to 5-lobed to 12" across, 6–8" long, cordate at base, pubescent as they emerge; bright yellow in fall.

Flowers: Calyx showy, lemon-yellow to ½" across, lobes often reflexed, on 10–15" terminal panicles; in June-July.

Fruit: Wrinkled green fruits that separate into 4 or 5 leaf-like lobes with 2–3 black pea-sized seeds on inner edge.

Winter aspect: Smooth, lustrous green bark; branches arranged in accentuated whorls.

CULTURE Grows best in full sun in fairly moist soil, away from strong winds. Self-sown seedlings should be removed first year since they are deep-rooted.

Disease and insect problems: None serious.

Transplanting: Easy; root system deep.

Propagation: By seed sown as soon as collected.

LANDSCAPE VALUE A fast-growing shade tree with large ornamental leaves, flowers in showy upright clusters, unusual pods and attractive bark. A tree of interest for all seasons. May be used as a street, shade or lawn specimen. Needs to develop freely on all sides to do justice to its beauty. Its wood is used for furniture.

Cultivar:
   'Variegata'—leaves mottled with white

Plant may be observed at: *Arboreta*—Los Angeles, National; *Botanical Gardens*—Atlanta, Birmingham, Brooklyn, Huntington, U. of Georgia; *Gardens*—Bok Tower, Fairchild Tropical, Longwood.

J. GREEN

J. GREEN

N. BREWSTER

Franklinia alatamaha H. Marshall [*Gordonia alatamaha* (H. Marshall) C. Sargent].
FRANKLIN TREE. *Theaceae.* U.S.D.A. Zone 5–8. U.S.A. (Georgia).
Introduced into cultivation 1765 by John Bartram.

DESCRIPTION **Deciduous** small tree of upright spreading habit; grows slowly to 10–20′ (30′ in southern U.S.). Casts medium shade.

Leaves: Alternate, serrate, oblanceolate to obovate, to 6″ long, lustrous bright green in summer, orange and red in fall.

Flowers: White, 5-petaled, frilled and cup-shaped, with center of yellow stamens, 3″ diam. Fragrant.

Fruit: A woody capsule, subglobose, ½–¾″ across, with 6–8 wingless seeds in each cell.

Winter aspect: Bark smooth and thin, young branchlets silky; branching habit upright, spreading.

CULTURE Needs full sun for best bloom and fall color; will tolerate partial shade. Intolerant of environmental stresses. Grows in acid peat and loam, well drained but with constant moisture. Will tolerate mildly alkaline soils.

Disease and insect problems: Few; fusarium wilt.

Transplanting: Difficult because of fibrous roots; move when young in container or balled and burlapped.

Propagation: By softwood cuttings taken in late summer, by hardwood cuttings, by seed which is kept moist, or by layering.

LANDSCAPE VALUE Highly ornamental as specimen or in mixed plantings. Fragrant blossoms resemble single camellias and are borne over a long period in late summer. New growth crowds toward tips, giving the tree its airy, leggy look. Hardy in southern New England if sheltered; farther north it is better grown as a tall shrub.

This tree has an interesting history: it was discovered by John Bartram and his son William near Fort Barrington at the mouth of the Altamaha River in Georgia in 1765, and was found again by William Bartram in 1773. A few were seen in 1803 by John Lyon, nurseryman and plant hunter, in the same area, and then disappeared from the wild. All known specimens today are direct descendants of those collected by Bartram and planted at his home in Philadelphia. He named the tree for Benjamin Franklin and for the river near which he discovered it growing.

Plant may be observed at: *Arboreta*—American Horticultural Society-River Farm, Arnold, Dawes, Holden, National, Planting Fields, Spring Grove, U. of Washington; *Botanical Gardens*—Birmingham, Brooklyn, Chicago, Missouri, Palmgarten, U. of Georgia; *Gardens*—Longwood, Old Westbury, Winterthur.

M. DIRR

R. HEBB

M. DIRR

Fraxinus oxycarpa Willdenow 'Raywood'. RAYWOOD ASH. *Oleaceaae.* USDA Zones 5–8. Eastern Mediterranean, the Caucasus and Asia Minor. Introduced 1815.

DESCRIPTION   *Deciduous* tree growing at a fast rate to 40′ (occasionally to 80′) with a 25′ spread; straight trunk and narrow habit when young, but opening with age.

Leaves: 7–9 slender leaflets ovate-oblong to lanceolate, each 2½″ long, sharply serrated, light green on both surfaces and glabrous, midrib and lower veins downy; leaves turn a rich claret in fall.

Flowers: Inconspicuous.

Fruit: Obovate-oblong to lanceolate, to 1½″ long.

Winter aspect: Winter buds dark brown; sturdy branching habit.

CULTURE   Needs sunny position. Grows in clay, loam or sand. Tolerates wind, wet conditions and drought, although it prefers dry situation.

Disease and insect problems: None; appears to be resistant to anthracnose foliage disease and ash lygusbug which attack other ashes.

Transplanting: Easy.

Propagation: Budded onto *F. oxycarpa* rootstock in July-August.

LANDSCAPE VALUE   An elegant tree known chiefly for its rich plum-purple foliage in autumn. Its tolerances of a wide range of soils, drought and heat and its resistance to disease and insect problems create a beautiful and tough tree that deserves more attention. An excellent substitute for the troublesome Modesto Ash. Cultivar 'Raywood' which originated in the Raywood Gardens at Bridgewater near Adelaide, Australia, is often known as the 'Claret Ash.'

Plant may be observed at: *Arboreta*—U. of Washington; *Botanical Gardens*—Birmingham, Brooklyn, Huntington, Saratoga Horticultural Foundation.

S. MacBRIDE

A. BUSSEWITZ

N. BREWSTER

Fraxinus quadrangulata Michaux. BLUE ASH. *Oleaceae.* USDA Zones 4–7. U.S.A.: Iowa, Michigan, Arkansas, Tennessee. Introduced 1823.

DESCRIPTION

Deciduous tree with rapid growth to 50–70'; develops a straight, slender trunk that supports an irregular, narrowly oval crown. Casts moderate to dense shade.

Leaves: Opposite, pinnately compound, 7–12" long, composed of 5–11 lance-shaped leaflets, each 3–5" long; margins coarsely toothed; dull green and smooth above, smooth to pubescent beneath; pale yellow fall color.

Flowers: Clusters of tiny purple flowers in mid-spring, persisting for short time.

Fruit: Broad, flat samaras, borne in dense, drooping clusters, which fall over a period of several weeks in autumn.

Winter aspect: Bark consists of elongate, loose-fitting gray scales; moderately coarse branching habit with some twisting.

CULTURE

Grows in sun in clay and loam with a pH range of 6.5–8.0. Tolerates wind and drought; somewhat tolerant of salt and soil compaction.

Disease and insect problems: None serious. May be attacked by lilac leaf miner, fall webworm, lilac borer and ash borer.

Transplanting: Easy because of fibrous root system.

Propagation: By seed, grafting or budding.

LANDSCAPE VALUE

Useful large shade and street tree that retains dense foliage for many years. Becomes somewhat coarser in branching habit as it gets larger and older. Quite tolerant of urban conditions and grows well in alkaline soils. Extends as far north as southern Ontario, and south to Arkansas and Alabama. May live 125–150 years. Four conspicuous parallel wings on coarse twigs make winter identification easy. Fruits source of food for quail, turkey and song birds. Wood used commercially for interiors and flooring.

Plant may be observed at: *Arboreta*—Arnold, Dawes, Minnesota Landscape, Morton, Spring Grove, U. of Wisconsin-Madison; *Botanical Gardens*—Brooklyn, Chicago, Missouri, New York, Royal/Kew.

MORTON ARB.

E. HASSELKUS

K. KOHOUT

Fraxinus texensis (A. Gray) C. Sargent. TEXAS ASH. *Oleaceae.* USDA Zones 7–9. U.S.A.; from Oklahoma to central and west Texas. Introduced 1901.

DESCRIPTION *Deciduous* tree with short trunk, contoured branches and rounded crown. Grows at medium rate to 50' at maturity. Casts medium shade.

Leaves: Pinnately compound, 7" long; 1–3" leaflets (5–7), opposite, on long, slender petioles; blades elliptic to oblong. Margins serrate on upper half of leaflet, entire toward base. Upper surface olive to dark green, paler beneath.

Flowers: Minute, inconspicuous; appear with or just before leaves from axils of last year's leaves, in large panicles; buds with brown to orange-brown scales.

Fruit: Distinctive, single-bladed samara; oblong to 1", body rounded; wing terminal on seed body.

Winter aspect: Bark gray to brown with deep horizontal furrows. Branches extremely contorted.

CULTURE Grows in sun, in well-drained soils on slopes. Will adapt to drought and wet conditions if soil is extremely well-drained. Prefers loam or sand, and alkaline pH. Will tolerate some soil compaction and moderate air pollution. More adaptable than *F. velutina* (Arizona Ash) and should be planted in its place.

Disease and insect problems: None serious.

Transplanting: Difficult after second year; root system is deep.

Propagation: By seed.

LANDSCAPE VALUE An excellent shade tree in arid climates. Valuable as street or parkway tree. A better tree for city planting than *F. velutina*, which is smaller and a rapid grower but short-lived and more susceptible to borers. Less useful as windbreak or specimen shade tree than *F. pennsylvanica* (Green Ash), which is a larger tree with a greater breadth. *F. texensis* is less susceptible to fungi than *F. pennsylvanica* and should be cultivated more extensively. It is considered by some botanists to be a variety of *F. americana*, or White Ash.

Plant may be observed at: *Botanical Gardens*—Royal/Kew.

P. COX

B. TRAMMELL

B. TRAMMELL

Geijera parviflora Schott. AUSTRALIAN WILLOW, DESERT WILLOW. *Rutaceae.*
USDA Zones 9–10; possibly Zone 8. Australia. Introduced 1927 Santa
Monica.

DESCRIPTION *Evergreen,* small graceful tree to 30′ with 30′ spread and oval, upright
shape. Growth rate moderate. Casts light shade.

Leaves: Narrow, linear, 3–6″ long, olive-green.

Flowers: Creamy white, in short terminal panicles in summer;
inconspicuous.

Fruit: Inconspicuous.

Winter aspect: Evergreen; looks much the same year-round.

CULTURE Grows in sun or light shade. Will tolerate wind and/or dry conditions.
Grows in clay soil or loam.

Disease and insect problems: Fairly pest-free; occasional scale under stress
conditions.

Transplanting: Easy.

Propagation: By seed.

LANDSCAPE
VALUE A medium-sized evergreen with few pests, deep, non-invasive roots, hard
wood and strong branch angles that prevent breakage in storms. Narrow
drooping leaves cast light shade and give effect of graceful willow.
Tolerates hot sun, low nutrient soils and high temperatures. Drought
resistant when established. Not often seen in landscape. Has been used as
a street tree in Los Gatos, California.

Plant may be observed at: *Arboreta*—Los Angeles; *Botanical Gardens*—
Huntington.

SARATOGA HORT. FDN.

P.K. THOMPSON

P.K. THOMPSON

Gordonia lasianthus (L.) Ellis. LOBLOLLY BAY. *Theaceae.* USDA Zones 7–9. U.S.A., coastal plain from North Carolina to central Florida and southern Mississippi. Introduced 1768.

DESCRIPTION
Broadleaved evergreen with fast rate of growth to 35–60' high; upright tree with compacted crown. Casts light shade.

Leaves: Alternate, simple, 2–7" long, narrowly elliptic; shiny dark green, lustrous and leathery; fine, blunt teeth along margin; turn scarlet and drop at end of second year.

Flowers: Single, white, tea-like blooms of 2–3" with yellow stamens; 5 large petals; fragrant. Blooms July-September.

Fruit: Woody, egg-shaped capsules contain flattened, winged seeds.

Winter aspect: Gray to red-brown bark has shallow to deep furrows; erect to slightly spreading habit.

CULTURE
Grows in sun (with sufficient moisture) and shade in loam or sand. Prefers acid conditions; tolerates wet conditions.

Disease and insect problems: None.

Transplanting: Difficult unless in container; root system shallow.

Propagation: By seed; easy from cuttings in late summer.

LANDSCAPE VALUE
Attractive, medium-sized evergreen with especially showy white flowers in summer, beautiful reddish foliage in fall and winter. Sometimes used as ornamental specimen. Found growing in moist, swampy areas; does not grow as well under cultivation. Similar to *Franklinia* which was once considered to be in *Gordonia* genus; however, *Franklinia* later proved to be sufficiently distinct to warrant its own genus.

Plant may be observed at: *Arboreta*—National; *Botanical Gardens*—Birmingham, U. of Georgia; *Gardens*—Bok Tower, Callaway.

M. DIRR

J. GREEN

L. WRINKLE

Guaiacum officinale L. LIGNUM-VITAE, GUM GUAIACUM. *Zygophyllaceae.* USDA Zone 10. USDA Zone 10. Dry coastal parts of Central America; northern South America, West Indies.

DESCRIPTION
Broadleaved evergreen growing slowly to 30–40'; crooked trunk, round crown. Casts light shade.

Leaves: Opposite, each leaf with 2–3 pairs of smooth, stemless, oval and leathery leaflets, 1–2" long; medium-dark green; at its base, each leaf has a tiny spot of orange: considerable variation in size and shape of leaves.

Flowers: Large clusters of felty, deep blue flowers at branch tip; old flowers fade to pale silver; each flower has five ½" petals surrounding 10 erect, yellow-tipped stamens, longer than the five sepals; year-round bloom.

Fruit: Yellow, broad, heart-shaped berries, about ¾" long, somewhat flattened, with angled edge; two-celled, each cell with one seed.

Winter aspect: Smooth bark, variegated in shades of gray and beige; branches furrowed and ashy; knotty, angular branches.

CULTURE
Grows in sun and shade and in clay, loam and sand with a wide pH range. Tolerates wind and wet conditions and is very drought-resistant. Resistant to salt spray in seaside plantings.

Disease and insect problems: None.

Transplanting: Move when young; difficult when mature; spreading root system.

Propagation: By seed.

LANDSCAPE VALUE
Lovely ornamental tree, especially in flower when the whole crown becomes swathed with a cast of silvery blue. In late summer the tree is enhanced with clusters of golden berries. Bark is handsome. Useful for small garden or patio, or as a container plant or bonsai. In silhouette is typical of an artist's conception of a tree. The fine-grained, extremely hard wood is the heaviest of all commercial woods and will not float in water. It is used for propeller shafts of steamships, bowling balls, mallets, bearings, etc. The wood, gum and bark all have medicinal qualities. The tree has many names in different regions of the world. Lignum vitae means "wood of life." Often called "Tree of Life."

Plant may be observed at: *Botanical Gardens*—Pacific Tropical; *Gardens*—Fairchild Tropical.

P. NOTTAGE

P. NOTTAGE

P. NOTTAGE

Gymnocladus dioicus (L.) K. Koch [G. canadensis de Lamarck]. KENTUCKY COFFEE TREE. *Leguminosae*. USDA Zones 4–8. Native eastern and central U.S. Introduced 1748.

DESCRIPTION *Deciduous* tree growing slowly to 60–100' high and 45–50' wide, with globose crown. Casts light shade.

Leaves: Alternate, up to 36" long and 19" wide, oval to ovate and acuminate; stalks persist after leaves have fallen. Leaves pink-tinted when unfolding, then blue-green in summer. Fall color not usually effective, but sometimes a pleasant warm yellow.

Flowers: Dioecious, green-white, 5-petaled symmetrical flowers in terminal panicles 8–12" long, 3–4" wide on female trees; panicles 3–4" long on male tree. The female tree has lovely fragrance. Blooms in spring.

Fruit: Red-brown, leathery, leguminose pods, 5–10", contain large brown-black, hard-shelled seeds which ripen in October.

Winter aspect: Gray bark tinged with red, deeply fissured and roughened by small scales; vertically ascending habit.

CULTURE Prefers moist, deep, rich soil but will adapt to a wide range of conditions: drought, limestone, pH range of 4.6–7. Needs sun for good growth. Tolerant of air pollution and some wind. Should be pruned in winter or early spring.

Disease and insect problems: None serious.

Transplanting: Balled and burlapped.

Propagation: By seed, scarified in sulfuric acid 6–8 hours; by cuttings of radical shoots taken in December.

LANDSCAPE VALUE Bold architectural habit creates an attractive tree that has been neglected in the landscape. Beautiful foliage in summer, handsome, textured gray bark and stubby branches create distinctive winter interest. Tolerates severe climates and city conditions. An excellent, tough tree for parks and golf courses, even though the falling pods can create litter. At one time the people of Kentucky and Tennessee roasted the seeds to make a coffee-like beverage, hence the common name. There is considerable variation in the species, thus it is preferable to select trees from seedlings grown from nearby seed trees.

Plant may be observed at: *Arboreta*—Arnold, Morton, National; *Botanical Gardens*—Brooklyn, Chicago, Missouri, New York; *Gardens*—Longwood, Winterthur.

M. DIRR

M. DIRR

M. DIRR

Halesia monticola C. Sargent. 'Rosea' MOUNTAIN SILVER BELL. *Styracaceae.* USDA
Zones 5–9. U.S.A., North Carolina to Tennessee and Georgia—mountains.
Introduced 1897.

DESCRIPTION *Deciduous* tree growing rapidly to 30–80', sometimes to 100'; large tree
that usually maintains central leader; conical habit. Casts light shade.

Leaves: To 7" long, elliptic to oblong-obovate; bright dark green, smooth,
often densely pubescent when young; pale yellow fall color.

Flowers: ¾–1" long, light pink bells in drooping, axillary clusters; in
spring.

Fruit: 4-winged, brown 1–2" pod; persists into winter.

Winter aspect: Smooth, bluish-gray bark with long buff streaks, becoming
rough and ridged in old specimens. Wide-spreading habit.

CULTURE Grows in sun and shade; prefers acid, loamy soil. Able to withstand urban
conditions.

Disease and insect problems: None serious.

Transplanting: Easy.

Propagation: By seed, stem cuttings.

LANDSCAPE
VALUE Graceful, refined tree with delicate bell-like flowers pendulous on
branches. Decorative in spring as it flowers before leaves; fruit attractive,
used for garlands. Good urban tree. Grows well in Boston.

Plant may be observed at: *Arboreta*—U. of Wisconsin-Madison; *Botanical
Gardens*—U. of Georgia.

E. HASSELKUS

A. BUSSEWITZ

E. HASSELKUS

Hoheria populnea A. Cunningham. LACEBARK. *Malvaceae.* USDA Zones 8–9. New Zealand. Planted by E. Walther and J. McLaren in San Francisco's parks in first half of this century.

DESCRIPTION *Evergreen,* growing at moderate to rapid rate to 30' high (45' in wild); rounded, narrow habit. Casts moderate shade.

Leaves: ¾" long, half as wide; serrated, elliptic, somewhat pendulous, glabrous; some stellate down on young leaves.

Flowers: White, star-shaped flowers, ¾–1" across in profuse clusters; in late summer.

Fruit: Dry, brown fruit in fall; does not persist.

Winter aspect: Interesting poplar-like bark.

CULTURE Grows in sun and shade in loam and sand. Tolerates wind.

Disease and insect problems: None.

Transplanting: Easy when young; root system deep.

Propagation: By seed.

LANDSCAPE VALUE Lovely, ornamental specimen tree, somewhat pendulous in habit. Profuse clusters of white flowers are extremely attractive. Handsome trunk on older trees. In cool, moist conditions of Golden Gate Park it produced a profusion of seedlings; however, this does not seem to be a problem in other environments.

Cv. 'Osbornii'—Flowers have purple-blue stamens; leaves are purple beneath.

Plant may be observed at: *Botanical Gardens*—Palmgarten; *Parks*—Golden Gate.

P.K. THOMPSON

P.K. THOMPSON

P.K. THOMPSON

Hovenia dulcis Thunberg [*H. dulcis* var. *glabra* Makino]. JAPANESE RAISIN TREE. *Rhamnaceae.* USDA Zones 5–8. China. Cultivated in Japan and India; introduced 1820. Named in honor of David Hoven (1724–87), senator of Amsterdam.

DESCRIPTION *Deciduous* tree growing at medium rate to 30' high; spread ⅔ of height; upright, oval to rounded habit. Casts light shade.

Leaves: Alternate, oval 4–7" long; glossy, medium-green in summer.

Flowers: Pale green to white, ⅓" dia., produced abundantly in many-flowered cymes near the ends of branches.

Fruit: ⅓", brown globular capsules.

Winter aspect: Flat gray-brown bark with wide ridges in shallow furrows; ascending main branches with few laterals.

CULTURE Grows in sun or light shade in loam and sand in wide pH range. Tolerates wind but not wet conditions.

Disease and insect problems: None serious.

Transplanting: Easy.

Propagation: By seed soaked in sulfuric acid 2 hours; softwood or hardwood cuttings.

LANDSCAPE VALUE An unusual and still uncommon ornamental in American gardens, grown for its handsome, glossy green foliage and full habit. As the fruit capsules mature, they become red and edible, tasting like a sweet raisin. They are considered a delicacy by Oriental peoples. When the flowers are ripe, they have a strong, sweet fragrance which attracts insects. Has potential as a container plant.

Plant may be observed at: *Arboreta*—Arnold, Los Angeles, National; *Botanical Gardens*—Brooklyn, Canton, Huntington, Missouri, Palmgarten, Royal/Kew; *Parks*—Forest Parks-Ibaraki, Japan.

N. BREWSTER

M. DIRR

N. BREWSTER

Idesia polycarpa Maximowicz. IIGIRI TREE. *Flacourtiaceae.* USDA Zones 7–9. Japan, China. Introduced into Europe by Maximowicz, the Russian botanist who found tree in Japan in 1860.

DESCRIPTION
Deciduous, dioecious tree, growing at medium rate to 40–50' high; spreads horizontally in distinct tiers as it grows. Casts medium shade.

Leaves: Alternate, cordate to ovate, 6–10" long and about as wide; long-stalked, widely spaced teeth, heart-shaped base and pointed on end; dark green glabrous above, glaucous beneath.

Flowers: Fragrant, tiny yellow flowers, ⅓", without petals, borne in large terminal panicles; unisexual and produced on different trees; male panicles 5–6" long, females in longer, looser panicles and with prominent globular ovaries; June-July blooms.

Fruit: Fleshy, many-seeded, bright red berries, 5/16" diam., borne in large pendent clusters, 6–10" long (only on female trees); showy in autumn and effective into mid-winter.

Winter aspect: Grayish, speckled bark; horizontal habit.

CULTURE
Grows well in full sun, partial shade, and slightly acid, loamy soil; will withstand wind and some air pollution.

Disease and insect problems: None serious.

Transplanting: Easy.

Propagation: By root and greenwood cuttings, and by seed; since tree is dioecious, vegetative propagation is essential if plants of known sex are to be produced.

LANDSCAPE VALUE
Interesting and seldom used tree. Little is accurately known about its hardiness range and its tolerances. In general appearance, it resembles the *catalpa,* but the leaves are not as large and are thicker. The attractive fruits, which hang like a bunch of grapes, create fall and winter interest. *Idesia* was named in honor of Eberhart Ysbrant Ides, 17th century Dutch traveler. The tree was later reintroduced from China by Wilson and Forrest. Most of the trees now cultivated are probably derived from those seedlings.

Plant may be observed at: *Arboreta*—Strybing; *Botanical Gardens*—Birmingham, Brooklyn, Huntington; *Parks*—Golden Gate, Forest Parks-Ibaraki, Japan.

N. BREWSTER

N. BREWSTER

N. BREWSTER

Ilex x altaclerensis (Dallimore) Rehder 'James G. Esson' (*I. aquifolium* L. x *I. perado* W. Aiton). ESSON HOLLY (female). *Aquifoliaceae.* USDA Zones 6–9. Eastern U.S.A. Introduced 1949 and named by T. H. Everett; seedling raised by J. G. Esson of Great Neck, Long Island.

DESCRIPTION   *Broadleaved evergreen* growing rapidly to 15' by 25' at maturity; growth habit broadly pyramidal. Casts dense shade.

Leaves: Oblong or elliptic, 2¼–4" long and 1½–2" wide, with 4–5 well developed spines; glossy, rich green.

Flowers: Inconspicuous, white petals united at base; in axillary clusters on previous year's growth.

Fruit: Large, shiny globose red berries, in fall.

Winter aspect: Smooth bark; compact branching habit; fruit persistent through winter.

CULTURE   Grows in sun or shade in well-drained loam or sandy soil in pH range of 5.0–7.0. Needs some protection from wind; moderately tolerant of drought, air and salt pollution and soil compaction. Fertilize yearly in February-March with mixed fertilizer containing 10% nitrogen.

Disease and insect problems: Some scale; seems resistant to holly leaf miner.

Transplanting: Easy; root system shallow.

Propagation: By cuttings taken in late fall.

LANDSCAPE VALUE   One of the hardiest cultivars, of vigorous habit and heavily berried, this is excellent as a specimen tree or in an evergreen border. Berries remain on the tree through winter, since birds do not enjoy the fruit until after a heavy frost. Must have male of the same species in the vicinity to ensure fruit production. The *I. x altaclerensis* group of hollies is thought to have originated from a natural crossing of the Azores and Canary Island hollies (*I. perado*) and the English hollies (*I. aquifolium*).

Other good varieties are 'Camelliifolia', introduced from France in 1858, and 'Wilsonii', introduced from England in 1899.

Plant may be observed at: *Arboreta*—Los Angeles, U. of Washington; *Botanical Gardens*—New York, Van Dusen; *Gardens*—Callaway.

N. BREWSTER

N. BREWSTER

N. BREWSTER

Ilex x aquipernyi Gable ex W. Clarke 'San Jose' (*I. aquifolium* L. x *I. Pernyi* Franchet).
SAN JOSE HOLLY (female). *Aquifoliaceae.* USDA Zones 6–8. U.S.A.
Introduced in 1950s; source unknown.

DESCRIPTION *Broadleaved evergreen,* growing at a relatively rapid rate to 20–25′ high; pyramidal habit.

Leaves: Small, averaging ¾–1½″ long, strongly spined, twisted; highly glossy, dark green in color.

Flowers: Inconspicuous white petals united at base; axillary clusters on previous year's growth.

Fruit: Bright red globose berries ripen in fall.

Winter aspect: Smooth bark, compact branching habit. Evergreen leaves and fruit persistent through winter.

CULTURE Grows in full sun or light shade in fertile, well-drained loam or sandy soil with pH range of 5.0 to 7.0. In northern areas of its range, a moist soil is advisable before ground freezes, and protection from winter winds and sun is desirable. Will tolerate some drought and high air pollution, some salt pollution and soil compaction. Hollies should be fertilized every year in February or March with mixed commercial fertilizer containing 8–10% nitrogen.

Disease and insect problems: None.

Transplanting: Easy; root system shallow.

Propagation: By both hardwood and softwood cuttings taken in fall.

LANDSCAPE VALUE Excellent as specimen tree or as hedge; interestingly textured due to small, glossy leaves. Plant is dioecious and needs male of same species, or either *I. aquifolium* or *I. pernyi* in vicinity, to ensure fruit production.

Other good varieties are 'Brilliant' (female clone) and 'Aquipern' (male clone); they should be planted in same vicinity to ensure fruit production.

Plant may be observed at: *Arboreta*—Bernheim Forest, National, Planting Fields, U. of Washington; *Botanical Gardens*—Brooklyn.

N. BREWSTER

N. BREWSTER

N. BREWSTER

Ilex opaca W. Aiton. 'Miss Helen' MISS HELEN HOLLY (female). *Aquifoliaceae.* USDA Zones 5–7. Eastern U.S.A. Introduced 1944 by Stewart H. McLean.

DESCRIPTION   *Broadleaved evergreen* growing relatively rapidly to 40–50′ at maturity; pyramidal habit.

Leaves: Average in size, 2¼″ long x 1¼″ wide, elliptic to oval with stout, rigid spines; dull yellow-green in color.

Flowers: Inconspicuous, creamy white, petals united at base, axillary on current year's growth; solitary or in 2–3 flowered cymes.

Fruit: Dark, glossy, globose red berries; mature November-December.

Winter aspect: Smooth bark, short branches; spreading, compact habit. Fruit persistent through winter.

CULTURE   Grows in either sun or shade in well-drained loam or sandy soil in pH range of 5.0–7.0. Protection from winter winds and sun is advisable. Will withstand some drought, salt pollution and soil compaction, and high air pollution. Should be fertilized yearly in February-March with mixed fertilizer containing 8–10% nitrogen.

Disease and insect problems: Holly leaf miner and holly berry midge are the most common.

Transplanting: Easy; root system shallow.

Propagation: By both hardwood and softwood cuttings taken in fall from current season's growth.

LANDSCAPE VALUE   Excellent as a specimen tree, in an evergreen border, or as hedge. Beautifully shaped. Plant is dioecious and therefore needs male of same species in vicinity to ensure fruit production. Wood from *I. opaca* has been used for making canes, scroll work and furniture. Stained black, it is substituted for ebony and used for inlay. The American Indians preserved holly berries and used them as decorative buttons; these were eagerly traded with tribes that did not grow hollies. They planted holly around their dwellings for protection, and, as the tree was strong and evergreen, as an emblem of courage and everlasting life.

There are many good varieties of *I. opaca* with red fruit; others with yellow fruit include 'Canary' and 'Morgan Gold'.

Plant may be observed at: *Arboreta*—Bernheim Forest, Dawes, National, Planting Fields; *Botanical Gardens*—Birmingham, Missouri; *Gardens*—Longwood.

N. BREWSTER

N. BREWSTER

N. BREWSTER

Ilex pedunculosa Miquel [*I. fujisanensis* Sakata]. LONG-STALK HOLLY. *Aquifoliaceae.*
USDA Zones 5–8. China and Japan. Introduced in 1893 in England by
Miquel.

DESCRIPTION *Broadleaved evergreen*, generally of broadly upright habit, growing slowly
to 25–30′. Casts dense shade.

Leaves: 1½–3″ long and ¾–1¼″ wide; alternate, simple, acuminate, entire,
ovate or elliptic; smooth, lustrous green above, paler beneath. Foliage
resembles that of Mountain Laurel (*Kalmia latifolia*). Leaves persist for 3
years.

Flowers: Inconspicuous, white or greenish, petals combined at base,
peduncles 1–2″ long, axillary on current year's growth.

Fruit: ¼″ dia., long-stalked, pendent, globose, bright red, in fall.

Winter aspect: Bark smooth, branching fairly compact. Fruit persists into
November. In exposed areas, develops yellow cast in winter.

CULTURE Grows in full sun or light shade in loam or sand in pH range of 5.0–7.0;
prefers good drainage and some protection from wind. Not adaptable to
chalky soils. Will withstand high air pollution, some salt pollution and soil
compaction. Has survived in harsh conditions of Midwest: heavy soils,
strong, dry winds and intense summer heat.

Disease and insect problems: None observed.

Transplanting: Easy; root system shallow.

Propagation: By cuttings or by seed.

LANDSCAPE VALUE An interesting, handsome small tree with beautiful, smooth, lustrous dark
green leaves and long-stalked bright red berries; valued as a specimen
tree. Branching habit not quite as dense as that of most other hollies; thus,
its form seems more graceful. One of the hardiest of the evergreen hollies
and one of the few grown in northern gardens. Fruits are relished by
birds. Being dioecious, it needs a male of the same species in the vicinity
to ensure fruit production. Should be fertilized yearly in February-March
with a mixed commercial fertilizer containing 8–10% nitrogen.

Plant may be observed at: *Arboreta*—Arnold, Bernheim Forest, Dawes,
National, Planting Fields, U. of Washington; *Botanical Gardens*—Brooklyn,
Chicago, Denver, Missouri, Van Dusen; *Gardens*—Brookgreen, Longwood,
Callaway; *Parks*—Forest Parks-Ibaraki, Japan.

G. AVERY

PLANTING FIELDS ARB.

A. BUSSEWITZ

Kalopanax pictus (Thunberg) Nakai. (*K. septemlobus* G. Koidzumi) CASTOR-ARALIA. *Araliaceae.* USDA Zones 5–7. China, Manchuria, Japan. Introduced 1865 by Maximowicz. Native of Japan, forests of Hokkaido, also found on other islands. Native also to Sakhalin Island, Russian Far East, Korea and China.

DESCRIPTION
Deciduous, round-headed tree; can grow to 80–90' in wild with trunk to 4' in dia.; under cultivation more typically 40–60' high with equal spread. Casts dense shade.

Leaves: Palmate, 7–12" across, 5–7 lobes, toothed, coarse; dark green above, light green and pubescent beneath; similar to Sweet Gum but larger. Fall color reddish.

Flowers: Produced in many 1"-dia. umbels which form large, 12–24" terminal panicles; 5 petals, white.

Fruit: Small black drupe in early fall. Fruits every other year.

Winter aspect: Mature trunk is ridged and black. Young stems have stout, yellowish prickles. Branching habit is round-headed, with massive, open branches.

CULTURE
Grows in sun in deep, rich, moist loam. Needs moisture but will also tolerate very dry soil when established.

Disease and insect problems: Seems pest- and disease-resistant.

Transplanting: Ball and burlap and move when young; prune during spring.

Propagation: Seeds take two years to germinate but they germinate approximately 90% second spring. Seeds should be stratified 60–90 days (warm plus cold stratification).

LANDSCAPE VALUE
An elegant, large shade tree. Flowers are enjoyed by bees; fruit attractive in fall, eaten by birds. This extremely hardy, trouble-free tree has very tropical-looking foliage, is long-lived and tolerant of alkaline soils.

Var. *'maximowiczii'* has more deeply loped leaves.

Plant may be observed at: *Arboreta*—Arnold, Dawes, U. of Washington, U. of Wisconsin-Madison; *Botanical Gardens*—Chicago, Royal/Kew.

M. DIRR

M. DIRR

M. DIRR

Koelreuteria bipinnata Franchet. CHINESE FLAME TREE. *Sapindaceae.* USDA Zones 6–9. China. Introduced about 1900.

DESCRIPTION   *Deciduous* tree with spreading crown, growing moderately fast to 30–40′ at maturity. Casts medium shade.

Leaves: Compound, alternate, bipinnate, to 18″ long, with 7–12 ovate-oblong serrate leaflets to 5″ long; dark green above, light green and usually pubescent beneath.

Flowers: Small, 5-lobed with 4–5 petals, yellow; borne in large, showy terminal panicles; fragrant; blooms early summer.

Fruit: Capsules 2–2½″ long with 3 ovate papery segments, rose-pink, in late summer to fall.

Winter aspect: Bark light brown, smooth; ridged and furrowed on older trunks.

CULTURE   Prefers full sun or filtered shade; withstands wind, drought, heat and air pollution. Adaptable to wide range of soils.

Disease and insect problems: None serious.

Transplanting: Easy when young, balled and burlapped; root system deep.

Propagation: By seed stratified 90 days at 40°F; seeds germinate within 6–8 days.

LANDSCAPE VALUE   One of the few yellow-flowering trees; flowers are showy and bloom later than most. Bladder-like fruits of papery texture are very decorative, resembling Chinese lanterns. The tree has a beautiful textural pattern, almost like that of a tree fern. Excellent as a small lawn tree, street tree, or as a specimen tree in limited space. It needs no pruning except for occasional shaping and to remove dead wood. Not as hardy as *K. paniculata.*

Plant may be observed at: *Arboreta*—Los Angeles, National; *Botanical Gardens*—Royal/Kew, U. of Georgia.

W. ADAMS

J. RAULSTON

G. COURTRIGHT

Koelreuteria paniculata Laxmann. [*K. paniculata* var. apiculata (Rehder & E. H. Wilson) Rehder] GOLDEN RAIN TREE. *Sapindaceae.* USDA Zones 5–9. China and Korea. Introduced 1763.

DESCRIPTION *Deciduous* tree growing moderately to 30–40' with equal or greater spread; round-headed, open branching habit. Casts fairly dense shade.

Leaves: Alternate, pinnate to 18" long; 7–15 leaflets 1½–3" long; ovate, crenate, serrate; glabrous, medium green above, pubescent on vein areas beneath. Yellow fall color lacks vibrance.

Flowers: 8–14" long clusters of small yellow flowers, each about ½" wide, carried above foliage; fragrant. Blooms in June in South, in summer in northern states.

Fruit: 1½–2" long, bladder-like greenish capsules, which turn brown, contain black, hard seeds; clusters persist into winter.

Winter aspect: Light brown, ridged, furrowed bark; branches spreading and ascending.

CULTURE Grows in sun and shade in clay, loam and sand with a wide pH range; performs best in full sun. Withstands heat, wind and drought; tolerates city conditions, air pollution.

Disease and insect problems: None serious; leaf spot, canker, coral-spot fungus and root rot reported.

Transplanting: Easy; best moved as small tree, balled and burlapped.

Propagation: By seed, cuttings.

LANDSCAPE VALUE Excellent small lawn or patio tree; adaptable to diverse soils and environmental stress. Suggested as a street tree. Showy, late, yellow flowers create lovely ornamental specimen. May also be grown as an understory tree for woodland areas.

Cv. 'Fastigiata'—strongly upright to 25' with 6' spread
'September'—late flowering, not so hardy as species.

Plant may be observed at: *Arboreta*—American Horticultural Society-River Farm, Arnold, Bernheim Forest, Dawes, Los Angeles, Morton, National, U. of Washington, U. of Wisconsin-Madison; *Botanical Gardens*—Brooklyn, Chicago, Denver, Missouri, Munich, New York, Palmgarten, Royal/Kew, U. of Georgia, Van Dusen; *Gardens*—Brookgreen, Callaway; *Parks*—Forest Parks-Ibaraki, Japan.

M. DIRR

N. BREWSTER   M. DIRR

Laburnum x watereri (Kirchner) Dippel 'Vossii' (*L. alpinum* Berchtold & J. Presl x *L. anagyroides* Medicus). GOLDEN-CHAIN TREE. *Leguminosae.* USDA Zones 6–7. Holland. Introduced 1864.

DESCRIPTION   *Deciduous* tree growing at medium rate (12–20″ per year) to 12–15′ high and 9–12′ wide at maturity; upright, vase-shaped habit. Casts light shade.

Leaves: Alternate, stalked leaves with 3 leaflets, elliptic to elliptic-ovate, 1-3″ long; bright blue-green in summer.

Flowers: Yellow, ¾″, on silky racemes up to 2′ in length, in spring; wisteria-like blooms, larger than those of parents.

Fruit: Pod, of no ornamental consequence.

Winter aspect: Olive-green bark on young branches and trunk; vase-shaped habit.

CULTURE   Needs full sun for best flowering; prefers moist, well-drained loam with peat added; tolerant of high pH. Adaptable to many conditions but will not tolerate standing water; plant in protected area.

Disease and insect problems: Mildew, aphids, black spot, twig blight; plant in sites with good air circulation.

Transplanting: Balled and burlapped; few problems once established.

Propagation: By scarified seeds sown as soon as ripe in cold frame; by root sprout cuttings.

LANDSCAPE VALUE   Superb small tree. Extremely effective in bloom and when planted in groups. When in full flower, the streaming racemes of golden color are strikingly beautiful. Widely planted in Europe, but relatively uncommon in the United States. The German popular name Goldregen (Golden Rain) is extremely descriptive. Tree can be grown in containers in colder climates and forced into bloom in greenhouses; excellent choice for pleached arch. Easy to cultivate, raised readily from seed. Thrives in a wide variety of soils and conditions. Should be grown more widely in the United States. Care should be exercised when using this tree in a public garden, since seeds are poisonous.

Plant may be observed at: *Arboreta*—Los Angeles, National, Planting Fields, U. of Washington; *Botanical Gardens*—British Columbia, Brooklyn, Munich, Royal/Kew, Van Dusen; *Gardens*—Filoli, Longwood.

A. MacBRIDE

H. FLINT

A. MacBRIDE

Lagerstroemia indica L. 'Alba' [*L. elegans,* Wallich ex Paxton]. WHITE CRAPE MYRTLE. *Lythraceae.* USDA Zones 7–9. China, Korea. Introduced to Royal Botanic Garden-Kew in 1759.

DESCRIPTION
Deciduous tree growing rapidly to 20′ at maturity; upright to round-headed habit. Casts light shade.

Leaves: Opposite, fine-textured, privet-like, oblong-elliptic to rounded, 3¾″, dark green, lustrous; foliage dense on upper third of tree.

Flowers: White crinkled petals borne in terminal panicles 6–8″ long; August-September blooms on current year's wood.

Fruit: Loculicidal capsule longer than calyx tube, persisting through winter; seeds winged.

Winter aspect: Very smooth, mottled, gray, pink and cinnamon bark exfoliating in irregular patches; often multi-stemmed.

CULTURE
Grows in sun (best for flowering) or light shade; performs best in well-drained soil supplemented with peat moss, and with good water-holding capacity. Plant will usually persist but suffers from frequent die-back north of Washington, D.C. Does not tolerate wet conditions or drought. Needs good air circulation to control mildew.

Disease and insect problems: Mildew, aphids, scale; Japanese beetle can be a problem where prevalent.

Transplanting: Difficult since sensitive to root disturbance; plant balled and burlapped in late spring before new growth.

Propagation: Softwood cuttings from leafy summer shoots; by seed, but flowers may be of inferior colors.

LANDSCAPE VALUE
Strikingly beautiful specimen tree with profuse summer bloom and extremely attractive winter bark. Amenable to heavy winter pruning, which creates compact growth. May be pruned for use as hedge; good container plant, E.H. Wilson found *L. indica* in open, grassy lands and on cliffs from central to west China.

Cultivars:
  The National Arboretum has introduced mildew-resistant cultivars:
  'Cherokee'—brilliant red flowers
  'Potomac'—pink flowers
  'Seminole'—medium pink flowers
  'Natchez'—white flowers with magnificent cinnamon bark
  'Near East'—delicate pink flowers

Plant may be observed at: *Arboreta*—National, Planting Fields; *Botanical Gardens*—Birmingham, Canton, Pacific Tropical, Palmgarten, U. of Georgia; *Gardens*—Bok Tower, Brookgreen, Dixon; *Parks*—Forest Parks-Ibaraki, Japan.

J. RAULSTON

N. BREWSTER

N. BREWSTER

Larix decidua P. Miller [*L. Europaea* de Candolle]. EUROPEAN LARCH. *Pinaceae.* USDA Zones 2–6. North and Central Europe. Introduced 1910.

DESCRIPTION *Deciduous conifer.* Grows moderately rapidly to 80–100' or more. Has single trunk with horizontal branches and graceful pendulous branchlets. Pyramidal in habit. Casts moderate to light shade.

Leaves: Soft, flat, short, bright green needles 1¼" long, in clusters on spurs and in spirals on terminal branches. Fall color yellow to rust before needles drop.

Flowers and fruit: Male cones solitary; purplish female cones ovoid, 1–1½" long and ¾–1" wide when young, maturing in one year.

Winter aspect: Bark has small loose reddish elongate plates. Tree has dominant single trunk with pendulous newer branches and persistent cones in clusters.

CULTURE Grows in clay, loam or sand with pH of 6.0–7.2, in sun, shade and wind and even wet conditions. Tolerant of most stresses; soil compaction may be detrimental. Intolerant of salt.

Disease and insect problems: Needle rust *(Melampsora paradoxa)* uncommon, but known to occur. Larch canker is known in Europe.

Transplanting: Moderately easy; roots are shallow to deep.

Propagation: By seed, grafts, and cuttings.

LANDSCAPE VALUE A long-lived large tree. Bright green needles in springtime make a beautiful contrast with verdure of other plants. Tree has an attractive habit of growth: horizontal branching with pendulous new growth is unusual and arresting. Cones attract birds in winter. This tree is one of the few deciduous conifers. It is attractive planted in groups as screening, and excellent as a specimen tree for parks. Its only unfavorable characteristics are that it can accumulate cones and debris on the ground and is somewhat susceptible to ice breakage.

Plant may be observed at: *Arboreta*—Arnold, Cary, Dawes, Holden, Minnesota Landscape, Morton, Planting Fields, U. of Washington, U. of Wisconsin-Madison; *Botanical Gardens*—Chicago, Munich, New York, Palmgarten, Royal/Kew, Van Dusen; *Gardens*—Longwood.

M. DIRR

M. DIRR

M. DIRR

Larix kaempferi (Lambert) Carriere [*L. leptolepis* (Siebold & Zuccarini) Gordon]. JAPANESE LARCH. *Pinaceae.* USDA Zones 5–7. Japan. Introduced 1861 by John Gould Veitch.

DESCRIPTION
Deciduous conifer of very open, conical habit. Rate of growth medium to fast; reaches 80–90' at maturity, with 30–40' spread and trunk 3–4' thick. Casts light shade.

Leaves: Needle-like to 1½" long, underside keeled with white glaucous bands. Fall color yellow-gold.

Flowers: Insignificant, monoecious.

Fruit: Stalked cones 1–1½" long, scales keeled, forming a rosette.

Winter aspect: Bark peeling off in long strips, showing red underneath; branching habit ascending. Young shoots glabrous to downy.

CULTURE
Grows in sun; tolerates wet conditions well. Also tolerates shallow, acid soils; is intolerant of chalky soils, polluted and shaded areas. Needs free air circulation; is likely to grow well on north-facing slopes.

Disease and insect problems: Larch case bearer, woolly aphid, sawfly, tussock and gypsy moth, leaf-cast, needle rusts. Less susceptible to canker than other larches.

Transplanting: Easy.

Propagation: By seed, cuttings or grafting onto seedling understock.

LANDSCAPE VALUE
This is one of the handsomest and fastest growing larches and has good fall color. It is more open in habit than *L. decidua,* but less hardy and more susceptible to drought. Distinguishing features from *L. decidua: L. kaempferi* has red-brown shoots, blue-green leaves to glaucous, wider needles, broader cones. An excellent candidate for parks, golf courses and large areas.

Plant may be observed at: *Arboreta*—Arnold, Bernheim Forest, Holden, Minnesota Landscape, Morton, National, Planting Fields, U. of Washington, U. of Wisconsin-Madison; *Botanical Gardens*—Brooklyn, Chicago, Munich, Royal-Kew, Van Dusen; *Gardens*—Longwood, Old Westbury; *Parks*—Forest Parks-Ibaraki, Japan.

E. HASSELKUS

M. DIRR

E. HASSELKUS

Luma apiculata (de Candolle) Burret [*Eugenia apiculata* de Candolle; *Myrceugenia apiculata* (de Candolle) Niedenzu]. *Myrtaceae.* USDA Zones 8–10. Chile. Introduced in 1912. Golden Gate Park.

DESCRIPTION *Evergreen,* small tree to 25', wider than high at maturity. Growth rate moderate. Casts moderate shade.

Leaves: ½–1" long, ovate, rounded, pointed at end; dark green, new growth light green.

Flowers: ½" in dia., creamy white; in profusion in summer and early fall.

Fruit: Black globose berries in fall/winter, ⅜" across.

Winter aspect: Evergreen shiny foliage and striking cinnamon-red colored bark.

CULTURE Grows in sun; will tolerate some shade, wind and wet conditions if well-drained; drought-resistant when established. Prefers loamy soil but will grow in sandy or clay soil. Tolerates high acidity.

Disease and insect problems: None noted.

Transplanting: Easy when young.

Propagation: By seed or semi-hardwood cuttings.

LANDSCAPE VALUE Handsome small specimen tree or can be used as screen. Often grows as multi-trunked tree with graceful appearance. Late summer bloom and striking orange bark make it valuable addition to any garden. The year-round appearance is neat and handsome.

Plant may be observed at: *Arboreta*—Strybing; *Gardens*—Filoli; *Parks*—Forest Parks-Ibaraki, Japan.

S. MacBRIDE

S. MacBRIDE

M. GALLAGHER

Maackia amurensis Ruprecht & Maximowicz [*Cladrastis amurensis* (Ruprecht & Maximowicz) K. Koch]. AMUR MAACKIA. *Leguminosae.* USDA Zones 3–7. Manchuria. Named for Richard Maack, Russian naturalist who died in 1886.

DESCRIPTION
Deciduous tree growing slowly (12′ in 20 years) to 20–30′ high in cultivation and 40′ in wild; wider than tall, with small, rounded head.

Leaves: Alternate, compound, pinnate-ovate to elliptic, 3–8″ long; 7–11 leaflets 1½–3″ long; glabrous, dark green in summer; fall color of no consequence.

Flowers: Dull white tinged with palest slate-blue; set on stiff, erect and dense racemes 4–6″ long; in July.

Fruit: Flat pod 2–3″ long, ⅓″ wide; in September-October.

Winter aspect: Shiny copper brown bark peeling with maturity; lateral branching habit.

CULTURE
Performs best in sunny location in good, loose, well-drained acid or alkaline soil. Will tolerate some wind but not extreme wet or dry conditions. All pruning should be done when tree is young and branches small as cuts and wounds to older trees do not heal readily.

Disease and insect problems: None serious.

Transplanting: Easy.

Propagation: By seed soaked in hot water (190°F) 24 hours; by cuttings.

LANDSCAPE VALUE
Very hardy, durable and adaptable, slow growing small tree; a potential street tree. Attractive, clean foliage and late summer flowers produced on young plants. Valued especially for its wide hardiness range.

Plant may be observed at: *Arboreta*—Bernheim Forest, Holden, Minnesota Landscape, Morton, National, Planting Fields, Spring Grove, U. of Washington, U. of Wisconsin-Madison; *Botanical Gardens*—Brooklyn, Missouri, New York, Palmgarten, Royal/Kew; *Gardens*—Winterthur; *Parks*—Forest Parks-Ibaraki, Japan.

M. DIRR

M. DIRR

M. DIRR

Magnolia acuminata (L.) L. CUCUMBER TREE, INDIAN BITTER. *Magnoliaceae.* USDA Zones 4–9. Eastern U.S. forests of Carolinas and Tennessee. Introduced 1726 by John Clayton, Virginia's early botanist; later sent to England by John Bartram.

DESCRIPTION *Deciduous* tree growing rapidly to 60–90' with comparable spread at maturity. Pyramidal when young, broader when mature. Blooms in early June. Casts dense shade unless limbed up.

Leaves: Alternate, 5–10" long, elliptic to oblong-ovate, coarse; light green and downy beneath, dark green above. Insignificant fall color; some develop ash-brown color.

Flowers: 3", yellow-green, erect, bell-shaped; inconspicuous because color blends with young foliage. Flowers slightly fragrant.

Fruit: In early fall, pink to red, 3" long, cucumber-like shape, hence name.

Winter aspect: Thin, scaly, gray-brown bark; young branches erect, wide; arching branches when mature.

CULTURE Grows in full sun or partial shade in calcareous soils of Midwest; likes slightly acid, moist, well-drained loam; does not tolerate excessive moisture, drought or pollution. Prune after flowering.

Disease and insect problems: Essentially pest-free; occasional scale.

Transplanting: Has fleshy root; plant in early spring, not too deeply.

Propagation: Seed, stratified 90 days; cuttings.

LANDSCAPE VALUE Specimen tree; hardy, mature trees have beautiful, gracious, spreading branches. Does not look well when restrained by pruning, so should only be used where it can develop naturally. Excellent tree for parks, golf courses and large estates. One of the fastest growing magnolias. The wood, which closely resembles that of the tulip tree, is often sold as poplar and is used for lumber. Francois Michaux collected seeds to send to Europe. They were kept viable by putting them in damp moss. In July 1802, he observed, "The inhabitants of the remotest parts of Pennsylvania and Virginia pick the cones when green to infuse in whiskey, which gives it a pleasant bitter."

Cultivar 'Elizabeth' (*M. acuminata x M. heptapeta*) patented by the Brooklyn Botanic Garden in 1977; habit pyramidal, flowers primrose yellow.

Plant may be observed at: *Arboreta*—Arnold, Dawes, Morton, National, Planting Fields, U. of Washington; *Botanical Gardens*—Berry, Brooklyn, Canton, Chicago, Missouri, Munich, New York, Palmgarten, Royal/Kew, U. of Georgia; *Gardens*—Brookgreen, Callaway, Longwood, Old Westbury, Winterthur.

M. DIRR

R. HEBB

K. KOHOUT

Magnolia heptapeta (Buc'hoz) Dandy [*M. conspicua* Salisbury; *M. denudata* Desroysseaux; *M. Yulan* Desfontaines]. YULAN MAGNOLIA. *Magnoliaceae.* USDA Zones 5–7. Central China. Introduced 1789.

DESCRIPTION **Deciduous** tree with irregular habit; grows relatively fast to 30–40' with equal spread.

Leaves: Alternate, simple, obovate-oblong, 4–6" long, 2–3½" wide; dark green above, light green beneath, slightly pubescent; no conspicuous fall color.

Flowers: 9 petals, ivory-white, fragrant, 5–6" across; tulip-shaped bud, saucer-shaped when open; blooms before *M. x soulangiana.*

Fruit: Green pods, turning brown, oblong to 5"; open early fall; red seeds within.

Winter aspect: Interesting magnolia pewter bark; interesting spreading habit.

CULTURE Grows in sun and some shade; prefers rich soil with some moisture; does not tolerate extreme drought or moisture. Hardy to cold, but does poorly in very hot, dry, windy areas. Does well in Los Angeles-Pasadena area.

Disease and insect problems: None serious; magnolia scale.

Transplanting: Difficult, unless moved in early spring, balled and burlapped; root system thick, fleshy.

Propagation: Difficult to root from cuttings; often grafted on *M. x soulangiana.* Seeds quickly lose viability; should be sown as soon as ripe.

LANDSCAPE VALUE Early-blooming small to medium specimen tree. Magnificent flowers before leaves; used effectively in flower arrangements. Excellent foliage, interesting seed pods and winter branches. Can be grown as multi-stemmed tree. Early spring warm spells may produce early flowering, which can be injured by late frosts.* Magnolia bark easily damaged; should not be used as street tree. In cultivation in China 1,300 years before introduction to England in 1789. Received Award of Garden Merit from Royal Horticultural Society in 1936. Not often found in nurseries and should be grown more.

Was used as parent of 'Elizabeth' (*M. acuminata x M. heptapeta*) patented by the Brooklyn Botanic Garden in 1977. Cv. 'Japanese Clone' has larger flowers, hardier buds; Cv. 'Lacey' has larger flowers, up to 8" across.

Plant may be observed at: *Arboreta*—Arnold, Dawes, Los Angeles, National, Planting Fields, Strybing, U. of Washington; *Botanical Gardens*—Brooklyn, Canton, Huntington, Missouri, Palmgarten; *Gardens*—Filoli, Longwood; *Parks*—Golden Gate.

*Site carefully to avoid frost damage—survives better on North facing sites. Adapted to city use—good for small enclosed city (urban) garden.

N. BREWSTER

N. BREWSTER

PLANTING FIELDS

Magnolia x *loebneri* Kache 'Merrill' (*M. kobus* de Candolle x *M. stellata* Maximowicz). *Magnoliaceae.* USDA Zones 4–8. U.S.A. Introduced 1939 at Arnold Arboretum.

DESCRIPTION   *Deciduous* tree with spreading, pyramidal habit; grows rapidly to 20–30' (25' in 17 years) at maturity. Casts dense shade.

Leaves: 2–4" long, oval to oblong, dark green above, lighter beneath; insignificant fall color; slightly larger than *M. stellata.*

Flowers: 8–15 petals, white with blush of pink at base, 4–6", fragrant; slightly larger than *M. stellata;* blooms mid to late April in Midwest.

Fruit: Knobby, cucumber-like pods to 3" long, containing red seeds.

Winter aspect: Pewter bark, winter buds and spreading, irregular branching habit add interest.

CULTURE   Grows in sun and light shade in acid loam. Tolerates wind if not strong and some drought; prefers good drainage; does not tolerate wet conditions.

Disease and insect problems: None evident.

Transplanting: Early spring, balled and burlapped; roots fleshy, must not dry out.

Propagation: By cuttings of new wood, layering or grafting on *M. kobus.*

LANDSCAPE VALUE   Vigorous growing, picturesque, flowering tree with spectacular blooms, bright green foliage. Blooms at young age; a late freeze may ruin early blooms. Tree has performed well at Minnesota Landscape Arboretum. 'Merrill' is one of the taller cultivars of *M. x loebneri.*

Other cultivars:
'Ballerina'—hybrid from seeds of *M. x loebneri* and perhaps back-crossed by *M. stellata.* Flowers unusual, 30 or more petals, longer lasting than most.
'Leonard Messel' —lilac-pink flowers.
'Spring Snow'—fragrant, long lasting flowers; slightly less susceptible to frost damage than 'Merrill'.

Plant may be observed at: *Arboreta*—Arnold, Dawes, Morton, National, Planting Fields, Strybing, U. of Washington, U. of Wisconsin-Madison; *Botanical Gardens*—Atlanta, Birmingham, Brooklyn, Chicago, Missouri, Royal/Kew; *Gardens*—Longwood; *Parks*—Golden Gate.

R. HEBB

M. DIRR

R. HEBB

Magnolia virginiana L. [*M. glauca* L.]. SWEET BAY MAGNOLIA, SWAMP BAY MAGNOLIA. *Magnoliaceae.* USDA Zones 5–9. Coastal area of eastern U.S., Massachusetts to Florida and Texas. Introduced 1688.

DESCRIPTION *Deciduous* in North, nearly *evergreen* in South. Pyramidal, upright tree in South, more shrublike in North. Grows at medium to fast rate to 15–25' high with 10–15' spread in North, to 60' high in South.

Leaves: Alternate, simple, oblong to 5"; glaucous-gray under surface, dark lustrous green above; very little fall color.

Flowers: 9–12 white petals, water lily shape, 2–3" across; very fragrant, lemon scent; flowers appear with leaves. Bloom late May-early June to September; slow to flower when young.

Fruit: Interesting and attractive cucumber-like pods to 2", which hang suspended by threads before falling; contain red seeds.

Winter aspect: Gray to brown, smooth bark; spreading, low branches.

CULTURE Grows in sun and some shade; requires acid soil; prefers loam. Does well in wet, almost swampy soils; does not like dry situations. Grows best in warm climate; winter damage possible in northern Zone 5.

Disease and insect problems: Few.

Transplanting: Best done in early spring, when young; fleshy root system requires tree to be balled and burlapped.

Propagation: By cutting, grafting, or seed, which should be stratified.

LANDSCAPE VALUE Excellent specimen tree with handsome, lustrous green foliage, lovely creamy white flowers and attractive red fruit pods. Blooms off and on all summer. Can be grown as multi-stemmed tree. Can be rejuvenated by selective pruning, which is not possible with all magnolias. More tolerant of wet soil than most magnolias; also tolerates some shade and wind. Tends to chlorosis in calcareous soils of Midwest. Bark at one time was source of official drug for treatment of rheumatism and malaria; use has been abandoned. Flowers used in perfume manufacture and leaves as flavoring for meat.

Cv. 'Henry Hicks' remains evergreen at temperatures low as −17°F.

Plant may be observed at: *Arboreta*—Arnold, Bernheim Forest, Dawes, Morton, National, Planting Fields, U. of Washington; *Botanical Gardens*—Berry, Birmingham, Brooklyn, Denver, Missouri, Royal/Kew, U. of Georgia; *Gardens*—Brookgreen, Callaway, Dixon, Longwood.

N. BREWSTER

J. GREEN

HOLDEN ARB.

Malus 'Adams'. ADAMS CRAB APPLE. *Rosaceae.* USDA Zone 5–8. U.S.A. Introduced c. 1947 by Walter Adams, Adams Nursery, Inc., Westfield, Mass.

DESCRIPTION *Deciduous*, rounded dense tree to 20–25' at maturity; rate of growth moderate. Casts dense shade.

Leaves: 2–3" long, elliptical, serrulate; light green with reddish tinge on new growth; fall color yellow.

Flowers: Carmine buds and flowers fading to pink, single, with 5 petals, 1½" in diameter.

Fruit: Red, ⅝" in diameter. Color develops about mid-July, peaking in September to October.

Winter aspect: Fruit persists with good color even after frost. Bark and branching habit typical of *Malus.*

CULTURE Does best in full sun in well-drained loam in pH range of 5.0–7.5. There is little information as to its tolerance of environmental stresses except that it does tolerate drought and soil compaction.

Disease and insect problems: Very resistant to major diseases and major insect pests, but is subject to minor pests such as aphids, mites, scale, borers, and caterpillars.

Transplanting: No major problems with either balled and burlapped or bare root.

Propagation: Mainly by budding, also by root grafting.

LANDSCAPE VALUE When a crab apple is being chosen on the basis of red flowers, 'Adams' should be considered at the top of the list. Few red crabs are resistant to disease: 'Adams' is resistant to scab, fire blight, and cedar apple rust, and only slightly susceptible to powdery mildew. It has good form, annual flowers and attractive fruit. Can be used for mass planting or as a specimen tree.

Plant may be observed at: *Arboreta*—Arnold, Holden, Morton, National, U. of Wisconsin-Madison; *Botanical Gardens*—Chicago, Missouri.

E. HASSELKUS

E. HASSELKUS   T. GREEN

Malus 'Donald Wyman'. DONALD WYMAN CRAB APPLE. *Rosaceae.* USDA Zones 5–8. U.S.A. Introduced in 1940s by Arnold Arboretum.

DESCRIPTION **Deciduous** tree of compact, rounded form, growing at a moderate rate to 15–20' at maturity. Casts dense shade.

Leaves: Dark green, 2–3" long, elliptical, serrulate. Fall color attractive yellow.

Flowers: Pink buds, white flowers, single, with 5 petals, 1¾" in diam.; blooms annually.

Winter aspect: Typical apple bark. Fruit persists through most of winter, attracting winter birds.

CULTURE Does best in full sun and well-drained loam in pH range of 5.0–7.5, though will grow in clay or sand. Most crabs tolerate drought, salt, air pollution and soil compaction fairly well, but do not tolerate wet soils.

Disease and insect problems: Resistant to scab, cedar apple rust and fire blight; slightly susceptible to powdery mildew. No major insect pests but numerous minor pests.

Transplanting: No major problem with either balled and burlapped or bare root.

Propagation: Usually by budding; also by root grafting and cuttings.

LANDSCAPE VALUE The shape, size, disease resistance, extremely attractive fruit, abundant annual flowering and warm green foliage make 'Donald Wyman' one of the best ornamental trees in North America. Can be used as a specimen in the landscape, in mass planting, and for wildlife. It is difficult to understand why there are only a few nurseries growing it.

Plant may be observed at: *Arboreta*—Arnold, Bernheim Forest, Holden, Minnesota Landscape, Morton, National, U. of Wisconsin-Madison; *Botanical Gardens*—Brooklyn, Chicago, Missouri.

R. HEBB

A. BUSSEWITZ

A. BUSSEWITZ

Malus hupehensis (Pampini) Rehder [*M. theifera* Rehder; *Pyrus hupehensis* Pampanini; *P. theifera* (Rehder) L. H. Bailey]. TEA CRAB APPLE. *Rosaceae*. USDA Zones 4–8. China, Assam. Introduced 1900 by E. H. Wilson for Veitch Nursery, England.

DESCRIPTION **Deciduous** tree, broadly vase-shaped and arching, growing to mature size of 25'. Casts light shade.

Leaves: 2–4" long, 1–1½" wide, ovate-elliptic, serrulate; purplish when young, deep green in summer changing to yellow and copper in autumn.

Flowers: Soft pink in bud, opening to white; single (5 petals), rotate form, about 1½" diam. in May. Fragrant.

Fruit: Small, ½" diam., yellowish with red cheek in autumn.

Winter aspect: Bark typical of most *Malus;* long wand-like branches form spreading vase shape.

CULTURE Grows in sun or light shade in well-drained soil. Tolerance of wind usually good, of drought moderate. Probably not very tolerant of salt, air pollution or soil compaction.

Disease and insect problems: Fairly resistant to most *Malus* problems, though moderately susceptible to fire blight in some seasons.

Transplanting: Excellent; root system shallow and normal.

Propagation: By seed.

LANDSCAPE VALUE Superlative tree, not surpassed by new or hybrid crabapples. It is most picturesque of all, with long-reaching, single branches spreading up and out from the trunk; flowers are produced on spurs up and down the entire length of the branches. This species comes true from seed and usually acts as an apomict—not hybridizing with other *Malus* nearby. At late-bud stage the "paper lantern" effect is delightful and distinct from all usual *Malus*. Consistently beautiful every year, delightfully fragrant; strong, sturdy habit and constitution. Fruit usually produced in abundance, excellent early winter food for wildlife, occasionally persisting and highly esteemed by late robins, mockingbirds, etc.

Plant may be observed at: *Arboreta*—Arnold, Holden, Morton, National, Strybing, U. of Washington, U. of Wisconsin-Madison; *Botanical Gardens*— Brooklyn, Chicago, Munich, Palmgarten, Royal/Kew; *Gardens*— Longwood; *Parks*—Golden Gate.

HOLDEN ARB.

A. BUSSEWITZ

K. KOHOUT

Malus 'Mary Potter' (*M.* × *atrosanguinea* × *M. sargentii* var. *rosea*) MARY POTTER CRAB APPLE. *Rosaceae.* USDA Zones 5–8. U.S.A. Introduced 1947 by Dr. Karl Sax of the Arnold Arboretum.

DESCRIPTION **Deciduous** small tree of dense, spreading, low-branched habit; mature size is 10–15′ high. Casts dense shade.

Leaves: 2–3″ long, elliptical, serrulate, dark green in color, fall color yellow.

Flowers: Pink buds open to white, single, 5-petaled blossoms, 1″ in diam.

Fruit: ½″ in diam., begins to redden in early August, reaching a peak of bright red in September-October; post-frost color is attractive.

Winter aspect: Bark is typical *Malus* bark. Fruit is persistent and attractive to wildlife.

CULTURE Grows in full sun in loam in pH range of 5.0–7.5. Intolerant of wet conditions; tolerates drought and is believed tolerant of salt, air pollution and soil compaction. Moderately adaptable to clay or sandy soils.

Disease and insect problems: Moderately susceptible to scab, powdery mildew and fire blight.

Transplanting: Easy, balled and burlapped or bare root.

Propagation: Mostly by budding, also by root grafts and seed.

LANDSCAPE VALUE Excellent small tree where shrubby form and crab apple larger than *M. sargentii* is desired. Valued for its attractive shape, disease tolerance, annual masses of bloom and fruit, and post-frost color. Use with caution where fire blight is a problem.

Plant may be observed at: *Arboreta*—Arnold, Bernheim Forest, Holden, Morton, National, U. of Washington, U. of Wisconsin-Madison; *Botanical Gardens*—Chicago, Missouri.

T. GREEN

T. GREEN

E. HASSELKUS

Malus 'Professor Sprenger' *sieboldii* var. *zumi* (Matsumura) Asami. PROFESSOR SPRENGER CRAB APPLE. *Rosaceae.* USDA Zone 5–7. Netherlands. Introduced in 1950 by S.G.A. Doorenbos of The Hague.

DESCRIPTION **Deciduous** small tree of dense rounded to spreading habit; grows at medium rate to 20' at maturity. Casts dense shade.

Leaves: 2–3" long, elliptical, serrulate; warm green, attractive yellow in fall.

Flowers: Pink bud opening to white, 5-petaled, single, about 1½" in diameter.

Fruit: Profuse, ½–⅝" in diameter, shining amber changing to coral in October. Fruit retains color after frost.

Winter aspect: Bark typical of *Malus;* branching dense and spreading. Fruit persistent.

CULTURE Grows best in full sun in well drained loam in pH range of 5.0–7.5. Intolerant of wet conditions, somewhat tolerant of clay and sandy soils. Tolerates drought, road salt, air pollution, and soil compaction.

Disease and insect problems: Highly disease resistant. No major pests but numerous minor pests.

Transplanting: No major problems; balled and burlapped and bare root.

Propagation: Mostly by budding.

LANDSCAPE VALUE Its shape, size and disease resistance, its extremely attractive annual abundant white flowers and fruit, its warm green foliage and nice fall color make 'Professor Sprenger' one of the best ornamental trees in North America. A very useful specimen tree for the landscape. It is hard to understand why this tree is not available in the trade. One commercial grower objected to its name; if necessary, the name should be changed. This tree should be included in our landscape.

Plant may be observed at: *Arboreta*—Arnold, Morton, National, U. of Wisconsin-Madison.

T. GREEN

T. GREEN

T. GREEN

Metasequoia glyptostroboides H. H. Hu & Cheng. DAWN REDWOOD. *Taxodiaceae.*
USDA Zones 5–8. Eastern Szechuan and Western Hupeh, China.
Described 1941 from fossils found in Japan.

DESCRIPTION
Deciduous conifer with a very fast growth rate of 50' in 15–20 years; 70–115' high and 25' spread at maturity. Pyramidal, conical, straight trunk when young; develops broadly rounded crown in maturity. Casts medium shade.

Leaves: Opposite, ½" long, 1/16" broad; upper surface bright green spring and summer, warm orange-brown to red-brown in fall.

Flowers: Monoecious, male flowers in racemes or panicles.

Fruit: Round cones, pendulous on long stalks, 3/5–4/5" across; deep brown and mature first year.

Winter aspect: Red-brown bark, turning to gray, fissured and exfoliating with age; trees become heavily buttressed at base as they mature.

CULTURE
Grows in sun; prefers moist, deep, well-drained, slightly acid soil. Grows best in areas with a combination of plenty of rain and long growing season.

Disease and insect problems: Some canker infections; Japanese beetles will feed on foliage.

Transplanting: Easy.

Propagation: From seed, also from softwood or hardwood cuttings.

LANDSCAPE VALUE
A graceful, ornamental tree that seldom requires pruning; good for large areas, lining streets or walkways. Well-suited to parks and golf courses. A fast growing, attractive tree with soft, light green feathery foliage, it creates an effective screen when planted in groups. By stemming it up, Maplewood, N.J. uses it as a street tree. Has tendency to grow late in summer, which sometimes creates a problem in areas with early frosts. Similar to *Taxodium distichum* but faster growing and less demanding. In China, the wood is used for interior finishes. Species has been growing and reproducing itself for 50 million years. It was part of the landscape at the time of the dinosaurs. In 1944 the Arnold Arboretum provided a grant which enabled Dr. H. H. Hu to collect seeds from wild specimens discovered in China. Seeds were distributed by the Arnold to many arboreta around the world where trees can be seen today.

Plant may be observed at: *Arboreta*—Arnold, Bernheim Forest, Dawes, Holden, Los Angeles, Morton, National, Planting Fields, Strybing, U. of Washington; *Botanical Gardens*—Atlanta, Berry, Birmingham, British Columbia, Brooklyn, Canton, Chicago, Huntington, Munich, Missouri, Palmgarten, Royal/Kew, Shanghai, U. of Georgia, Van Dusen; *Gardens*—Brookgreen, Callaway, Filoli, Longwood, Old Westbury, Winterthur; *Parks*—Golden Gate, Forest Parks-Ibaraki, Japan.

SHANGHAI BOT. GARD.

N. BREWSTER

E. HASSELKUS

Metrosideros excelsus Solander ex J. Gaertner [*M. tomentosus* A. Richard]. NEW ZEALAND CHRISTMAS TREE. *Myrtaceae.* USDA Zones 9–10. New Zealand. Introduced 1840.

DESCRIPTION *Broadleaved evergreen* of erect, much-branched habit; grows at moderate rate to 30′ at maturity. Casts dense shade.

Leaves: Opposite, simple, elliptic to oblong, 2–4″ long and half as wide. Foliage on young plants smooth, glossy green, gray-hairy beneath.

Flowers: Showy, brilliant crimson, in dense cymose clusters, with reddish stamens 1″ or more long, producing "bottle-brush" effect, covering branches in summer.

Fruit: A leathery capsule, inconspicuous.

Winter aspect: Bark gray and smooth, becoming rough with age. Branches erect and profuse.

CULTURE Grows in full sun in clay, loam or sand; not fussy as to soil. Extremely tolerant of wind, salt air and salt spray, and of drought when established.

Disease and insect problems: None.

Transplanting: Easy when young, balled and burlapped or container-grown. Root system extensive and somewhat invasive.

Propagation: By cuttings.

LANDSCAPE VALUE An attractive accent, specimen or street tree; also excellent for seaside planting. It is easily trained into many shapes, and makes a fine large shrub for the border, or in hedges as an alternative to *Myoporum* or *Pittosporum.* Very hardy, always green, no diseases or pests, and will take a lot of wind and salt air. Its limitations are that its roots can break up sidewalks if it is planted in too restricted an area, and that frost and dry air limit its success inland.

Plant may be observed at: *Arboreta*—Los Angeles; *Botanical Gardens*—Huntington; *Parks*—Golden Gate.

R. JONES

R. JONES

R. JONES

Michelia doltsopa Buchanan ex de Candolle [*M. excelsa* (Wallich) Blume ex Wallich]. *Magnoliaceae.* USDA Zones 8–10. Asia. Introduced from western China by Forrest in 1918.

DESCRIPTION
Evergreen, upright, occasionally bushy tree growing moderately to 25–40′ in cultivation; much larger in Asia. Casts light shade.

Leaves: Elliptic to oblong, 6–12″ long, 1¼–3″ wide, nearly glabrous; leathery, dark glossy green above, pale beneath.

Flowers: 3–4″ across, 12–16 petals, obovate to oblanceolate, rounded at apex. Soft pale yellow to white magnolia-like blooms from January through March. Flowers reach bud stage in fall but do not open until following spring; very fragrant.

Fruit: On cone, 2″ long, containing usually three seeds.

Winter aspect: Evergreen winter beauty.

CULTURE
Grows in sun or shade. Will tolerate wet conditions. Thrives in rich soil and needs ample water.

Disease and insect problems: Relatively pest-free.

Transplanting: Balled and burlapped in spring.

Propagation: Cuttings of ripe wood under glass, seed, grafting on *Magnolia grandiflora.*

LANDSCAPE VALUE
Handsome evergreen with beautiful flowers. An excellent lawn tree, easily pruned to desired shape. Not readily available commercially. Its appearance is good the entire year. It should be used more often in suitable climates. A valuable timber tree in the Himalayas.

Plant may be observed at: *Arboreta*—Los Angeles; *Botanical Gardens*—Huntington; *Parks*—Golden Gate.

S. MacBRIDE

CARDOZA

G. COURTRIGHT

Nothofagus antarctica G. (Forster f.) Oersted *Fagus antarctica* Forster f; *N. montagnei* (Hombron & Jacquinot) Reiche. NIRRE. *Fagaceae.* USDA Zone 8. South America, Cape Horn into the Andes. Introduced in 1830.

DESCRIPTION

Deciduous tree growing at medium rate to 40–50'; slender trunk, thin and open irregular branches, often occurring as dense shrub in exposed places. Casts light shade.

Leaves: Alternate, ½–1½" long, broadly ovate to somewhat triangular, rounded at tip, sometimes slightly lobed, irregularly and minutely toothed, glabrous on both sides except for minute down on midrib; orange-yellow fall color.

Flowers: Monoecious, male flowers single to threes in basal leaf axils of small twigs, about 1/6" across, pendulous; April-May blooms.

Fruit: ¼", 4-valved capsule, very fragrant.

Winter aspect: Scaly and very attractive bark, young shoots downy; irregular, angular branching habit striking in winter; may be very dense in exposed locations.

CULTURE

Needs open, sunny position, prefers acid loam. Tolerates wind (it comes from Tierra del Fuego) and drought when established. Tolerant of air pollution and possibly salt-tolerant.

Disease and insect problems: Disease-free.

Transplanting: Easy.

Propagation: By seed, cuttings.

LANDSCAPE VALUE

A tree of great distinction and elegance. Valued for its delicate branching habit and bright green, fine-textured leaves often arranged in a single plane. It is prevalent as a "subalpine" tree above the evergreen beech forests, but also occurs in the lower valleys. It grows on large tracts east of the Andes, on the edge of the Patagonian steppe. Rarely seen in gardens. Some of the oldest trees in cultivation derive from seeds collected in Argentina in 1902.

Related species:
  Nothofagus dombeyi—grows to 70'; a handsome, hardy (in Pacific Northwest) broadleaved evergreen tree notable for its graceful branching habit, enhanced by the fine texture of its small leaves.

The Univ. of Washington Arboretum is growing an upright, more compact form that it is considering naming and placing in the nursery trade. This plant came into the collections in a batch of seedlings, and plants propagated from it are now about 15' high. It grows rapidly, with a very interesting branching pattern.

Plant may be observed at: *Arboreta*—U. of Washington; *Botanical Gardens*—Royal/Kew.

U. OF WASHINGTON ARB.

U. OF WASHINGTON ARB.

U. OF WASHINGTON ARB.

Nyssa sylvatica Marshall [*N. multiflora* Wangenheim, *N. villosa* Michaux; *N. aquatica* L.].
TUPELO, PEPPERIDGE, SOUR GUM, BLACK GUM. *Nyssaceae*. USDA
Zones 4–9. Maine to Florida and Texas. Introduced before 1750 by
Bannister or Tradescant and again by John Bartram and Michaux.

DESCRIPTION
Deciduous tree, 30–50′ in height, with spread of 25–30′; may grow to 100′
in wild. Medium to slow rate of growth. Casts light shade.

Leaves: Alternate, simple, variable, 2–5″ long, 1½–3″ wide, elliptical to
obovate, lustrous dark green above, glaucescent beneath, turning brilliant
flame in autumn.

Flowers: Inconspicuous, ½″ or less across, greenish-yellow; male and
female on separate heads.

Fruit: Blue-black ovoid drupes ½″ long, especially attractive when
observed close by.

Winter aspect: Very distinctive and often spectacular for right-angle
branching from main trunk.

CULTURE
Grows in loam in sun or shade; tolerates wind and swampy conditions.
Moderately drought resistant. Probably not tolerant of environmental
stresses.

Disease and insect problems: Few.

Transplanting: Reputation for being difficult presumably originated in
collecting wild trees with erratic root systems.

Propagation: By seed.

LANDSCAPE
VALUE
Superior, outstanding tree because of vibrant autumn coloring and
pattern of branching, especially when featured against evergreens. Not to
be used in heavily polluted areas but acceptable as street tree; excellent
for naturalized areas or for use as a specimen. Bears and foxes are
attracted to the fruit, as are wood duck and other birds.

Plant may be observed at: *Arboreta*—Arnold, Bayard Cutting, Bernheim
Forest, Cary, Dawes, Holden, Minnesota Landscape, Morton, National,
Planting Fields, U. of Washington, U. of Wisconsin-Madison; *Botanical
Gardens*—Birmingham, Brooklyn, Chicago, Huntington, Missouri, New
York, Palmgarten, Royal/Kew, U. of Georgia; *Gardens*—Brookgreen,
Callaway, Longwood, Winterthur.

E. HASSELKUS

K. KOHOUT

A. BUSSEWITZ

Olmediella betschleriana (Göppert) L. Loesener. COSTA RICA HOLLY, GUATE-
MALAN HOLLY, MANZANOLE. *Flacourtiaceae.* USDA Zones 9–10.
Guatemala. Introduced 1932 in Guatemala.

DESCRIPTION *Broadleaved evergreen* growing moderately fast to 20–25' (occasionally to
45') with 10–15' spread.

Leaves: Alternate, dense, dark green, elliptic-oblong to 6" long; new
growth has bronze cast. Resemble English Holly leaves but have less
prominent spines.

Flowers: Small and inconspicuous.

Fruit: Berry; female trees capable of producing a few inedible fruits about
size of a small orange.

Winter aspect: Bark interesting in all seasons. Single- or multi-trunked
and bushy habit.

CULTURE Grows in sun or shade on coast, or in partial shade with ample water
inland. Prefers well drained, fertile soil.

Disease and insect problems: None.

Transplanting: Balled and burlapped.

Propagation: By seed, which produces sturdier plants, or by cuttings.
Sometimes it self-sows.

LANDSCAPE
VALUE An interesting evergreen, dioecious tree with coarse, leathery leaves
resembling those of the hollies. May be planted as a specimen lawn tree or
a background landscape.

Plant may be observed at: *Arboreta*—Los Angeles, Strybing; *Parks*—
Golden Gate.

Olmediella betschleriana COSTA RICA HOLLY, GUATEMALAN HOLLY, MANZANOLE

P. THOMPSON

P. THOMPSON

P. THOMPSON

Ostrya virginiana (P. Miller) K. Koch. AMERICAN HOP HORNBEAM, IRONWOOD. *Betulaceae.* USDA Zones 4–9. Eastern North America: Ontario to Minnesota, south to Florida, Texas and into northern Mexico. Introduced 1692 by Compton, Bishop of London.

DESCRIPTION **Deciduous** tree growing slowly to 25–40'; pyramidal when young, forming a rounded habit at maturity, with dense canopy. Casts dense shade.

Leaves: Alternate, 2½–4½" long, 1½–2" wide; oval-lanceolate, rounded, sometimes heart-shaped at base; sharply toothed, doubly serrate, dark green above, paler and more pubescent beneath.

Flowers: Monoecious, male flowers in cylinder-shaped catkins, light, red-brown; female, slender catkin, light green with red cast; spring bloom (immature male flowers visible in winter).

Fruit: Pods, 1½–2½" long, in pendulous clusters; nutlet, ⅓" long; resembles fruit of hop vine, hence name Hop Hornbeam; green, turning brown at maturity.

Winter aspect: Gray-brown bark in narrow, plate-like strips, finely shredded, that may peel away from trunk; slender branches drooping at ends.

CULTURE Grows in a variety of soil conditions (moist and fertile to sandy soils); however, prefers well-drained sites, slightly acid soil and full sun or partial shade; intolerant of salt, so should not be used in roadside plantings in northern areas.

Disease and insect problems: None serious.

Transplanting: Somewhat difficult; move when small and use container-grown plants when available.

Propagation: By seed; warm followed by cold treatment is best.

LANDSCAPE VALUE Attractive, medium-sized, high-quality tree that deserves greater exposure in the landscape. It is almost trouble-free, withstands harsh winds and ice storms and requires little maintenance. Excellent specimen for lawns, parks, golf courses and naturalized areas and a good candidate for cities where it is not exposed to salt spray. The light brown wood is durable and extremely hard (hence name Ironwood) and is often used for handles of tools, as the tree is not large enough to be of major commercial importance. *O. virginiana* differs from its close relative *O. carpinifolia* in the larger nut, in the glandular hairs on twigs, in fewer ribs of the leaf and in darker brown bark.

Plant may be observed at: *Arboreta*—Bernheim Forest, Cary, Minnesota Landscape, Planting Fields, Spring Grove, U. of Washington, U. of Wisconsin-Madison; *Botanical Gardens*—Brooklyn, Chicago, Huntington, New York, Royal/Kew, Royal/Ontario, U. of Georgia; *Gardens*—Longwood.

E. HASSELKUS

E. HASSELKUS   A. BUSSEWITZ

Oxydendrum arboreum (L.) de Candolle [*Andromeda arborea* L.; *Lyonia arborea* (L.) D. Don]. SOURWOOD, SORREL TREE. *Ericaceae.* USDA Zone 5-8. U.S.A.: Pennsylvania to Florida, west of Indiana and Louisiana. Introduced 1747.

DESCRIPTION
Deciduous graceful narrow tree with rounded top and drooping branches. A slow grower to 40' or more at maturity, with spread of 20'. Casts medium shade.

Leaves: Alternate, 5–8" long, acuminate, serrulate, resembling peach tree leaves, lustrous leathery green in summer, brilliant scarlet to plum in fall, pale beneath.

Flowers: Small, bell-shaped, creamy white, in compound clusters of slightly hanging panicles 7–10" long. Fragrant.

Fruit: Dehiscent capsules borne in profuse panicles, persistent into winter.

Winter aspect: Bark smooth gray to deeply furrowed at maturity; branching of irregular form, with individual branches often twisted.

CULTURE
Grow in full sun for best flowering and fall color; will tolerate light shade. Does best in peaty loam well-drained but moist, in pH range of 4.0–6.0. Intolerant of environmental stresses.

Disease and insect problems: No serious problems; fall webworm in some years.

Transplanting: Roots deep and fibrous. Must be transplanted young, balled and burlapped or container-grown.

Propagation: By fresh seed in moist peat, or by softwood heel cuttings in sand and peat, treated with IBA, in late July.

LANDSCAPE VALUE
One of our finest native flowering trees. A three-season tree that blooms at an unusual time in mid-summer with pendulous terminal bouquets of bloom resembling lily-of-the-valley or *Pieris japonica*. Has spectacular fall color of brilliant scarlet to plum, conspicuous attractive hanging racemes of fruiting capsules in winter, and handsome glossy foliage in spring. Will not grow in neutral or alkaline soil, hence is of restricted use.

Its name is derived from the Greek *oxys* (acid) + *dendron* (tree), referring to the sour taste of the leaves. In the southern Appalachians one can buy Sourwood honey.

Plant may be observed at: *Arboreta*—Arnold, Bernheim Forest, Cary, Holden, Morton, National, Planting Fields, U. of Washington; *Botanical Gardens*—Birmingham, Brooklyn, Missouri, New York, Royal/Kew, U. of Georgia; *Gardens*—Brookgreen, Callaway, Dixon, Longwood, Old Westbury, Winterthur.

P. KINGSLEY

R. HEBB

N. BREWSTER

Parkinsonia aculeata L. JERUSALEM THORN, MEXICAN PALO VERDE. *Leguminosae.*
USDA Zones 9–10. Tropical America. Introduced ???

DESCRIPTION *Deciduous* tree growing rapidly when young to 40'; loose, open habit with spreading head. Casts light shade.

Leaves: Alternate, twice compound, 7–12" long, with up to 50 very small leaflets.

Flowers: Fragrant, bright yellow tinged with orange; 1" diam., borne in large numbers, each produced on short stalk and loosely clustered on an elongated spike. Long blooming period begins in spring, with intermittent bloom throughout year. Sometimes important as a food for bees.

Fruit: Pods 2–4" long, leathery; brown seeds.

Winter aspect: Yellow-green, thin, smooth bark, turning red-brown on older trunks; slender, spiny twigs with thorns.

CULTURE Tolerates sun and shade and a moderate amount of wind; very tolerant of drought. Prefers moist, sandy or gravelly alkaline soils with good drainage. Requires minimum attention once established. Resistant to salt spray in seashore site.

Disease and insect problems: None.

Transplanting: Moderately easy; root system deep.

Propagation: By seed.

LANDSCAPE VALUE A highly picturesque tree; its many tiny leaflets create light, filtered shade. The fragrant, bright yellow flowers borne in great numbers bloom intermittently throughout the year. Easily trained for high or low branching. Can be clipped and formed into an excellent hedge. Also valued for its tolerance of drought and salt spray. Used as a street tree in California because it grows in light sandy soil; however, leaflets fall easily in cold or drought, which can become a litter problem. The hard wood is sometimes used for fuel. Trees of this genus are easily recognized by their leaves, which look like long, narrow streamers. Genus name *Parkinsonia*, refers to the English botanical author John Parkinson.

Plant may be observed at: *Botanical Gardens*—Huntington, Pacific Tropical, San Antonio.

R. JONES

R. JONES

W. ADAMS

Parrotia persica C. A. Meyer. PERSIAN PARROTIA. *Hamamelidaceae.* USDA Zones 5–8. Iran. Introduced 1840; named for F.W. Parrott, German naturalist.

DESCRIPTION *Deciduous* tree growing at medium rate (10' in 6–8 years) to 20–40' high with 15–30' spread; oval-rounded head of upright branches; sometimes multi-trunked. Casts medium shade.

Leaves: 2–4" long, alternate, short-petioled, sinuate-dentate, oval to obovate-oblong; reddish, unfolding to dark green; brilliant yellow to orange-scarlet in fall.

Flowers: 1/2–3/4" diam., without petals, clustered in dense heads surrounded by bracts; conspicuous for numerous red stamens. Flowers in spring before leaves.

Fruit: Seed vessels nut-like; seeds 3/8" long, bright brown.

Winter aspect: Gray, green, white and brown exfoliating bark; horizontal habit; branches low.

CULTURE Grows best in full sun but will tolerate light shade; prefers loam or sand in pH range of 6.0–6.5; does not withstand wet conditions or drought.

Disease and insect problems: Pest-free.

Transplanting: Balled and burlapped in spring.

Propagation: By cuttings in July; by seeds stratified for 5 months at warm temperature, then 3 months at 40°F.

LANDSCAPE VALUE An outstanding specimen tree valued for its pest resistance, its wide hardiness range and its attractiveness in all seasons. Its showy crimson stamens and rich brown bracts create a hazy and pleasant effect on the leafless branches in early spring. The interesting bark is an asset in the winter landscape. The greatest charm of this tree is the glowing tints of gold and crimson in the fall. It is one of the most effective trees for autumn color.

Plant may be observed at: *Arboreta*—Bernheim Forest, Cary, Dawes, Holden, Morton, National, Planting Fields, Strybing; *Botanical Gardens*—Berry, British Columbia, Brooklyn, Missouri, Munich, New York, Palmgarten, Royal/Kew, U. of Georgia, Van Dusen; *Gardens*—Dixon, Longwood; *Parks*—Golden Gate.

M. DIRR

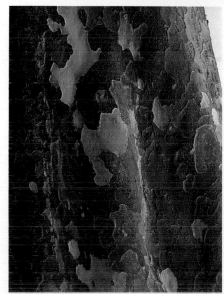

A. BUSSEWITZ

PLANTING FIELDS

Phellodendron amurense Ruprecht. AMUR or CHINESE CORK TREE. *Rutaceae.* USDA Zones 3–7. China (Amur region, Manchuria), Japan. Introduced around 1856 by Arnold Arboretum.

DESCRIPTION *Deciduous*, broad-leaved, broadly spreading tree, with medium fast growth to 30–45' high and wide spread. Casts light shade.

Leaves: Compound, 5–13 leaflets, ovate to ovate-lanceolate, 2½–4½" long; glossy dark green above, glabrous beneath; bright yellow in fall.

Flowers: Small white panicles, dioecious.

Fruit: Black, berry-like, 5-seeded pods only on female trees; ripen in October, persist into winter.

Winter aspect: Bark oak-like, gray-brown on short trunk; older bark has corky texture; horizontal, spreading habit.

CULTURE Grows in sun in clay or loam with pH range of 5.0–7.0. Heavy feeder, prefers deep, rich soil; will withstand wind, some air pollution, salt and soil compaction. Does not do well in warm climates. Best pruned in winter.

Disease and insect problems: None.

Transplanting: Easy; root system shallow, fibrous.

Propagation: Seed germinates readily.

LANDSCAPE VALUE Lustrous dark green leaves, unique and beautiful oak-like bark, and broad spreading habit make this a handsome, tough, small shade tree. Bark and structure of massive branches provide winter interest. Once considered a good city tree, it may not be as tolerant as believed. An excellent specimen may be seen in the courtyard of St. Bartholomew's Church in New York City. A grafted male clone, with no pods to be removed, might be considered best for city planting.

Related species:
  P. lavallei, Lavalle Cork Tree. More upright habit. Introduced from Japan 1862. Hardy to Zone 5. Can be seen at Arnold Arboretum.
  P. sachalinense, Sakhalin Cork Tree. More vase-shaped. Similar to American elm, taller than *P. amurense,* with less cork-like bark. Introduced 1877 from Korea, western China, northern Japan. USDA Zone 3. Difficult to find in nurseries. Can be seen at Arnold Arboretum.

Plant may be observed at: *Arboreta*—Arnold, Bernheim Forest, Minnesota Landscape, Morton, Planting Fields, U. of Wisconsin-Madison; *Botanical Gardens*—Brooklyn, Chicago, Huntington, Missouri, Munich, New York, Palmgarten, Royal/Kew, Van Dusen; *Gardens*—Old Westbury; *Parks*—Forest Parks-Ibaraki, Japan.

M. DIRR

E. HASSELKUS

M. DIRR

Picea omorika (Pancic) Purkyne. SERBIAN SPRUCE. *Pinaceae.* USDA Zones 4–7. Southeastern Europe (Yugoslavia). Introduced to cultivation 1881 by Froebel of Zurich.

DESCRIPTION *Evergreen conifer*, conical, almost columnar tree with short ascending branches. Grows slowly to 60–100' high with 20–25' spread. Casts dense shade.

Leaves: Flattened needles to ½" long, glossy dark green above, distinct white bands beneath.

Flowers: Inconspicuous, purple, monoecious.

Fruit: Egg-shaped cones to 2½" long; male cones catkin-like, female cones woody, pendulous, blue-black when young, cinnamon when mature.

Winter aspect: Deep brown, thin, scaling bark; pendent, drooping lower branches when old.

CULTURE Grows in sun in loam with pH range of 5.0–7.0. Tolerant of drought; needs shelter from winter winds.

Disease and insect problems: Occasional borer in terminal shoot or leader; budworm.

Transplanting: Easy when balled and burlapped; root system deep.

Propagation: By seed.

LANDSCAPE VALUE Probably the handsomest of the spruces—graceful, ornamental. The silvery undersides of the needles are very effective as they move in the wind. The pendent branchlets create a lovely effect. An elegant and adaptable tree, it can be used as a specimen, in groups, or as a street tree. Subject to winter burn if planted in a site too exposed. Tree has scientific interest because it is an undoubted relic from Tertiary period and is one of the few spruces with flat needles like a hemlock, not four-sided needles of most spruces. Strong, light wood can be used for paper pulp.

Cultivar 'Pendula' is graceful, slender tree with pendent branches.

Plant may be observed at: *Arboreta*—Arnold, Bayard Cutting, Bernheim Forest, Cary, Dawes, Holden, Minnesota Landscape, Missouri, Morton, National, Planting Fields, U. of Washington, U. of Wisconsin-Madison; *Botanical Gardens*—British Columbia, Brooklyn, Chicago, Munich, New York, Palmgarten, Royal/Kew, Royal/Ontario, Van Dusen; *Gardens*—Longwood

M. DIRR

M. DIRR

E. HASSELKUS

Picea orientalis (L.) Link. ORIENTAL SPRUCE. *Pinaceae.* USDA Zones 5–7. Caucasus and Asia Minor. Introduced 1837.

DESCRIPTION

Evergreen conifer growing slowly to 50–60' in cultivation, up to 120' in wild; dense pyramidal shape of common spruce, but more slenderly branched. Casts dense shade.

Leaves: ¼–½", lustrous dark green; 4-sided with 1–4 lines of stomata on each surface.

Flowers: Inconspicuous, monoecious.

Fruit: Short-stalked, ovoid, cylindrical cone, 2–4" long; beautiful purple when young, turning cinnamon brown with age.

Winter aspect: Brown bark exfoliating in thin scales; stiffly horizontal habit; often pendulous, with branches to ground level.

CULTURE

Grows in sun and light shade; prefers clay or loam but will tolerate poor, gravelly soils; adaptable to wide pH range. Will not withstand wind, wet conditions, drought, or air pollution; suffers from browning of leaves in cold climates.

Disease and insect problems: Spruce bud worm.

Transplanting: Easy when balled and burlapped; large trees may be transplanted because of shallow root system.

Propagation: By seed.

LANDSCAPE VALUE

One of the most handsome of all the spruces. Its graceful and attractive dense habit makes it an excellent choice for small areas. The needles are smaller than those of most spruces and are brilliant dark green. It is highly ornamental when bearing a crop of its colorful cones. An adaptable specimen.

Cultivars:
'Gracilis'—densely branched, slow growing, small, 18–20' conical tree; needles bright green and radially set.
'Pendula'—slow growing with pendulous branches.
'Aurea'—young shoots warm yellow; often has golden cast over all leaves.

Plant may be observed at: *Arboreta*—Arnold, Bayard Cutting, Bernheim Forest, Dawes, Holden, Morton, National, Planting Fields, Spring Grove, U. of Washington; *Botanical Gardens*—Chicago, Munich, New York, Palmgarten, Royal/Kew, Van Dusen; *Gardens*—Longwood, Winterthur.

E. HASSELKUS

E. HASSELKUS

PLANTING FIELDS

Pinus bungeana Zuccarini ex Endlicher. LACEBARK PINE. *Pinaceae.* USDA Zones 5–8. Northwest China. Introduced 1846 by Robert Fortune. First discovered by Dr. A. A. von Bunge in a temple garden near Peking 1831.

DESCRIPTION   *Evergreen conifer* growing slowly to 20–45' up to 80'; pyramidal when young, flat-topped and broad-spreading at maturity. Casts dense shade that becomes lighter in maturity.

Leaves: 4" long in fascicles of 3; stiff, sharp, light green with stomatic lines on both sides; remain 3–5 years.

Flowers: Monoecious, clustered.

Fruit: Cone, 2–2½" long, 1¼–1½" wide, shortly stalked; seeds ⅓" long with a short wing.

Winter aspect: Bark exfoliating in irregular plates of gray-green to chalky white; many-trunked; open in maturity.

CULTURE   Requires sun; prefers acid soil but tolerates limestone; will not withstand wet conditions or drought.

Disease and insect problems: Blister rusts, cankers, twig blight, bark beetles.

Transplanting: Balled and burlapped after root pruning.

Propagation: By seed, grafting.

LANDSCAPE VALUE   Hardy, slow-growing specimen evergreen especially valued for its beautifully marbled and interesting bark, which displays colors from yellow, when freshly exposed, to gray-green and/or purple-brown. Has the desirable trait of holding its needles about 5 years. Cultivated in China for its spectacular bark; often seen on the grounds of Buddhist temples. Grows wild in the mountains west of Peking. *P. bungeana* was named for Alexander von Bunge, Russian author who researched and recorded information about the plants of northern and northeastern Asia.

Plant may be observed at: *Arboreta*—Bayard Cutting, Bernheim Forest, Dawes, Holden, Morton, National, Planting Fields, U. of Washington, U of Wisconsin-Madison; *Botanical Gardens*—Birmingham, Brooklyn, Canton, Missouri, New York, Palmgarten, Royal/Kew, U. of Georgia; *Gardens*—Longwood; *Parks*—Central/New York.

M. DIRR

HOLDEN ARB.

HOLDEN ARB

Pinus cembra L. SWISS STONE PINE, AROLLA PINE. *Pinaceae.* USDA Zones 3–7.
Alps, from France to lower Austria. Introduced 1746 into Britain.

DESCRIPTION

Evergreen conifer, growing slowly to 35–40′ with spread of 15–20′; may grow to 100′; densely columnar in youth, becoming more open and spreading with age.

Leaves: Bundles of 5 needles, 2½–5″ long, margins finely toothed; lustrous dark green above, white stomatic lines beneath; persist 3–5 years.

Flowers: Monoecious, clustered and inconspicuous.

Fruit: Egg-shaped cone, 2–3″ long; green-purple at first, turning purple-brown when mature.

Winter aspect: Interest in all seasons; drooping branches when mature.

CULTURE

Prefers full sun and well-drained, loamy soil; will tolerate wind.

Disease and insect problems: Relatively trouble free.

Transplanting: Easier than most pines.

Propagation: By seed, with stratification.

LANDSCAPE VALUE

Well-proportioned, hardy pine of slow growth and dense habit. Useful in small-scale gardens, formal landscapes and as excellent screenage.

Cultivar 'Columnaris' more columnar in habit than species.

Plant may be observed at: *Arboreta*—Arnold, Bernheim Forest, Cary, Holden, Minnesota Landscape, Morton, National, Planting Fields, U. of Washington, U. of Wisconsin-Madison; *Botanical Gardens*—Brooklyn, Chicago, Denver, Missouri, Munich, New York, Palmgarten, Royal/Kew; *Gardens*—Longwood, Winterthur; *Parks*—Central/New York.

M. DIRR

J. POOR

M. DIRR

Pinus flexilis James. LIMBER PINE. *Pinaceae.* USDA Zones 5–7. USA, Rocky Mountains from Alberta to northern New Mexico and Arizona. Introduced to Harvard Botanic Garden in 1861 by Dr. Parry.

DESCRIPTION
Coniferous evergreen, 40–60′, occasionally 80′, 15–35′ spread. Pyramidal growth habit when young, spreading with age, the young parts so flexible they can be easily bent without breaking. A slow grower. Casts dense shade.

Leaves: Stout, rigid, dark green, in clusters of 5, 1½–3½″ long, persisting for four years. All sides are marked with 3 or 4 white lines of stomata.

Flowers: Male red, female clustered, bright purple.

Fruit: Cones 3–6″ long, 1½″ in diam., yellow to buff when developing, with narrow and more or less reflexed scales.

Winter aspect: Bark of young branches smooth, silvery gray; on old trunks dark brown and deeply fissured. Stout long-persistent branches ultimately form a low, wide, round-topped head. Cones persistent.

CULTURE
Grows in clay, loam or sandy soils, in pH range of 5.0–7.4. Intolerant of wet conditions and most environmental stresses, but tolerant of drought and probably tolerant of soil compaction. Prefers sun or partial shade. Adaptable to rocky slopes.

Disease and insect problems: Shoe-string fungus (*Armillaria*) may affect distressed trees.

Transplanting: Moderately easy; root system shallow to deep.

Propagation: By seed or by grafts.

LANDSCAPE VALUE
A long-lived tree, with a solid, stable mien due to density of foliage. Makes fairly good growth on well-drained sites but slow on poor, sodden sites. Since it is native to windswept ridges in Nebraska, South Dakota and Wyoming, its tolerance of clay soils, drought and open windy areas makes this an excellent candidate for urban plantings in the Midwest and Plains states.

Recommended cultivars:
 P. flexilis 'Columnaris'—upright habit good for limited space.
 P. flexilis 'Glauca'—needles more blue-green than the species. Attractive.
 P. flexilis 'Nana'—slow growing dwarf form.

Plant may be observed at: *Arboreta*—Arnold, Bernheim Forest, Cary, Dawes, Holden, Minnesota Landscape, Morton, National, Planting Fields, U. of Washington, U. of Wisconsin-Madison; *Botanical Gardens*—Brooklyn, Chicago, Missouri, New York, Palmgarten, Royal/Kew; *Gardens*—Longwood.

E. HASSELKUS

M. DIRR

M. DIRR

Pinus koraiensis Siebold & Zuccarini. KOREAN PINE. *Pinaceae.* USDA Zones 4–7. Korea, Japan, Manchuria and Russian Far East. Introduced in 1861 by J.G. Veitch.

DESCRIPTION
Evergreen conifer growing slowly to 35–50'; may grow over 100'; dense, pyramidal habit.

Leaves: In bundles of 3 or 5, each needle 3½–4½'' long; dark green with stomated lines on both surfaces; margins toothed.

Flowers: Inconspicuous.

Fruit: Cones short-stalked, yellow-brown; scales with recurved obtuse apex; 3½–6'' long, 2–2½'' wide.

Winter aspect: Scaly gray-brown or gray bark; relaxed branching to ground.

CULTURE
Grows in full sun but will tolerate partial shade; grows in heavy soil but perhaps prefers well-drained site. Extremely cold hardy.

Disease and insect problems: None serious.

Transplanting: Balled and burlapped.

Propagation: By seed, usually without pretreatment.

LANDSCAPE VALUE
Handsome evergreen. An excellent candidate for small gardens because of its slow growth. Its lustrous, dark green foliage creates a picturesque, dramatic appearance against a winter landscape. It is becoming recognized as one of the most useful and attractive pines for northern regions. Closely allied to *P. cembra,* but leaves are more spreading and blunter, the cones longer and the growth habit more open.

Plant may be observed at: *Arboreta*—Bernheim Forest, Holden, Minnesota Landscape, Morton, National, Planting Fields, U. of Washington, U. of Wisconsin-Madison; *Botanical Gardens*—Brooklyn, Chicago, Munich, New York, Royal/Kew; *Gardens*—Old Westbury; *Parks*—Forest Parks-Ibaraki, Japan.

MORTON ARB.

MORTON ARB.   E. HASSELKUS

Pinus parviflora Siebold & Zuccarini. 'Glauca' *P. parviflora* var. *pentaphylla* (Mayr) A. Henry; *P. pentaphylla* Mayr. JAPANESE WHITE PINE. *Pinaceae.* USDA Zones 4–7. Japan. Introduced 1861 by John Gould Veitch.

DESCRIPTION

Evergreen conifer, wide spreading. Growth rate variable from slow to 21″ per year; height at maturity 60–90′ with same or greater spread. Casts medium shade.

Leaves: Slender needles in bundles of 5, 2–3″ long, blue-green with 3–4 silver bands on inner sides of needles, on 1-year-old and older branches (smooth the first year) and in whorled tufts at ends of branchlets.

Fruit: Upright ovoid cones, solitary or in clusters, 2–4″ long, nearly terminal on branches and branchlets, almost sessile, very abundant on young trees, less so with maturity. Scales few, woody, and undulated. Cones open widely, resembling small waterlilies, and persist on tree 6 to 7 years. Very decorative.

Winter aspect: Bark purplish; branching habit open, spreading and graceful. Striking foliage color.

CULTURE

Grows in sun in moist, well-drained loam or clay soils. Tolerant of most soils, wind, drought, salt air (not road salt), and of soil compaction. No data available on tolerance of air pollution.

Disease and insect problems: None serious.

Transplanting: Best when very young, container-grown or balled and burlapped. Root system deep.

Propagation: By stratified seed (germination rate low due to large percentage of empty seeds), or by grafting.

LANDSCAPE VALUE

P. parviflora 'Glauca' would seem to be highly variable throughout its range. Some are small trees 50′ in height, some are 90′; some grow slowly, some very fast; some are dense, some open. The specimen grown in New Jersey was labeled *P. parviflora glauca* 'nana'; it grew 18″ the first year, and has grown 21″ every year since and is now over 40′. Variable or not, this tree is hardy and a beauty. Its form grows more picturesque every year, and at all seasons the color of its foliage is a sharp contrast with other conifers including the bluest *Picea pungens.* Its undulating branches with their long-persistent open cones are eye-stoppers (and when cut have lasted six months in water and put out new growth). It is too little known, and should be planted in areas where it can show to advantage as a specimen.

Plant may be observed at: *Arboreta*—Bernheim Forest, National, Planting Fields, U. of Wisconsin-Madison; *Botanical Gardens*—Berry, Chicago, Missouri, Van Dusen; *Gardens*—Longwood, Winterthur; *Parks*—Forest Parks-Ibaraki, Japan.

M. DIRR

H. MULLIGAN

N. BREWSTER

Pinus wallichiana A.B. Jackson [*P. excelsa* Wallich ex D. Don; *P. griffithii* A. B. Jackson; *P. nepalensis* Chambray]. HIMALAYAN PINE, BHUTAN PINE. *Pinaceae.* USDA Zones 5–7. Himalayan Mountains west to Afghanistan. Introduced 1823 by A. B. Lambert.

DESCRIPTION *Coniferous evergreen* growing to 150′ in natural habitat, with spread of half or more of its height. Growth habit is upright and conical when young, but broadens quickly to open pyramid. Casts dense shade.

Leaves: Needles to 9″ long in clusters of 5, dark green in color with silvery blue cast, long, very slender and pendulous, as windblown as a willow.

Flowers: Inconspicuous.

Fruit: Cones solitary or in bunches, banana-shaped, 6–12″ long, 1½ to 1¾″ wide, with stalks somewhat longer than *P. strobus.*

Winter aspect: Bark gray-brown, flaking. Branching habit is sparse whorls; cones are persistent.

CULTURE Grows in full or half-day sun, in clay, loam or sandy soil in pH range of 5.5–7.2. Reasonably wind-tolerant. Tolerates seasonal wet soil conditions as well as seasonal drought, but not wet feet year-round. Surprisingly tolerant of city air pollution, more so than most white pines.

Disease and insect problems: Few. Pine aphid; possibly blister rust in New England.

Transplanting: Easy when young; should be moved to permanent site when not over 3′. Roots shallow.

Propagation: By seed.

LANDSCAPE VALUE A beautiful lawn specimen, this lovely tree belongs in backgrounds, on campuses and in industrial, park and other large-scale plantings. In very mild climates it grows too fast and can become gangly and sparse, but where the climate and space are suitable it is a beautiful pine, widely hardy and environmentally tolerant. On the northern edge of its range severe winter winds can result in needle burn and often in partial top-kill, but the tree speedily recovers. On some sites this annual pruning by nature can be an advantage in stabilizing the tree's height.

Recommended cultivar:
  P. Wallichiana 'Zebrina', a rarely obtainable cultivar whose needles are uniformly and regularly marked with bands of gold. When windblown the tree shimmers in arresting beauty.

Plant may be observed at: *Arboreta*—Arnold, Bernheim Forest, Dawes, Los Angeles, Minnesota Landscape, Morton, National, U. of Washington; *Botanical Gardens*—Berry, Chicago, Huntington, Munich, New York, Palmgarten, Royal/Kew, Van Dusen; *Gardens*—Longwood; *Parks*—Central/New York, Golden Gate.

N. BREWSTER

P. KINGSLEY

N. BREWSTER

Pithecellobium flexicaule (Bentham) J. Coulter [*Ebenopsis flexicaulis* (Bentham) Britton & Rose]. TEXAS EBONY. *Leguminosae* (subfamily *Mimosoideae*). USDA Zone 9. Temperate to warm U.S.A. and Mexico.

DESCRIPTION *Evergreen* with spiny, wide, rounded head to 35–50′ at maturity. Grows very slowly. Casts medium shade.

Leaves: Twice pinnately compound, alternate, composed of 1–3 pairs of pinnae; leaflets 3–5 pairs per pinnae, 2″ long and 3″ broad; dark lustrous green.

Flowers: Small, ¼″ long, in dense, slender spikes; white and fragrant, blooming June-August.

Fruit: Legume 4–6″ long, 1–1¼″ wide, dark brown to black; straight to falcate and woody. Ripens in fall; remains on branches until after flowering season the following year.

Winter aspect: Spiny tree with short, forked branches; spines usually in pairs at nodes and persistent. Fruit and leaves also persistent. Wood dark red to purple-brown, sapwood yellow.

CULTURE Grows in sun and drought conditions. Withstands winds and soil compaction. Prefers well-drained loam to sandy soils with high alkalinity.

Disease and insect problems: None serious.

Transplanting: Difficult after second year. Best transplanted from 3–5 gallon container; root system deep.

Propagation: Mainly by seed. Seed coat thick and hard; scarify or soak in warm water.

LANDSCAPE VALUE Good, hardy, drought-resistant evergreen. Long-lived and adaptable to dry, well-drained locations. Spines are its most unfavorable characteristic. Only adaptable to warm-temperate regions of southern U.S. and Mexico. Planted along streets of Brownsville, Texas, as ornamental shade tree. Seeds eaten in Mexico and their shells have been used to brew a coffee substitute. Wood used for cabinet making and fuel. Often considered the most valuable native tree in lower Rio Grande Valley.

Plant may be observed at: *Arboreta*—Los Angeles; *Botanical Gardens*—Huntington, San Antonio; *Gardens*—Fairchild Tropical.

W. ADAMS

S. WALKER

S. WALKER

Prunus maacki Ruprecht. AMUR CHOKECHERRY. *Rosaceae.* USDA Zones 3–6. Korea, Manchuria. Introduced 1878 by way of Leningrad.

DESCRIPTION *Deciduous* tree growing at medium rate to 35–45' high; rounded crown. Casts light shade.

Leaves: 3" long, oblong to elliptic-ovate, serrate; covered with glandular dots on lower surface.

Flowers: Small, white, 6–10 flowers on 2–3" irregular racemes which come from shoots of the previous year; in spring.

Fruit: Small, 1/5" diam. black fruit, ripening in August.

Winter aspect: Handsome brown-yellow, sometimes cinnamon, bark exfoliating in thin strips; dense branching habit.

CULTURE Requires sun and well-drained loam and sandy soil in a neutral pH range; prefers cold climates.

Disease and insect problems: Borers in warm climates, aphids, scale, leaf spot.

Transplanting: Easy.

Propagation: Best results by cuttings taken in the summer; by seed.

LANDSCAPE VALUE A rare, vigorous, small tree valued for its attractive, shiny, golden-brown, often flaking bark and its tolerance of extremely cold climates.

Plant may be observed at: *Arboreta*—Arnold, Minnesota Landscape, Morton, U. of Wisconsin-Madison; *Botanical Gardens*—Brooklyn, Chicago, Missouri, Munich, New York, Royal/Kew.

M. DIRR

R. HEBB

M. DIRR

Prunus 'Okame' (Incampi Group) *P. incisa* Thunberg x *P. campanulata* Maximowicz. OKAME CHERRY. *Rosaceae.* USDA Zone 5–8. England. Hybridized in England before 1947 by Capt. Collingwood Ingram.

DESCRIPTION
Deciduous, upright, oval tree which grows rapidly while young to a mature height of 25'. Casts medium shade.

Leaves: 1–2½" long, acuminate, dark green changing to yellow-orange-red in fall.

Flowers: Clear pink, profuse, very early spring.

Fruit: Inconspicuous.

Winter aspect: Cherry-like bark with prominent elongated lenticels; fine-textured branches.

CULTURE
Grows in sun in clay or loam.

Disease and insect problems: Few; canker worms.

Transplanting: Easy.

Propagation: By softwood cuttings.

LANDSCAPE VALUE
The little-known Okame Cherry is one of the finest flowering trees. A heavy annual bloomer, it bears small clear pink flowers profusely. Though it flowers a week or 10 days before Higan Cherry, its blossoms are resistant to late frost. Its flower buds are an attractive landscape asset for a week before it flowers, and later after the petals drop, the deep red calyx and stamens persist for another week. In all, Okame Cherry has an effective flowering period of 2–3 weeks, compared with a few days for many other cherries. Its branching habit is finer textured and more graceful than most cherries. It has dependably good orange-red fall color. It propagates easily from cuttings and grows rapidly when young. *P.* 'Okame' has been commended by the Pennsylvania Horticultural Society for outstanding garden merit.

Plant may be observed at: *Arboreta*—Morris, National, Planting Fields; *Botanical Gardens*—Atlanta, Brooklyn, Huntington, Palmgarten, Royal/Kew, U. of Georgia.

P. MEYER

P. MEYER

P. MEYER

Prunus sargentii Rehder. SARGENT CHERRY. *Rosaceae.* USDA Zones 4–7. North Japan, Korea. Introduced 1890 by Arnold Arboretum.

DESCRIPTION
Deciduous upright tree with rounded top; grows rapidly to 40–50' high and comparable width. Casts dense shade.

Leaves: Alternate, simple, 2–5" long and half as wide, elliptic to narrow-obovate, serrate. Young spring foliage colorful bronze, turning deep green when mature and orange to red in fall.

Flowers: Single, pink to deep pink, in 2–4 umbels, 1½" across on slender pedicels, blooming before the leaves.

Fruit: Inconspicuous, ⅜" ovoid, dark purple; ripens June-July.

Winter aspect: Brown to red-bronze bark marked with horizontal lenticels; spreading habit.

CULTURE
Grows in sun, in loam with pH range of 5.0–7.0; tolerant of wind but intolerant of smog.

Disease and insect problems: Tent caterpillars some years.

Transplanting: Easy; root system deep.

Propagation: By seed, grafting, budding.

LANDSCAPE
VALUE
Hardiest of the taller Japanese cherries and one of the finest of all cherry trees. Excellent, showy flowers, dense deep green foliage, lustrous cherry bark, good fall color make a distinctive ornamental specimen. Can be used as street tree or in parks; rather large for average small property. Wood has been used for timber in Japan for many years. Oldest specimen in America, grown from seed in 1890 at Arnold Arboretum, had to be taken down because of storm damage.

'P. sargentii 'Columnaris', noted at Arnold Arboretum in 1914, also excellent tree; narrower and more upright; good as street tree.

Plant may be observed at: *Arboreta*—Arnold, Bernheim Forest, Cary, Morton, Planting Fields, U. of Washington, U. of Wisconsin-Madison; *Botanical Gardens*—Brooklyn, Chicago, Missouri, Royal/Kew, Palmgarten, Van Dusen; *Gardens*—Winterthur; *Parks*—Forest Parks-Ibaraki, Japan.

M. DIRR

M. DIRR

M. DIRR

Prunus subhirtella Miquel. 'Autumnalis' DOUBLE-FLOWERED HIGAN CHERRY.
Rosaceae. USDA Zones 5–8. Japan. Introduced 1894 by Arnold Arboretum.

DESCRIPTION
Deciduous wide-spreading, short, rounded tree; grows rapidly when young to 20–40' high at maturity with 15–30' spread. Casts light shade.

Leaves: Alternate, simple, ovate-oblong, 1–4" long; pubescent on veins beneath, lustrous dark green above; yellow in fall.

Flowers: Partly double, pink, ¾"; in spring before leaves and sparse bloom again in fall, especially during warm spells.

Fruit: Fruits irregularly; small black berry when ripe, about ⅜" diam.

Winter aspect: Brown, smooth bark, forked trunk; spreading, erect, twiggy branches.

CULTURE
Grows in sun and some shade in any good soil with adequate moisture; prefers loam with pH range of 5.0–7.0. Intolerant of smog. Heavy winds, snow, or ice can cause damage as wood splits easily.

Disease and insect problems: Some borer and scale; should be sprayed yearly for leaf-eating insects such as tent caterpillars.

Transplanting: Easy when young.

Propagation: By cuttings or grafts.

LANDSCAPE VALUE
Excellent, neat and tidy small tree with two flowering seasons: heavy in spring, sparse in fall. Semi-double flowers remain effective for long time. One of earliest Oriental cherries to bloom and one of the most floriferous. Cv. 'Autumnalis' is hardier than any of the serrulata forms of Japanese Cherry.

Cv. 'Pendula', Weeping Higan Cherry, was one of first to come to U.S.; it was listed in 1846 catalogue of Ellwanger and Barry Nursery of Rochester, N.Y.

Plant may be observed at: *Arboreta*—Arnold, National, U. of Washington, U. of Wisconsin-Madison; *Botanical Gardens*—Birmingham, British Columbia, Chicago, New York, Palmgarten, Royal/Kew, U. of Georgia, Van Dusen; *Gardens*—Callaway, Dixon, Longwood, Winterthur; *Parks*—Forest Parks-Ibaraki, Japan.

M. HOPKINS

M. HOPKINS

HOLDEN ARB.

Pseudolarix kaempferi Gordon [*P. amabilis* (J. Nelson) Rehder; *Chrysolarix amabilis* (J. Nelson) H.E. Moore]. GOLDEN LARCH. *Pinaceae.* USDA Zones 5–7. Eastern China. Introduced 1854 by R. Fortune.

DESCRIPTION

Deciduous conifer with broad, pyramidal, open growth habit; grows slowly to 30–50' high (can grow to 120') and 20–40' spread.

Leaves: Needles 1½–2½" long; soft, light green above, bluish-green beneath; clear golden-yellow in fall.

Flowers: Monoecious, borne on separate branches of same tree; male flowers yellow in clustered catkins.

Fruit: Solitary 2–3" cones, borne upright; ripen in autumn of first year; green to purple in summer, golden-brown in fall.

Winter aspect: Bark lightly ridged, gray to red-brown; wide-spreading, horizontal habit.

CULTURE

Grows in sun in loam or sand; prefers light, moist, acid, deep, well-drained soil. Somewhat resistant to air pollutants; intolerant of limestone soil; needs protection from wind.

Disease and insect problems: None serious.

Transplanting: Easy when balled and burlapped.

Propagation: By seed, although trees generally produce good crop of seed only every 3–4 years.

LANDSCAPE VALUE

Beautiful foliage in spring and early summer, cones and dazzling fall color add extra dimension of interest; branching habit creates distinctive winter silhouette. A large handsome tree which should be grown more frequently in expansive, open areas; not a tree for small gardens. Has been growing at Arnold Arboretum since 1891. Found by Robert Fortune as a pot plant in China; 11 years later he found it growing naturally in a monastery garden. Distinguished from *Larix* in having acuminate rather than obtuse bud scales; leaves longer and wider than true larch. *P. kaempferi* 'Nana'—dwarf.

Plant may be observed at: *Arboreta*—Arnold, Bernheim Forest, Cary, Morton, National, Planting Fields, U. of Wisconsin-Madison; *Botanical Gardens*—Birmingham, Brooklyn, Missouri, Palmgarten, Royal/Kew; *Gardens*—Longwood; *Parks*—Central/New York.

J. RAULSTON

PLANTING FIELDS

J. RAULSTON

Ptelea trifoliata L. [*P. isophylla* Greene; *P. serrata* Small]. HOP TREE, WAFER ASH, WATER ASH. *Rutaceae.* USDA Zones 4–9. Ontario and New York to Florida, west to Minnesota. Introduced 1724.

DESCRIPTION *Deciduous* small round-headed tree, growing at moderate rate to 25′ high and 15′ wide at maturity. Casts medium shade.

Leaves: Trifoliate, leaflets nearly sessile, alternate, 2–6″ long. Lustrous dark green in summer changing to yellow in fall.

Flowers: Small, yellow-green, borne on slender stalks in corymbs 2–3″ across, pungent in spring.

Fruit: Light brown samaras ⅔–1″ wide in terminal clusters.

Winter aspect: Bark dark red-brown, open branching habit. Fruit may persist until spring if not eaten by wildlife.

CULTURE Grows in rich woods and thickets in moderately moist, fertile loam, and also in well-drained gravelly places. Tolerates sun, shade and wind but neither extreme of moisture. Adaptable plant.

Disease and insect problems: None serious; occasional leaf-hoppers.

Transplanting: Easy when dormant, in early spring or late fall.

Propagation: By seed (stratify 3 mos. at 40°); budding, layering, grafting.

LANDSCAPE VALUE Valuable small tree for residence, good in shelter belts and environmental plantings; provides wildlife food. Desirable because of picturesque habit, handsome foliage, fragrance of flowers resembling that of orange blossoms, and attractive light-colored fruit. Conspicuous and persistent fruit creates a spectacular appearance in fall and into winter. The bark, leaves and fruit have an aromatic scent when crushed; the fruit has been suggested as a substitute for hops because of its extreme bitterness. May need occasional pruning to keep in shape.

Plant may be observed at: *Arboreta*—Arnold, Holden, Morton, Planting Fields, U. of Washington, U. of Wisconsin-Madison; *Botanical Gardens*—British Columbia, Brooklyn, Munich, Royal/Kew, U. of Georgia.

E. HASSELKUS

K. KOHOUT

K. KOHOUT

Pterostyrax hispida Siebold & Zuccarini. EPAULETTE TREE. *Styraceae.* USDA Zones 5–7. Japan, China. Introduced in 1875.

DESCRIPTION *Deciduous* tree, branching very low, spread equal to height, with moderate rate of growth to 50' at maturity. Casts dense shade.

Leaves: Alternate, simple, elliptical, pointed, 5–11" long and 4" wide, very finely toothed. Light green, silvery beneath.

Flowers: Creamy white with 5 separate petals ⅜" long and fringe of stamens ⅝" long, in large panicles 9" long and 4" in dia. Fragrant.

Fruit: 10-ribbed, ½" long, dry, gray, hairy, in gracefully curved panicles.

Winter aspect: Gray snakeskin bark showing orange-tan at expansion breaks; branching habit, wide-reaching and gracefully upswept. Persistent fruit useful for dried arrangements.

CULTURE Full sun necessary: does poorly in shade. Tolerates windy site, drought and environmental stress in heart of city. Tolerates clay or sandy soil, prefers loam.

Disease and insect problems: None discovered in 9 years of experience or in reference books.

Transplanting: Reported to be moved easily balled and burlapped in spring.

Propagation: Easy by seed.

LANDSCAPE VALUE Has handsome and unusual tear-drop form, especially notable in winter, if allowed to keep its major branches near the ground. Its yellow leaves remain late into the fall. Should be a specimen plant, in full sun. Large size and light leaf color make good contrast with other plants in summer. Blooms when 4 years old, conspicuous at a distance. Contrary to some instructions, *P. hispida* is most notable when large, foot-high lower branches are permitted to sweep wide and exultantly upward, giving the tree a dropping-tear shape.

Plant may be observed at: *Arboreta*—Arnold, Bernheim Forest, Dawes, Holden, Morton, National, Spring Grove, U. of Washington; *Botanical Gardens*—Brooklyn, Missouri, Munich, Palmgarten, Royal/Kew; *Gardens*—Longwood, Winterthur.

M. DIRR

A. BUSSEWITZ

N. BREWSTER

Pyrus ussuriensis Maximowicz. USSURIAN PEAR. *Rosaceae.* USDA Zones 4-7. Manchuria (Northern China), Korea and Ussuri region of Russian Far East. Introduced 1855.

DESCRIPTION
Deciduous tree with moderately rapid growth to 30–40'; somewhat upright when young, spreading with age. Casts medium-dense shade.

Leaves: 2–4" long, rounded to oval; margin finely and regularly toothed; semi-glossy; mixed yellow-orange-red fall foliage.

Flowers: Showy flowers with conspicuous white petals, faintly pink in bud, 1⅓" across, in May.

Fruit: Greenish-yellow pome; slightly smaller than golf balls and becoming apparent in mid-summer, maturing and falling in September.

Winter aspect: Light gray bark with vertically peeling scales; ascending to broadly branching habit.

CULTURE
Grows in sun and shade in clay and loam with pH range of 6.0–7.4. Tolerates drought; soil compaction may hinder growth.

Disease and insect problems: Fire blight, but minimal.

Transplanting: Easy; root system shallow.

Propagation: By seed, cuttings, buds, grafts.

LANDSCAPE VALUE
Dependable, vigorous and attractive flowering tree. Excellent summer foliage and brilliant fall color. Hardiest of all the pears and one of the least susceptible to fire blight, it has a capacity to tolerate adverse soils. It is long-lived and requires minimal maintenance. Valued as a medium-sized ornamental for cold climates. The fruit is generally reported as not suitable for eating; however *P. ussuriensis* at the Morton Arboretum, Lisle, Illinois, is reported to have small, tasty, edible fruit.

Plant may be observed at: *Arboreta*—Dawes, Minnesota Landscape, Morton, U. of Wisconsin-Madison; *Botanical Gardens*—Denver, Royal/Kew.

P. KINGSLEY

K. KOHOUT

K. KOHOUT

Quercus acutissima Carruthers. SAWTOOTH OAK. *Fagaceae.* USDA Zones 6–9. Japan and China, Himalayas. Introduced 1862 by Richard Oldham.

DESCRIPTION
Deciduous tree growing at medium rate (fast in the South) to 35–45′ high; pyramidal when young, then oval-round to broad-round; some are wider than tall. Casts dense shade.

Leaves: Alternate, simple, 3½–7½″ long; oblong or narrowly oval, serrate, with bristle-like teeth, often confused with leaves of *Castanea*; upper surface lustrous and polished green in summer, lower surface paler green; yellow in fall.

Flowers: Inconspicuous.

Fruit: Stalkless acorns about 1″ long; tree often bears heavy crop.

Winter aspect: Ridged and furrowed bark; wide-spreading branching habit.

CULTURE
Grows in sun and light shade in clay and loam with a wide pH range. Tolerates soil compaction, wind and drought.

Disease and insect problems: None serious.

Transplanting: Easy when young (8–10′).

Propagation: By seeds sown as soon as ripe.

LANDSCAPE VALUE
Attractive, wide-spreading shade tree that needs adequate space for lateral development. Polished, chestnut-like leaves persist into winter. With its well rounded shape and its good, clean foliage, *Q. acutissima* makes an excellent lawn tree that should be planted more frequently.

Plant may be observed at: *Arboreta*—Bernheim Forest, Dawes, Los Angeles, Morton, National, Planting Fields, Spring Grove, U. of Washington, U. of Wisconsin-Madison; *Botanical Gardens*—Birmingham, Brooklyn, Canton, Missouri, New York, Royal/Kew, U. of Georgia; *Gardens*—Callaway, Longwood; *Parks*—Forest Parks-Ibaraki, Japan.

M. DIRR

M. DIRR

M. DIRR

Quercus bicolor Willdenow. SWAMP WHITE OAK. *Fagaceae.* USDA Zones 4–8. East and Central North America. Introduced c. 1800 into National Arboretum, Royal Botanic Garden; Hamilton, Canada.

DESCRIPTION   *Deciduous* tree with broad, open, round-topped crown and short trunk when mature; narrow, open crown when young. Size at maturity 60' tall with equal spread, occasionally taller. Spends several years slowly developing a substantial root system and then begins a moderately rapid growth rate. Casts dense shade.

Leaves: Alternate, simple, 4–6" long and 2–4" wide, obovate with sinuate margins; upper surface dark green and shiny, whitish-tomentose beneath. Fall color yellow-brown to red.

Flowers: Insignificant. Male and female in separate catkins.

Fruit: 1" acorn, usually paired, borne on slender peduncle; matures in one year and falls in October.

Winter aspect: Bark thick, gray-brown, deeply furrowed. Lower branches somewhat drooping, upper branches ascending.

CULTURE   Will tolerate sun, shade, wind and wet conditions; intolerant of salt and air pollution. May tolerate soil compaction. Prefers clay soil or loam, acid pH.

Disease and insect problems: Oak wilt (not serious in ornamental plantings), anthracnose, canker, gypsy moth, powdery mildew.

Transplanting: Not difficult; root system average, tap root is not well developed.

Propagation: By seed.

LANDSCAPE VALUE   Good in moist soils, for naturalizing, as shade tree. The specific epithet of "bicolor" derives from the two colors of foliage—green upper surface and whitish beneath. Found growing in the wild in low-lying swampy situations. Similar to white oak but grows in moister situations; also thrives on well-drained sites. Wood is important commercially for furniture, flooring, boat building. Acorn edible and attractive to mammals and birds. Moderately long-lived; may reach 300–350 years.

Plant may be observed at: *Arboreta*—Arnold, Bernheim Forest, Dawes, Holden, Minnesota Landscape, Morton, Planting Fields, U. of Washington, U. of Wisconsin-Madison; *Botanical Gardens*—Brooklyn, Chicago, Denver, Missouri, Munich, New York, Royal/Kew; *Gardens*—Brookgreen, Callaway, Longwood.

MORTON ARB

HOLDEN ARB.

E. HASSELKUS

Quercus imbricaria Michaux. SHINGLE OAK. *Fagaceae.* USDA Zones 5–8. Central U.S.: native of Ohio Valley, Pennsylvania to Georgia and Arkansas. Introduced 1724.

DESCRIPTION *Deciduous* tree with slow to medium rate of growth; 60–75' with comparable spread at maturity; pyramidal when young, round-topped and open when old. Casts medium to dense shade.

Leaves: Alternate, oblong to 6" long, 3" wide, not lobed or toothed; lustrous dark green above, pubescent beneath; laurel-like; sometimes remaining on tree late in fall; autumn color yellow to russet.

Flowers: Male flowers in drooping yellow-green catkins; female flowers in one to many flowered spikes; blooms mid-spring with or after leaves.

Fruit: Acorns, dark chestnut brown; thin, bowl-shaped cup encloses 1/3–1/2 of nut which is 5/8" long.

Winter aspect: Gray-brown bark, developing ridges and furrows with age; straight trunk and broad horizontal branching habit.

CULTURE Grows in sun; tolerant of clay soil but prefers moist, rich acid loam. Tolerates wind; is somewhat tolerant of city conditions and drought.

Disease and insect problems: Minimal, although can have borer, oak gall and powdery mildew.

Transplanting: Easy when young and balled and burlapped; easier than many oaks. Root system deep.

Propagation: By seed, stratified or sown outside in fall for spring germination; should be protected from rodents, who will eat seed.

LANDSCAPE VALUE Handsome specimen. One of the most beautiful of the oaks. Adaptable; performs well in Midwest as it tolerates calcareous soils. Can be used as street tree or for parks, golf courses, or other large areas, or can be pruned to form hedge or screen; used as windbreak as leaves persist into winter. Wood is hard and strong; does not split easily; can withstand summer storms; resistant to breaking under snow and ice. A long-lived tree. It is called Shingle Oak because the wood can be split into relatively thin sheets and is resistant to decay. It was used for shingles by early French colonists who settled at Kaskaskia, Illinois. Andre Michaux discovered this tree on one of his trips west to collect plants. He translated the word shingle into Latin and so called it "Quercus imbricaria." It is said that shingles are still made from the wood in Tennessee.

Plant may be observed at: *Arboreta*—Arnold, Bernheim Forest, Dawes, Holden, Morton, National, Planting Fields, U. of Washington, U. of Wisconsin-Madison; *Botanical Gardens*—Brooklyn, Chicago, Missouri, New York, Palmgarten, Royal/Kew, U. of Georgia; *Gardens*—Longwood.

E. HASSELKUS

E. HASSELKUS

E. HASSELKUS

Quercus macrocarpa Michaux [*Q. macrocarpa* var. *oliviformis* (Michaux f.) A. Gray; *Q. oliviformis* Michaux f.]. BUR OAK, MOSSYCUP OAK. *Fagaceae.* USDA Zones 3–8. Nova Scotia to Pennsylvania, west to Manitoba and Texas. Introduced 1811.

DESCRIPTION   *Deciduous* tree growing slowly to 70–80' with equal spread; can grow to 150' in wild; weakly pyramidal to oval when young; in maturity, develops a broad crown of stout branches and a massive trunk. Casts dense shade.

Leaves: Alternate, simple, 6–12" long, 3–6" wide, obovate; shallowly to deeply lobed and broader above middle; 5–9 lobes; terminal lobe the largest, tapering to a narrow base; dark green and usually lustrous above, gray-white, tomentulose beneath; fall color dull yellow to yellow-brown.

Flowers: Male flowers in slender yellow-green catkins; female flowers very small, reddish, usually in clusters at the junction of the leaves and branchlets; spring bloom.

Fruit: Acorn ¾–1½" long, half covered with heavy cup; broadly ovoid. Tree is sometimes called Mossycup Oak because of the fringe on the acorn cup.

Winter aspect: Gray-brown, deeply furrowed bark; stout, hairy branchlets smooth with age.

CULTURE   Needs full sun; tolerant of varying moisture and soil conditions, but prefers rich bottomlands.

Disease and insect problems: Oak galls, anthracnose, canker, oak lace bug, oak mite. None a serious threat to its usually long life.

Transplanting: Difficult because of coarse root system; move when young, balled and burlapped.

Propagation: By seed; no pretreatment required but suggest 30–60 days at 41°F. in moist peat or sand.

LANDSCAPE VALUE   Aristocratic and impressive major tree. Lends beauty, interest and large canopy of shade to the garden in summer. In the dormant season, the magnificent branching pattern adds architectural beauty to the winter sky. Adaptable to a wide variety of soils and harsh growing conditions. More tolerant of urban conditions than most oaks. Excellent park tree. Often occurs in pure stands but also grows with many other hardwoods. Does not begin to flower or fruit until about 30 years old, but may produce fruit and flowers for 200–300 years. Large seed crops produced every 2–3 years important to wildlife. White-tail deer, wood duck, turkeys, squirrels, feed on acorns. Very hard, durable, strong wood used for boat decks, flooring, furniture. There is a great variation within the species.

Plant may be observed at: *Arboreta*—American Horticultural Society-River Farm, Arnold, Bernheim Forest, Dawes, Minnesota Landscape, Morton, National, U. of Washington, U. of Wisconsin-Madison; *Botanical Gardens*—Chicago, Missouri, New York, Palmgarten, Royal/Kew, U. of Georgia; *Gardens*—Brookgreen, Longwood.

M. DIRR

M. DIRR

HOLDEN ARB

Quercus robur L. 'Fastigiata'. [*Q. pedunculata* J. F. Ehrhart] ENGLISH OAK. *Fagaceae.*
USDA Zones 5–8. Germany, Europe. Introduced 1783.

DESCRIPTION *Deciduous* tree growing at a medium rate to 50–60' high, 10–15' wide; narrow fastigiate habit.

Leaves: Alternate, simple, 2½–5" long, ¾–2½" wide, obovate to obovate-oblong; 3–7 pairs of rounded lobes; dark green; no fall color as leaves drop late in fall while still green.

Flowers: Male flowers in slender catkins; female flowers clustered in small groups of 2–5.

Fruit: Acorns, approximately 1" long, with a cap covering about ⅓ of their length; ripen in autumn.

Winter aspect: Dark brown-black, deeply furrowed bark; upright branching habit; persistent fruit.

CULTURE Prefers good, well-drained soil and full sun, but is tolerant of wide pH range.

Disease and insect problems: Powdery mildew.

Transplanting: Move balled and burlapped.

Propagation: Comes partly true (80-90%) from seed.

LANDSCAPE VALUE Handsome specimen with narrowly pyramidal growth. Excellent choice where vertical plant is needed. The most famous oak of this kind was found growing in the wild in a forest at Haareshausen near Frankfurt-am-Main. A tree was then propagated by grafting in 1783. Most of the fastigiate oaks cultivated in Germany, and perhaps in other countries, are believed to be descended from this tree. Similar in shape to Lombardy Poplar, but a superior tree. The timber is used in ship construction.

Plant may be observed at: *Arboreta*—Bernheim Forest, Cary, Holden, Los Angeles, Morton, National, Planting Fields, U. of Washington, U. of Wisconsin-Madison; *Botanical Gardens*—British Columbia, Brooklyn, Huntington, Missouri, Munich, New York, Palmgarten, Royal/Kew, Royal/Ontario; *Parks*—Golden Gate.

E. HASSELKUS

PLANTING FIELDS

M. DIRR

Quercus shumardii Buckley. SHUMARD OAK. *Fagaceae.* USDA Zones 5–8. South and Central U.S.A. Introduced 1907.

DESCRIPTION **Deciduous** large tree growing moderately fast to 60–80' in cultivation, over 100' in bottomland forests. Habit globose and wide-spreading. Casts medium-dense shade.

Leaves: Ovate or obovate, 4–8" long, deeply lobed; 5–9 lobes with needle tips and 2–4 rounded sinuses between lobes. Red to orange color in fall often spectacular.

Flowers: Male catkins, often reddish in color.

Fruit: Acorns ovoid to oblong, ½–1¼" long, enclosed at base by saucer-shaped scaly cup to 1¼" diam. Mature in early fall.

Winter aspect: Bark gray to red-brown in small scaly plates; branching, medium-compact when young, open-spreading as tree matures.

CULTURE Grows in sun in clay, loam or sandy soil in pH range of 6.9-7.8. Tolerates wind and both wet and dry conditions, and appears to be extremely stress-tolerant.

Disease and insect problems: Susceptible to oak wilt; this does not appear to be a serious drawback.

Transplanting: Moderately easy; root system shallow, deep only in light soils.

Propagation: By seed (acorns); grafting not usually effective.

LANDSCAPE VALUE A handsome tree that tolerates adverse sites. A good street or park tree, with attractive, deep green, glossy foliage and rounded, moderately dense crown. Fall color is a distinct asset; tolerance of alkaline clay soil is valuable. Pin Oak (*Q. palustris*) is widely planted as a shade and ornamental tree, yet it commonly develops chlorosis and slowly declines. Shumard Oak grows well where Pin Oak won't. A Shumard Oak leaf is pictured on the cover of Gray's Manual of Botany; it is a favorite of Dr. L. C. Chadwick, distinguished horticulturist of Columbus, Ohio.

Plant may be observed at: *Arboreta*—Arnold, Bernheim Forest, Dawes, Holden, Planting Fields, Spring Grove, U. of Washington; *Botanical Gardens*—Missouri, Royal/Kew; *Gardens*—Brookgreen, Longwood.

M. DIRR

N. BREWSTER

PLANTING FIELDS ARB.

Roystonea regia (HBK) O. F. Cook [*Oreodoxa regia* HBK; *R. Jenmanii* (C. H. Wright) Burret; *R. ventricosa* (C. H. Wright) Burret]. ROYAL PALM. *Palmae.* USDA Zone 10. Cuba. Introduced into Hawaii in 1850 by seed brought from West Indies.

DESCRIPTION *Evergreen* tree growing at moderate rate to 50–70'; single, erect, unbranched trunk, enlarged at base and tapering upward; nearly globose crown. Casts light shade.

Leaves: Crown of dark green leaves arching in all directions from a large, 4' long, green cylinder of leaf sheaths.

Flowers: Many-branched violet flower clusters develop off trunk; male and female flowers separate on same tree, but males are larger and open first year-round blooms.

Fruit: Ovoid, nearly ½" diam.; ordinarily one-seeded; dark red to purple.

Winter aspect: Year-round interest; pale gray bark, smooth and evenly ringed; tuft of numerous, long, arched leaves emanating from a green column formed by the leaf sheaths.

CULTURE Grows in full sun in clay and loam. Not tolerant of drought; needs constant watering. Can tolerate pollution from automobiles but will not tolerate salt. Trunks may grow irregularly under adverse conditions (drought, etc.).

Disease and insect problems: None.

Transplanting: Easy; root system shallow and spreading.

Propagation: By seed.

LANDSCAPE VALUE An elegant, stately and highly ornamental palm, known for its striking appearance. Used for its great symmetry and formal effect in parks and along boulevards. The tender top portion is cooked and eaten as a vegetable, and the leaf sheaths are often used as sleeping mats. Named for General Roy Stone.

Plant may be observed at: *Botanical Gardens*—Pacific Tropical; *Gardens*—Fairchild Tropical.

P. NOTTAGE

P. NOTTAGE

P. NOTTAGE

Sapindus drummondii W. Hooker & G. Arnott. WESTERN SOAPBERRY, CHINA-BERRY. *Sapindaceae.* USDA Zones 6–9. Southwest Missouri to southern Colorado and central Arizona, south to Louisiana and northern Mexico. Cultivated since 1900 in U.S.A. Introduced into Britain in 1915.

DESCRIPTION

Deciduous tree growing to 40–50' with almost equal spread; trunk up to 2' wide; rounded crown.

Leaves: Alternate, pinnate to 8" long, 4–9 pairs of short stalked leaflets, each 1½–4" long, ½–¾" wide; lanceolate, entire, veiny, glabrous, yellow-green above, downy beneath.

Flowers: Yellow-white in pyramidal terminal panicles, 6–10" long; each flower about ¼" diam., with 4–5 obovate, rounded petals; spring bloom.

Fruit: Drupe-like berry ½" thick with thin, semi-translucent, yellow-orange flesh that ultimately turns black; black, round seeds, ¼–⅓" wide.

Winter aspect: Gray-brown to red-brown bark, furrowed into long scaly plates; low-branched and erect habit; fruit remains on tree through winter.

CULTURE

Grows in full sun and partial shade; adaptable to varied soils, but prefers sandy, loamy soil; withstands high pH. Tolerant of wind, drought and urban conditions.

Disease and insect problems: None serious.

Transplanting: Easy.

Propagation: By seed; thick seed coat makes stratification or scarification necessary (germination rate is 31%); also by hardwood cuttings.

LANDSCAPE VALUE

Excellent shade and ornamental tree especially recommended for dry sites. Its adaptability to varied soils, harsh winds and urban conditions makes it a good candidate for a street tree; the only disadvantage is the litter from the fruit. The great clusters of translucent fruit look like yellow grapes or cherries and create an unusual and handsome appearance in the fall. The fruit has had many and varied uses over the years, including a medicinal remedy for rheumatism and fever, although it has been established that the fruits are poisonous, and it is probable that the nectar of the flower is also poisonous. Because the fruits contain 37% saponin, when macerated in water they create great quantities of suds; thus the Mexicans use it as a laundry soap. The wood is hard and strong, and the trees are sometimes used for shelter-belt planting. The species *drummondii* was named in honor of Thomas Drummond, botanist.

Plant may be observed at: *Arboreta*—National; *Botanical Gardens*—Brooklyn, Missouri, San Antonio.

M. DIRR

M. DIRR

M. DIRR

Sapium sebiferum (L.) Roxburgh [*Triadica sebifera* (L.)]. CHINESE TALLOW TREE. *Euphorbiaceae.* USDA Zones 8–10. China, Japan. Introduced 1850.

DESCRIPTION
Deciduous tree growing at rapid rate to 30–40' high; pyramidal, rounded, with airy crown. Casts medium, filtered shade.

Leaves: 3" long, poplar-shaped, glabrous and bright green; turn maroon-crimson-orange in fall.

Flowers: 4" terminal spikes, yellow-green and drooping; summer bloom.

Fruit: ½" wide brown capsule which opens to expose three large white seeds.

Winter aspect: Dark gray bark, ridged and furrowed; full, slightly irregular habit.

CULTURE
Adaptable to moist and dry, acid and alkaline soils, but needs full sun; tolerant of wind, wet conditions and drought.

Disease and insect problems: None known.

Transplanting: Easy when young.

Propagation: Easy; by seed (wash to remove fatty seed covering) and cuttings.

LANDSCAPE VALUE
Lovely ornamental tree which may be planted as a garden specimen or a street tree. It is quite drought-tolerant. The canopy is thin and airy, making it possible to cultivate a lawn beneath its branches. Exhibits beautiful fall color. The milky sap is poisonous. The waxy coat on the seeds is extracted by the Chinese for use in candles and soap. *S. sebiferum* is often called the "Popcorn Tree" because of the appearance of the seeds. *S. sebiferum* valued in California for its vibrant autumn color. In some areas of the South it seeds itself too profusely and becomes a "pest tree."

Plant may be observed at: *Arboreta*—Los Angeles; *Botanical Gardens*—Birmingham, San Antonio, U. of Georgia; *Gardens*—Fairchild Tropical.

A. MacBRIDE

A. MacBRIDE

M. DIRR

Sciadopitys verticillata (Thunberg) Siebold & Zuccarini. JAPANESE UMBRELLA PINE. *Taxodiaceae.* USDA Zones 6–8. Southwest and central Japan. Introduced 1861.

DESCRIPTION *Evergreen conifer* growing slowly when young (to 6″ a year), more rapidly with age; 20–30′ to 60–90′ high at maturity with 15–20′ or wider spread; compact, pyramidal when young, spreading with age. Dense shade of young tree becomes lighter with age.

Leaves: Leaves of two kinds: one small, scale-like, spirally arranged on twigs and crowded near tips; the other dark, glossy green whorls of 20–30 linear, flat needles 2–5″ long, ⅛″ wide.

Flowers: Inconspicuous, monoecious; female solitary, terminal; male flowers in 1″ long racemes.

Fruit: Cones 2–4″ long, 1–2″ wide; female ovoid-globose, subtended by a bract; male cones globose, clustered terminally on branches; green at first, ripening to brown, maturing second year; each scale bears 5–9 winged seeds.

Winter aspect: Thin orange to red-brown bark with exfoliating strips often hidden by foliage; horizontal branching habit becoming pendulous and spreading with age; sometimes multi-stemmed.

CULTURE Grows in sun and shade; prefers well-drained, acid soil. Needs some protection from wind; not tolerant of air pollution or drought; should not be planted in hot, dry locations.

Disease and insect problems: Few.

Transplanting: Best in spring, balled and burlapped.

Propagation: By seed or tip cuttings in late fall.

LANDSCAPE VALUE Almost prehistoric in appearance. Needles radiate around stem similar to ribs of an umbrella to create "umbrella" effect. A distinctive and handsome conifer valued for its dense habit and deep green foliage. Needles remain on tree 2–3 years before falling; lower branches persist for a long time. Makes a splendid accent tree in a border planting or used as a specimen. Tends to grow taller in native areas of Japan. Grows more slowly in U.S.; some plants at Arnold Arboretum only 25′ after 50 years.

Plant may be observed at: *Arboreta*—Arnold, Bernheim Forest, Dawes, National, Planting Fields, U. of Washington; *Botanical Gardens*—Brooklyn, Missouri, New York, Palmgarten, Royal/Kew; *Gardens*—Longwood, Old Westbury, Winterthur; *Parks*—Central/New York, Golden Gate, Forest Parks-Ibaraki, Japan.

NATIONAL ARB.

A. BUSSEWITZ

M. DIRR

Sophora japonica 'Regent' L. JAPANESE PAGODA TREE, CHINESE SCHOLAR TREE. *Leguminosea.* USDA Zones 5–8. China, Korea. Introduced to France 1747.

DESCRIPTION *Deciduous* tree, usually with upright spreading habit and broadly rounded, open crown. Grows slowly when young, medium to fast with age to 50–80' with comparable spread. Casts dense shade when young, more open at maturity.

Leaves: Deep green, lustrous above, glaucous, pale green beneath; pinnate, 6–10" long, composed of 7–15 leaflets, ovate to 2" long, 1" wide.

Flowers: Pale creamy yellow to greenish-white, ½" long in terminal panicles to 12" long; flowers open over period of several weeks in late summer.

Fruit: Yellow pods in October, 2–4" long, 1–6 seeded; remain late on tree, sometimes all winter.

Winter aspect: Bark downy when young, glabrous and dark gray-brown later; old bark corrugated and gray. Wide branching habit, tends to floppy growth; cv. 'Regent' has straight growth habit.

CULTURE Grows in sun and partial shade; prefers loamy, well-drained soil. When established, tolerant of pollution, heat and drought. Prune in fall.

Disease and insect problems: Some canker and potato leaf hopper; can kill young stems.

Transplanting: Best balled and burlapped when young.

Propagation: Seed, greenwood cuttings, grafts; when grown from seed does not flower until 10–12 years old.

LANDSCAPE VALUE Distinctively beautiful; one of the most outstanding of the leguminous trees. Showy, late summer bloom of yellowish pea-like flower; leaves remain green late in fall. Lovely shape creates handsome shade tree. Last of the larger trees to bloom. Important plus: can withstand city conditions; excellent candidate for street tree, parks, golf courses. Valued as a specimen residential tree. 'Regent', a fast grower; less floppy than species, Sophora is an Arabian name for a tree with pea-shaped flowers; common name Pagoda comes from fact that it was often used around Buddhist temples in Orient. Yellow dye is made from wood, bark and fruit.

Other cultivars.:
  'Pendula', Weeping Pagoda Tree with pendent branches
  'Fatigiata', an upright tree

Plant may be observed at: *Arboreta*—Bernheim Forest, Cary, Los Angeles, National, Planting Fields; *Botanical Gardens*—Birmingham, Chicago, U. of Georgia; *Parks*—Forest Parks-Ibaraki, Japan.

Sophora japonica 'Regent'   JAPANESE PAGODA TREE,
CHINESE SCHOLAR TREE

M. DIRR

N. BREWSTER

N. BREWSTER

Sophora secundiflora (Ortega.) Lagasca y Segura ex de Candolle. TEXAS MOUNTAIN LAUREL, MESCAL BEAN, MESCAL BEAN SOPHORA, FRIJOLITO. *Leguminosae.* USDA Zones 8–10. U.S.A. (Texas, New Mexico) and Mexico. Introduced 1800.

DESCRIPTION
Evergreen growing relatively slowly to 50′ in native habitat, more often 15–25′ in cultivation; narrow crown, regular shape.

Leaves: To 2″ long, elliptical, compound, alternate; leaflets in 3–5 pairs, odd-pinnate, margin entire; lustrous, thick, leathery, shiny dark green above, paler beneath.

Flowers: In large, dense, pendulous heads or terminal racemes; pea-shaped, with 5 unequal petals crowded on one side of stalk; individual flowers 1″ long, clusters 2–5″ long; violet-blue, very showy, very fragrant; similar to Wisteria. Blooming period March-April, along with new leaves.

Fruit: To 8″ long and ¾″ wide, on short pedicels; woody and hard, narrowing between the seeds; 1–8 seeds, ½″ long, often slightly flattened at one end, bright red in color, thought to be poisonous; maturing late summer to September.

Winter aspect: Dark gray to black bark; shallow fissures with narrow, flattened ridges; upright, dense habit.

CULTURE
Grows in sun and moderate shade in loam or sand; prefers alkaline soil high in calcium. Tolerates moderate wind and wet conditions, but must have good drainage. Can withstand moderate drought and some air pollution but not soil compaction. Withstands strong light, but immature trees benefit from shading from afternoon summer sun.

Disease and insect problems: None.

Transplanting: Difficult when large, plant when young; root system deep.

Propagation: By seed, greenwood cuttings, layering or grafting.

LANDSCAPE VALUE
This small evergreen native has dark green, lustrous foliage that is attractive all year; the fragrant, showy panicles of flowers rival the Wisteria in early spring. An excellent specimen tree for home or street planting, when a slow-growing, regularly shaped tree is required. *S. secundiflora* is larger in size than *S. affinis.* One of the most attractive, least planted natives, it can adapt to environment if planted, when small, high in bed with good drainage.

Plant may be observed at: *Arboreta*—Houston, Los Angeles, U. of Wisconsin-Madison; *Botanical Gardens*—Huntington, Royal/Kew, San Antonio.

E. DODD

J. RAULSTON

S. SQUIRE

Sorbus alnifolia (Siebold & Zuccarini) K. Koch [*Michromeles alnifolia* (Siebold & Zuccarini) Koehne]. *Rosaceae.* KOREAN MOUNTAIN ASH. USDA Zones 4–7. Korea, Japan, Central China. Introduced 1892 by Arnold Arboretum.

DESCRIPTION
Deciduous broadleaved tree with pyramidal, upright habit; rounded at maturity; medium to fast rate of growth to 40–60' high and 20–30' wide. Casts dense shade.

Leaves: Alternate, simple, ovate, unequally serrate, 2–4"; bright green, turning dark green in late summer; glabrous above, glabrous or pubescent beneath with 6–10 pairs of veins. Fall color warm orange to red.

Flowers: ½" small, white, in flat clusters; blooms late May; apt to flower heavily one year and lightly the next.

Fruit: ⅜" scarlet to orange berries in September-October, covering almost entire tree; persists until late fall.

Winter aspect: Smooth, gray beech-like bark; dense, upright when young, spreading with maturity.

CULTURE
Grows in sun, prefers loam with pH range of 5.0–7.0. Grows better in alkaline rather than acid soil; however fairly adaptable. Tolerates wind and wet conditions but will not tolerate air pollution. Prune in winter or early spring.

Disease and insect problems: Fire blight in areas where outbreaks of this disease severe. Has a few other problems in common with most members of the *Rosaceae* family. Borers, the most serious pest of *Sorbus* species, do not seem to be a problem with this species.

Transplanting: Easy when balled and burlapped; root system shallow.

Propagation: By stratified seeds, grafting.

LANDSCAPE VALUE
Best of Mountain Ashes; least susceptible to borer. Good specimen tree for lawns. Especially good for southern New York, New Jersey, Pennsylvania and coastal New England. Massive, rich green foliage throughout summer. Lovely in spring in full flower and again in fall when both fruit and leaves have excellent color. Scarlet-orange fruit against silvery gray bark creates highly ornamental plant. Handsome tree for gardens, but should not be used as street tree because of potential pests.

'Redbird' is an improved, more upright clone.

A related species, *S. cashmiriana*, Kashmir Mountain Ash, native to Himalayas, introduced in 1949 by Arnold Arboretum, has largest individual flowers, ¾–1", which open, tinged with blush pink. It grows to 20–40' with equal spread; foliage is dark green, turning red in fall. Cvs. of *S. cashmiriana*, 'Carpet of Gold', with yellow fruit, and 'Kirsten Pink' with dark pink fruits.

Plant may be observed at: *Arboreta*—Arnold, Bernheim Forest, Holden, Minnesota Landscape, **Morton**, Planting Fields, U. of Washington, U. of Wisconsin-Madison; *Botanical Gardens*—Brooklyn, Palmgarten, Royal/Kew; *Parks*—Forest Parks-Ibaraki, Japan.

R. HEBB

R. HEBB

A. BUSSEWITZ

Stewartia koreana Nakai ex Rehder. KOREAN STEWARTIA. *Theaceae.* USDA Zones 6–7. Korea. Introduced in 1917 by E.H. Wilson.

DESCRIPTION

Deciduous tree growing slowly to 20–25′ (45′ in wild); dense, pyramidal habit; maintains upright habit into old age. Casts dense shade.

Leaves: Alternate, to 4″; elliptic, somewhat serrulate; dark green turning orange-red to purple in fall.

Flowers: Solitary, white with gold stamens, 5–6 petals, to 3″ dia.; in leaf axils or near terminal shoots; July. Fall soon after bloom but flower continuously over 2-week period.

Fruit: Inconspicuous.

Winter aspect: Most important feature is irregular, flaking bark, which is smooth and gray to olive to cinnamon; zigzagging, ascending habit.

CULTURE

Grows in sun and very light shade; prefers well-drained, moist loam with peat in pH range of 4.5–5.5. Withstands heat and humidity well if roots are kept moist; does not tolerate wind, wet conditions, drought or environmental stress.

Disease and insect problems: None.

Transplanting: Difficult; should be container-grown and planted in permanent place.

Propagation: By seed stratified 90 days; by layering; by cuttings taken in late summer.

LANDSCAPE VALUE

The most hardy of the Stewartias. A perfectly beautiful ornamental specimen. Its most distinctive feature is its multi-colored flaking bark which heightens winter interest. Elegant in summer flower and rich in autumn color. Perhaps the best of the genus for small gardens. Similar to *S. pseudocamellia* but with larger, flatter, more open flowers. The genus was named in honor of John Stuart, Earl of Bute (1713–1792), an amateur botanist, who was chief advisor to Augusta, Dowager Princess of Wales, when she founded the Botanic Garden at Kew in 1759–60. *S. koreana* differs from trees of Japanese provenance in having flowers more widely open and broader leaves, broadly tapered at the base.

Plant may be observed at: *Arboreta*—Arnold, Bernheim Forest, Cary, Holden, Morton, Planting Fields, U. of Washington; *Botanical Gardens*—Chicago, Missouri, Royal/Kew; *Gardens*—Callaway, Longwood, Winterthur.

N. BREWSTER

R. HEBB

PLANTING FIELDS ARB.

Stewartia monadelpha Siebold & Zuccarini. TALL STEWARTIA. *Theaceae.* USDA Zone 6–8. Japan and Quelpart Island. Introduced about 1903.

DESCRIPTION *Deciduous* tree growing at a medium rate to 60–70′ in the wild, but smaller under garden conditions; slender, horizontal branches and irregular habit. Casts light shade.

Leaves: Alternate, ovate to ovate-lanceolate, 1½–3″ long, ⅝–1¼″ wide; finely serrate, downy beneath. Fall color orange to red to purple.

Flowers: 5 white, silky petals with violet anthers, solitary, 1–1⅜″ wide, numerous stamens; in early summer.

Fruit: Woody capsule, ovoid, beaked, ⅜″ long, covered with yellow hairs.

Winter aspect: Smooth, bright, orange-brown bark peeling in small, thin flakes; irregular habit.

CULTURE Grows in sun (faces toward the light); also likes shaded roots. Since it grows in beech forests of Japan, will take quite a bit of shade. Prefers sandy, lime-free loam.

Disease and insect problems: Disease-free.

Transplanting: Resents disturbance; therefore, plant in permanent place when young; root system shallow.

Propagation: By seed or semi-hardwood cuttings.

LANDSCAPE VALUE An all-season tree with soft, velvety, graceful leaves in spring and summer; summer flowers, however, are not conspicuous. The flowers and fruits are the smallest in the genus. It has gorgeous fall color and the most beautiful branching habit and winter bark of almost any tree. Named for John Stuart, Earl of Bute (1713–1792), Sometimes known as Stuartia.

Plant may be observed at: *Arboreta*—Bernheim Forest, National, Planting Fields, Spring Grove, University of Washington; *Botanical Gardens*—Brooklyn, Missouri, Royal/Kew; *Gardens*—Callaway; *Parks*—Forest Parks/Ibaraki, Japan.

J. PLATT

N. BREWSTER

P. KINGSLEY

Stewartia pseudocamellia Maximowicz. JAPANESE STEWARTIA. *Theaceae.* USDA
Zones 5–8. Japan. Introduced 1874.

DESCRIPTION *Deciduous* tree growing slowly to 30–50' (60' in wild); pyramidal habit.
Casts dense shade.

Leaves: Alternate, simple, ovate, 2–4" long, elliptic, finely toothed; bright
green, glabrous and sometimes silky beneath; turning red to purple-red in
fall.

Flowers: White with orange anthers, 2–2½" diam., united styles; cup-
shaped, 5 petals, with margins irregularly jagged.

Fruit: Broadly ovoid, hairy capsule, 1" long.

Winter aspect: Most colorful of Stewartias; gray-brown to orange bark,
exfoliating in large flakes; open, ascending habit.

CULTURE Grows best in sun but tolerates light shade. Prefers moist, well-drained
loam and peat with pH range of 4.5–5.5. Does not tolerate wind, drought
or environmental stress.

Disease and insect problems: None noted.

Transplanting: Difficult; plant small container-grown tree in permanent
place.

Propagation: Seeds stratified 5 months warm, 3 mos. at 40°; layering,
softwood cuttings in July-August.

LANDSCAPE
VALUE
A handsome year-round specimen tree that will enhance any garden in its
growing zone. The flaking bark is the most colorful of the Stewartias and
extremely attractive in the winter landscape. The blooms are the smallest
of the genus and are distinguished from other members of the genus
by the floral bracts that are considerably smaller than the silky, pubescent
sepals. They add color in the summer when few woody plants bloom.
Excellent, rich autumn foliage. The specific name refers to the
resemblance of the flowers to those of a single camellia.

Plant may be observed at: *Arboreta*—Arnold, Bernheim Forest, Cary,
Dawes, Holden, Morton, National, Planting Fields, U. of Washington;
Botanical Gardens—Berry, Birmingham, Brooklyn, Chicago, Missouri,
Munich, New York, Palmgarten, Royal/Kew, U. of Georgia, Van Dusen;
Gardens—Callaway, Dixon, Longwood, Old Westbury, Winterthur; *Parks*—
Forest Parks-Ibaraki, Japan.

M. DIRR

A. COOK

A. BUSSEWITZ

Styrax japonica Siebold & Zuccarini. JAPANESE SNOWBELL. *Styracaceae*. USDA Zones 5–8. China, Japan. Introduced 1862 by Arnold Arboretum.

DESCRIPTION   *Deciduous* tree growing at medium rate to 20–30′ high with equal spread; rounded crown, spreading when mature. Casts light shade.

Leaves: Alternate, simple, oval, tapering at both ends, occasionally obovate or round, 1–3½″ long, ½–1½″ wide, glabrous on both surfaces; glossy, rich green in summer, yellow in fall.

Flowers: White, bell-shaped, ¾″ long, 5-lobed, yellow stamens, slightly fragrant; each flower on pendulous stalk 1–1½″ long; blooms May-June.

Fruit: Drupe, ovoid, gray, ½″ long, in August; contains single hard brown seed.

Winter aspect: Smooth, gray-brown bark; irregular fissures with age; horizontal, low-branched, wide-spreading habit.

CULTURE   Grows in sun and partial shade in loamy, light soil in pH range of 5.0–7.0; prefers moist, acid, well-drained soil with peat and organic material added. Needs protection from winter wind; susceptible to injury by late spring frosts.

Disease and insect problems: Seemingly pest free.

Transplanting: Balled and burlapped in early spring; should be moved when young, as is slow to recover after transplanting.

Propagation: By softwood cuttings or seed which has double dormancy; seeds sown in fall germinate second spring.

LANDSCAPE VALUE   Handsome small tree with graceful habit; good for lawn or in shrub border. Also lovely near terrace; splendid tree to sit under and look up into. Very showy in spring when in flower; blooms later than many trees. Leaves extend from top of branches; flowers hang below so are very visible.

Cultivars soon to be available: 'Pendula', Weeping Snowbell; 'Rosea', with pink flowers.

Plant may be observed at: *Arboreta*—Arnold, Morton, National, Planting Fields, U. of Washington; *Botanical Gardens*—Berry, Birmingham, British Columbia, Brooklyn, Missouri, New York, Royal/Kew, Van Dusen; *Gardens*—Dixon, Filoli, Longwood, Old Westbury, Winterthur; *Parks*—Forest Parks-Ibaraki, Japan.

M. DIRR

M. DIRR

N. BREWSTER

Styrax obassia Siebold & Zuccarini. FRAGRANT SNOWBELL. *Styracaceae.* USDA Zones 5–8. China, Japan. Introduced 1879.

DESCRIPTION *Deciduous* small tree of rapid growth to 30'; habit almost pyramidal with ascending branches. Casts fairly dense shade.

Leaves: Alternate, simple, orbicular to 10" long and almost as wide, deep green and glabrous, pubescent beneath. Fall color undistinguished.

Flowers: White, ¾" in dia., bell-shaped, on pedicels 4" long, in drooping racemes 4–8" long, very fragrant, in May-June.

Fruit: Subglobose drupe ¾" long, silvery-green, in racemes in late summer.

Winter aspect: Bark smooth, light gray to gray-brown, with shallow vertical fissures. Dense, substantial, ascending branches. In second year shoots are chestnut-brown and exfoliating.

CULTURE Does best in full sun or light shade in acid, well drained, moist and porous loam enriched with organic matter.

Disease and insect problems: None noted.

Transplanting: When young, balled and burlapped, in early spring. Fairly difficult when larger.

Propagation: Easy from softwood cuttings taken in mid-July; seed more difficult.

LANDSCAPE VALUE An excellent ornamental when in flower; beautiful as specimen. The handsome, large foliage partially hides the long, fragrant racemes, which flower after *Cornus florida.* Bark and branching structure are arresting in winter.

Plant may be observed at: *Arboreta*—Bernheim Forest, National, Planting Fields; *Botanical Gardens*—Birmingham, British Columbia, Brooklyn, Missouri, New York, Royal/Kew; *Gardens*—Callaway, Dixon, Longwood, Old Westbury.

PLANTING FIELDS

E. HASSELKUS

A. BUSSEWITZ

Symplocos paniculata (Thunberg) Miquel [*S. crateagoides* F. Buchanan ex D. Don].
SAPPHIREBERRY. *Symplocaceae.* USDA Zones 5–8. Himalayas to Japan
and China, Formosa. Introduced 1875 by Thomas Hogg.

DESCRIPTION *Deciduous* tree growing slowly to 15–20' high and as wide; low-branched,
dense, twiggy habit, becoming widespreading at maturity. Casts dense
shade.

Leaves: Alternate, simple, variable, elliptic to obovate, 1½–3½" long and
half as wide, serrulate, tawny pubescent beneath, short-petioled, tapering
at both ends, dark green.

Flowers: Small, white, fragrant blooms in late spring, borne in panicles
approximately 2" long on previous year's growth; 5 petals and 30
stamens, the latter giving a fluffy look.

Fruit: ⅓" ovoid drupe, brilliant ultramarine turning dark violet-blue,
persistent in winter if not eaten by birds.

Winter aspect: Gray, furrowed bark; low-branched, widespreading habit.

CULTURE Grows best in sun, thrives in well-drained soil in pH range of 5.0–7.0. It is
necessary to plant two or more specimens (different clones) to obtain best
fertilization. Needs more than average summer heat to fruit well; best to
prune during winter even with loss of some flower buds. Withstands
some wind but does not tolerate wet conditions or drought.

Disease and insect problems: None serious.

Transplanting: Easy from container or balled and burlapped.

Propagation: By seed (germinate slowly as they need double dormancy),
or by layering, easiest from cuttings taken in summer from young wood.

LANDSCAPE
VALUE Handsome, small secondary tree to be used as a specimen or in a shrub
border. The dense foliage and low branching habit make it useful as a
screen. Although the foliage is attractive and the flowers effective, this tree
is valued primarily for its unique and colorful fruits; hence common name
Sapphireberry. Extremely attractive to birds. *S. paniculata* received the
Award of Merit from the Royal Horticultural Society in 1947.

Related Species:
  S. tinctoria—native of the southeastern U.S. Semi-evergreen foliage and
  attractive yellow flowers; fruit is inconspicuous. Little known tree.

Plant may be observed at: *Arboreta*—National; *Gardens*—Winterthur.

N. BREWSTER

N. BREWSTER

N. BREWSTER

Syringa reticulata (Blume) Hara [*S. amurensis* Ruprecht var. *japonica* (Maximowicz) Franchet & Savatier; *S. japonica* (Maximowicz) Decaisne]. JAPANESE TREE LILAC. *Oleaceae.* USDA Zones 4–7. Japan. Introduced 1876.

DESCRIPTION *Deciduous* tree with moderate growth rate to 30' high and 15–20' wide at maturity; erect habit with stiff, spreading branches; develops rounded crown. Casts medium shade.

Leaves: Opposite, simple, broad-ovate to 3-6" long, half as wide, with long, tapered tip; slightly downy underside, glabrous above.

Flowers: Creamy white in loose panicles to 12" long; privet-like fragrance; blooms at least 10 days.

Fruit: Gold capsules in clusters conspicuous through mid-winter; 4/5" long.

Winter aspect: Attractive, shiny, dark, cherry-like bark with horizontal lenticels; on old trunks gray and scaly; persistent fruit.

CULTURE Grows in sun in clay and loam; likes slightly acid, well-drained soil. Tolerates some drought. Prefers cool summers.

Disease and insect problems: Few; susceptible to scale and borers but is the most trouble-free lilac.

Transplanting: Moderately easy, balled and burlapped; root system shallow.

Propagation: By seed, cuttings, grafting.

LANDSCAPE VALUE A lovely flowering tree, especially valued for its late blooming flowers (May in South, June in New England, July in Midwest). Attractive, shiny, cherry-like bark adds interest in winter. Shapely, vigorous habit, large leaves and exquisite flowers make this a distinguished plant. May be used as specimen or in group planting as a screen.

Plant may be observed at: *Arboreta*—Arnold, Bernheim Forest, Dawes, Holden, Minnesota Landscape, Morton, National, Planting Fields, U. of Washington, U. of Wisconsin-Madison; *Botanical Gardens*—Brooklyn, Chicago, Missouri, Royal/Kew, Royal/Ontario; *Gardens*—Old Westbury, Winterthur; *Parks*—Forest Parks-Ibaraki, Japan.

E. HASSELKUS

J. POOR

F. GALLE

Tabebuia chrysotricha (Martius ex de Candolle) Standley [*Tecoma chrysotricha* Marticus ex de Candolle]. GOLDEN TRUMPET TREE. *Bignoniaceae.* USDA Zone 10. Brazil, tropical America, Mexico. Introduced 1964 by Los Angeles Arboretum.

DESCRIPTION *Deciduous,* sometimes evergreen tree, growing rapidly (4–5' a year) to 30–50' at maturity; open, spreading habit.

Leaves: Obovate-oblong to 4″ long; dark green with prominent veins; shiny appearance.

Flowers: 2½–8″ long, bright yellow, in umbellate clusters, late March-April-May; densely hairy.

Fruit: Long, brown, bean-like seed pods.

Winter aspect: Spreading habit, persistent seed pods.

CULTURE Grows in sun; thrives in rich loam but tolerant of light or heavy soils with good drainage. Tolerates a wide range of temperatures. Likes plentiful supply of water when becoming established; when older is able to tolerate some neglect and drought. Stake young plant to single leading shoot until 6–8', then allow to develop freely.

Disease and insect problems: None.

Transplanting: Moderately easy.

Propagation: Easy by fresh seed; by cuttings and air layering.

LANDSCAPE VALUE A versatile specimen tree. The spectacular flowers enhance garden or patio. Its tolerance of pests and diseases, a variety of soils, a wide range of temperatures and drought when mature, make it an excellent street tree. Needs little maintenance. Rarely available commercially.

Plant may be observed at: *Arboreta*—Los Angeles; *Botanical Gardens*—Huntington, Pacific Tropical.

D. KENT

M. GALLAGHER

M GALLAGHER

Tamarindus indica L. TAMARIND TREE. *Leguminosae* (subfamily *Caesalpinioideae*). USDA Zone 10. Tropical Africa and Asia. Introduced by Don de Francisco de Paulo Marin, an early-day horticulturist.

DESCRIPTION *Evergreen* tree growing slowly to 80'; open, spreading branches and graceful, feathery foliage. Casts light shade.

Leaves: Alternate, even pinnate, each leaf with 10–20 pairs of ½"-long evergreen leaflets.

Flowers: Small, red and yellow (1" diam.), with 3 petals which equal the four-lobed, narrow calyx; borne in terminal racemes.

Fruit: Red-brown, velvety, thick pod, 2–8" long, encloses a few seeds embedded in thick, sticky, brown pulp.

Winter aspect: Year-round interest; open, spreading branches.

CULTURE Grows in sun and shade in clay and loam but not sand; prefers deep soil with abundant moisture, but tolerates semi-arid sites when irrigated. Withstands wind and wet conditions; intolerant of salt.

Disease and insect problems: Beetles sometimes bore into seed pods.

Transplanting: Easy to moderate; root system not invasive.

Propagation: By seed.

LANDSCAPE VALUE One of the best ornamentals for tropical planting. It has an attractive habit and graceful foliage, and is a valued fruit tree. The edible pulp around the seed is used in India in chutney and curry. The pulp has cooling and laxative properties and is also used as a gargle. The rounded, starchy seeds and the flowers are edible. The very hard wood is used for making chopping blocks. Excellent dwarf variety (15') introduced by Dr. Horace Clay in 1963 from Tahiti.

Plant may be observed at: State Court Building, Ala Moana Park, Hawaii; *Botanical Gardens*—Pacific Tropical.

P. NOTTAGE

P. NOTTAGE

P. NOTTAGE

Taxodium distichum (L.) L. Richard. BALD CYPRESS. *Taxodiaceae.* USDA Zones 4–9. U.S.A., Delaware and south to Florida and Louisiana, west to Illinois and Arkansas. Introduced in 1640 by John Tradescant.

DESCRIPTION *Deciduous conifer* growing rapidly to mature height of up to 150′ (lower in north); pyramidal when young, broad-headed at maturity. Casts limited light shade.

Leaves: Needles ⅜–⅝″ long, alternate, spirally attached, linear, 2-ranked, not clustered, on deciduous branchlets. Color delicate light green in spring, gray-green in summer, yellow to bronze in fall. Foliage appears very late in season.

Flowers: Monoecious; brown catkins borne in early spring in slender 4–5″ panicles; female cones subglobose.

Fruit: Cones woody, globular or obovoid, ¾–1″ across, purplish when young, brown when mature at 1 year.

Winter aspect: Bark rough, gray to cinnamon-brown, with longitudinal narrow fissures. Trunk straight and buttressed at base, branches horizontal with pendulous lateral branchlets.

CULTURE Grows in sun or high shade in any acid soil (chalky soils result in chlorosis). Prefers deep sandy loam with plenty of moisture in upper layers and good drainage. Its natural habitat is swamps and stream banks, so it tolerates extremely wet as well as dry conditions. Also withstands winds of gale force and worse.

Disease and insect problems: Spider mite, gall-forming mite, cypress moth, twig blight.

Transplanting: Easy when balled and burlapped.

Propagation: Easy from softwood cuttings taken in summer, especially under mist.

LANDSCAPE VALUE A handsome, striking large tree for wet areas and compacted soils. Also has great potential as a large street tree. Too large for small areas; should be grown as a specimen. When grown near water it develops picturesque "cypress knees" which project above ground, as in the Florida Everglades where it is the dominant tree. Feathery foliage and neat habit resemble those of *Metasequoia*, of which it is a close relative. Requires almost no maintenance.

The "knees" are known as pneumatophores. It was once thought that they supplied air to the roots when the tree was immersed in water, but later research has shown that removing them makes no difference to the health of the tree. They do serve as an anchoring device when trees are growing in soft mud. The wood is highly valued for its water resistance; it will not rot, and is used in boats, docks, bridges.

Plant may be observed at: *Arboreta*—Arnold, Bayard Cutting, Bernheim Forest, Cary, Dawes, Holden, Los Angeles, Morton, National, Planting Fields, U. of Washington, U. of Wisconsin-Madison; *Botanical Gardens*—Atlanta, Birmingham, Brooklyn, Canton, Chicago, Missouri, Munich, Palmgarten, Royal/Kew, U. of Georgia, Van Dusen; *Gardens*—Brookgreen, Callaway, Fairchild Tropical, Longwood; *Parks*—Golden Gate, Forest Parks-Ibaraki, Japan.

M. DIRR

E. HASSELKUS

W. ADAMS

Thuja plicata J. Donn ex D. Don [*T. lobbii* Gordon]. GIANT ARBORVITAE, WESTERN RED CEDAR. *Cupressaceae.* USDA Zones 5–7. Western U.S.A. Introduced 1853 by William Lobb.

DESCRIPTION
Evergreen conifer, a large ornamental tree growing rapidly to 50–70′ high by 15–25′ wide in cultivation, to 200′ in wild in Pacific Northwest. Growth habit narrow pyramidal. Casts dense shade.

Leaves: Lustrous bright green, paler with whitish marks beneath, often glandular; carried in large, flattened, drooping sprays at ends of horizontal branches. Emit a fruity fragrance when crushed.

Flowers: Female cones erect, oblong, ½″ long with thin, leathery scales, ripening in early autumn; male cones ½″ long, egg-shaped, brown; both in clusters near ends of branchlets.

Winter aspect: Bark bright cinnamon-red in youth, dark reddish-brown tinged with purple in maturity, narrowly fissured in plate-like scales. Trunk straight, with a broad, tapering buttressed base as much as 15′ in diam. Lateral branchlets 5–6″ long, light green and lustrous on upper surface, turn yellow and drop usually in second year.

CULTURE
In the wild grows in sun or partial shade, singly or in groves, in moist bottomlands or near mountain streams. Prefers moist, well-drained, rich soils in pH range of 6.7–7.5, and moist air. Tolerates shallow chalk soils; susceptible to salt spray. Needs protection from strong winter winds.

Disease and insect problems: Heart rot and bagworm.

Transplanting: Easy balled and burlapped; root system shallow.

Propagation: By seed and by cuttings taken in cold weather.

LANDSCAPE VALUE
A large landscape tree that grows fast and retains good winter color. Useful as a specimen in parks and gardens, and also as a screen or hedge; tolerates trimming and light pruning. A splendid ornamental tree when properly grown. It is an important timber tree in the Pacific Northwest. Wood is light, soft, brittle and very durable; used for interiors, fences shingles and boats. Trunk used by the Indians in the Pacific Northwest for their canoes and totem poles.

Plant may be observed at: *Arboreta*—Arnold, Bayard Cutting, Morton, National, U. of Washington, U. of Wisconsin-Madison; *Botanical Gardens*— Berry, British Columbia, Chicago, Munich, New York, Palmgarten, Royal/Kew, Van Dusen; *Gardens*—Winterthur; *Parks*—Golden Gate.

M. DIRR

N. BREWSTER

A. BUSSEWITZ

Tilia tomentosa Moench [*T. argentea* de Candolle]. SILVER LINDEN. *Tiliaceae.* USDA Zones 4–7. Southeastern Europe, western Asia. Introduced 1767.

DESCRIPTION *Deciduous* broad, pyramidal tree when young, becomes upright and oval in old age; can be grown as multiple stemmed tree. Grows rapidly to 80' high by one-half to two-thirds that in spread. Casts dense shade.

Leaves: Simple, alternate, 2–5" long, usually rounded and heart-shaped at base, dark green above and silvery white beneath; margins sharp, sometimes double-toothed or even slightly lobulate. Fall color yellow.

Flowers: Cream-colored, small, pendulous and inconspicuous under large leaves but very fragrant in early summer.

Fruit: Inconspicuous; persists until winter; 1/3–3/8" long, egg-shaped.

Winter aspect: Bark dark gray, smooth; branches upright, often pendulous at tips.

CULTURE Grows in sun; moist loam or sand; pH range 6.5–7.5 preferred but tree is not particular as to soil. Tolerates wind as well as salt and air pollution.

Disease and insect problems: Subject to leaf-eating insects, especially aphids, but shunned by Japanese beetles.

Transplanting: Difficult in spite of shallow root system.

Propagation: By seed, layering, cuttings and budding. Seeds can take 2 years to germinate.

LANDSCAPE VALUE A beautiful specimen tree and superbly handsome street tree with its erect branches and sharply defined broad-pyramidal habit. The dense foliage with silver under-surfaces is particularly striking when blown by the wind. It is reported that *T. tomentosa*'s flowers are toxic, or perhaps intoxicating, to bees, although honey made from other *Tilia* species is unsurpassed in flavor and delicacy.

Plant may be observed at: *Arboreta*—Arnold, Bernheim Forest, Dawes, Holden, Los Angeles, Minnesota Landscape, Morton, Planting Fields, Spring Grove, U. of Wisconsin-Madison; *Botanical Gardens*—Brooklyn, Chicago, Royal/Kew.

PLANTING FIELDS

K. KOHOUT

K. KOHOUT

Torreya nucifera (L.) Siebold & Zuccarini. JAPANESE TORREYA, KAYA. *Taxaceae.*
USDA Zones 5 (with protection) to 8. Japan. Introduced before 1764 and
cultivated by Captain Cornwall. It was listed in 1775 as a plant then in
commerce.

DESCRIPTION   *Evergreen conifer* growing slowly to 40' in cultivation, 75' in wild;
pyramidal habit with slender, often shrubby, spreading to drooping
branches. Casts moderate to dense shade.

Leaves: ¾–1¼" long and abruptly narrowed near base; sessile, needle-
like, stiff and hard in texture; dark, glossy green on upper side, with two
white bands beneath.

Flowers: Inconspicuous.

Fruit: Ovulate reproductive organ matures into 1–1½" edible fruit, which
is subtly tinged with purple. When ripe, fruit splits into two parts.

Winter aspect: Young bark nearly smooth, pale gray to gray-brown; older
bark shallowly fissured into narrow strips which flake off. Branching habit
pyramidal to ovoid, with spreading branches. Fruit and needles persist.

CULTURE   Prefers moist, heavily shaded positions.

Disease and insect problems: None serious.

Transplanting: Easy to moderately easy.

Propagation: By seed or cuttings.

LANDSCAPE
VALUE   An attractive small, yew-like multi-stemmed tree with slow growth.
However, in its native habitat, this tree often reaches heights of over 75'.
Seeds of this species are edible, and the kernels of the nuts have a
pleasant, slightly resinous flavor. They produce an oil once used in the Far
East for cooking. *T. nucifera* is probably the hardiest of all species of
Torreya, but not reliably hardy in the very far northeastern U.S. It is similar
horticulturally to *Cephalotaxus* and *Taxus* genera, but distinguished from
Taxus by longer leaves, seeds enclosed in fleshy sac, and fruit that needs
two years to mature. *Torreya* is a small genus of rare species of North
America, China and Japan. Found infrequently in gardens, but has great
merit where hardy.

Plant may be observed at: *Arboreta*—Bernheim Forest, Morton, National,
Planting Fields; *Botanical Gardens*—Brooklyn, New York, Royal/Kew;
Parks—Forest Parks-Ibaraki, Japan.

N. BREWSTER

N. BREWSTER

A. BUSSEWITZ

Trochodendron aralioides, Siebold & Zuccarini. WHEEL TREE. *Trochodendraceae.* USDA Zone 8. Japan, South Korea, Ryukyus, and Formosa. Introduced from Japan in 1890s by Messrs. Veitch.

DESCRIPTION *Evergreen,* growing slowly to 60–80' in wild, smaller in cultivation; broad, shade-spreading habit. Casts light shade.

Leaves: Lustrous apple green, leathery, 5" long, obovate to lanceolate, shallowly toothed, new growth red to bronze; fall color bronze-green,

Flowers: Bright green, in erect terminal racemes, each flower on a slender stalk 1–1½" long, with numerous stamens but no sepals or petals, ¾" diam.; bloom April-June.

Fruit: Follicles (5–11) in clusters.

Winter aspect: Aromatic bark, spreading habit.

CULTURE Grows in sun and shade in any moist, fertile soil that is not excessively chalky; prefers neutral to acid soil. Requires conditions similar to Magnolia. Needs shelter from cold winds; tolerates wet conditions but not drought.

Disease and insect problems: None known.

Transplanting: Balled and burlapped; root system deep.

Propagation: By seed.

LANDSCAPE VALUE A striking broadleaved evergreen in demand by flower arrangers, but, unfortunately, a tree that is rarely seen. A handsome specimen in all seasons. Its long, leathery leaves resemble its relative, the Magnolia. It is interesting in bloom since it bears vivid green flowers in late spring and early summer, which are followed by attractive seedpods produced in clusters. Its bark is strongly aromatic. *T. aralioides* is the only member of its genus, and the generic name literally means "wheel tree," from the way in which the stamens radiate like the spokes of a wheel. The first record of its flower is in 1894 at the Coombe Wood Nursery of Messrs. Veitch.

Plant may be observed at: *Arboreta*—National, U. of Washington; *Botanical Gardens*—Canton, Chicago, Munich, Palmgarten; *Gardens*—Longwood; *Parks*—Forest Parks-Ibaraki, Japan.

J. PLATT

J. PLATT

J. PLATT

Ulmus japonica (Rehder) Sargent. JAPANESE ELM. *Ulmaceae.* USDA Zones 4–6. Japan, northern China. Introduced 1895.

DESCRIPTION *Deciduous* vase-shaped tree growing moderately rapidly to 60–80' at maturity, with 30–40' spread. Casts moderately dense shade.

Leaves: 3–5" long, obovate to elliptic, with doubly serrate margins; foliage green, yellow in fall.

Flowers: Tiny and inconspicuous.

Fruit: Appears simultaneously with leaves, drops in late spring.

Winter aspect: Bark light gray to gray with elongate furrowing; similar to *U. americana.* Branching habit erect and spreading.

CULTURE Grows in sun or shade in clay, loam or sand in pH range of 6.0–7.4; not particular as to soil. Tolerates wind and drought but not wet conditions. Apparently pollution tolerant; soil compaction slows growth but tree persists.

Disease and insect problems: None; moderately susceptible to elm-leaf beetle.

Transplanting: Easy; root system shallow to deep.

Propagation: By seeds, summer cuttings and grafting.

LANDSCAPE VALUE Japanese elm is a good substitute for American Elm, which it resembles, though it does not attain the great size of *U. americana.* It has good resistance to Dutch Elm Disease. There is no elm on lists of recommended trees for town and village planting. This elm has good potential for use as a street tree and in parks. Plants from Manchuria seem to be more useful for the Midwest than *U. japonica* from Japan; Manchuria's rigorous climate approximates that of the upper Midwest. This tree's only disadvantage is that its autumn color does not last very long; leaves drop somewhat early.

Plant may be observed at: *Arboreta*—Arnold, Morton; *Botanical Gardens*—Munich.

MORTON ARB.

G. WARE

MORTON ARB.

Ulmus parvifolia N. Jacquin [*U. parvifolia* var. *sempervirens* Hortorum]. CHINESE ELM, LACE-BARK ELM. *Ulmaceae.* USDA Zones 5–9. China, Japan. Introduced 1794.

DESCRIPTION
Deciduous broad, round-topped tree growing moderately rapidly to 40–50' at maturity. Casts moderately dense shade.

Leaves: Simple, alternate, small, lustrous and smooth above, somewhat leathery, ¾–2" long, ⅓ to 1⅓" wide, elliptic to ovate-lanceolate, margins evenly toothed. Fall color usually yellow; some forms turn red or purple. In warmer regions leaves are evergreen.

Flowers: In axillary clusters in August or September, abundant, inconspicuous.

Fruit: Samaras, about ⅓" long, appear in dense clusters in late summer to autumn.

Winter aspect: Bark reddish to light brown, in some forms attractively mottled, especially in older trees. Branches spreading, sometimes suggesting American elm.

CULTURE
Grows in sun or shade, in pH range of 6.0–7.5. Not fussy as to soil. Appears to be tolerant of all pollution adversities and of soil compaction; only moderately tolerant of wet conditions.

Disease and insect problems: Slightly susceptible to elm leaf beetle. Trunk cankers may develop on trees where soil is excessively wet.

Transplanting: Moderately easy; roots shallow to deep.

Propagation: By seed, summer cuttings, grafts.

LANDSCAPE VALUE
Certain forms of this elm are elegant, with deep green glossy summer foliage and spectacular bark, branches and silhouette in winter. There are many variations in form, leaf shape, size, and bark mottling; small-leaved forms are more fine-twigged than large-leaved, which need grooming for cleancut appearance.

Generally this is an excellent ornamental and well worth wider use in American gardens, parks and urban plantings. It combines attractiveness, durability, stress tolerance, and strong wood, and should be promoted. Specimen trees are often proudly pointed out, but still this tree is relatively unknown. It is indeed a meritorious plant. Not to be confused with *U. pumila.*

Plant may be observed at: *Arboreta*—Arnold, Bernheim Forest, Cary, Dawes, Holden, Los Angeles, Minnesota Landscape, Morton, National, Planting Fields, U. of Washington, U. of Wisconsin-Madison; *Botanical Gardens*—Birmingham, Brooklyn, Canton, Chicago, Missouri, Palmgarten, Royal/Kew, U. of Georgia; *Gardens*—Bok Tower, Brookgreen, Callaway, Longwood; *Parks*—Forest Parks-Ibaraki, Japan.

K. KOHOUT

M. DIRR

K. KOHOUT

Xanthoceras sorbifolium Bunge. YELLOWHORN. *Sapindaceae.* USDA Zones 5–7. Northern China. Introduced in 1866 by Pére David.

DESCRIPTION *Deciduous* tree growing to 20–25'; upright, stiff, erect habit.

Leaves: Alternate, pinnate, 5–8" long, glabrous; 9–17 leaflets, 1½–2½" long, lanceolate and sharply toothed.

Flowers: Terminal panicles 8–10" long, side panicles half as large; each flower, 1–1¼" across, is composed of 5 white petals, with a blotch at base that changes color as the flower ages—at first yellow, later carmine; spring bloom.

Fruit: Green capsule, 2" wide at top, tapering at base; 3-valved, with brown seeds, ⅓–½" wide; resembles a chestnut.

Winter aspect: Gray-brown bark with slightly purple cast; stiff and coarse branching habit. Shiny green leaves remain late in autumn.

CULTURE Prefers full sun but tolerates some shade. Prefers rich loam; tolerant of calcareous soil. Needs some protection from wind and requires a site not subject to late frosts, since flowers come out with young foliage.

Disease and insect problems: Coral spot fungus; prune off diseased branches.

Transplanting: Difficult because of fleshy roots.

Propagation: By seed, stratified and sown in spring; root cuttings over heat.

LANDSCAPE VALUE Strikingly beautiful, interesting and unusual tree which is virtually unknown in commerce. Only member of its genus and one of the few hardy members of the *Sapindaceae.* Pére David sent a seedling to the Paris Museum in 1866; it was successfully established and had fruited by 1873.

Plant may be observed at: *Botanical Gardens*—Missouri, Palmgarten; *Gardens*—Winterthur.

M. DIRR

K. KOHOUT

K. KOHOUT

Zelkova serrata (Thunberg) Makino 'Village Green' [*Z. keakii* (Siebold) Maximowicz]. JAPANESE ZELKOVA. *Ulmaceae.* USDA. Zones 5–8. Japan. Species introduced 1862 by J. G. Veitch. 'Village Green' patented by Princeton Nurseries in 1964.

DESCRIPTION **Deciduous** tree growing fast when young; reaches 90–100' at maturity; vase-shaped, with rounded top; short trunk has many ascending branches. Casts light shade.

Leaves: Alternate, simple, 2–5", acuminate, sharply-toothed, ovate or oblong-ovate; dark green turning to rusty-red in fall.

Flowers: Inconspicuous; produced in spring on short twigs.

Fruit: Small drupe, ⅛" diam.

Winter aspect: Smooth, gray bark when young, exfoliating with maturity; ascending habit.

CULTURE Grows in sun and light shade in clay or loam with a wide pH range. Tolerant of wind and will withstand drought after it is established. Tolerates air pollution and soil compaction.

Disease and insect problems: Highly resistant to Dutch Elm Disease and bark beetles.

Transplanting: Easy when young (8–10') and balled and burlapped.

Propagation: By seed, as soon as ripe, stratified at 40° for 60 days; softwood cuttings.

LANDSCAPE VALUE Handsome shade tree with the graceful and vigorous growth habit of the American Elm, interesting bark and beautiful foliage. Well suited as a lawn specimen or on urban streets. Cultivar 'Village Green' was selected for its symmetrical habit, its resistance to diseases and insects, its rapid growth, superior fall color, and its cold hardiness. Highly resistant to Dutch Elm Disease.

Related species *Zelkova sinica* has attracted attention in Midwest because of cold hardiness, but it lacks the handsome growth habit of *Z. serrata. Zelkova schneideriana,* excellent specimen with larger leaves than *Z. serrata,* introduced in 1920.

Plant may be observed at: *Arboreta*—Bernheim Forest, Planting Fields, Spring Grove, *Botanical Gardens*—Brooklyn, Canton, Denver, Missouri, New York; *Gardens*—Longwood.

M. DIRR

M. DIRR

M. DIRR

APPENDICES

APPENDIX I
ABORETA, BOTANICAL GARDENS, GARDENS, PARKS

American Horticultural Society, Dr. Charles A. Huckins, Executive Director
Box 0105, Mt. Vernon, VA 22121

Arnold Arboretum, Dr. Peter Ashton, Director
The Arborway, Jamaica Plain, MA 02130

Atlanta Botanical Garden, Ann L. Crammond, Executive Director
P.O. Box 77246, Atlanta, GA 30357

Bayard Cutting, Mr. Dan Tompkins, Director
Box 466 Montauk Hwy.
Oakdale, NY 11769

Bernheim Forest Arboretum, Mr. Clarence E. Hubbuch, Jr.
Clermont, KY 40110

Berry Botanic Garden, Mr. David Palmer, Director
11505 S.W. Summerville Ave., Portland, OR 97219

Birmingham Botanic Garden, Mr. Gary Gerlach, Director
2612 Lane Park Rd., Birmingham, AL 35223

Bok Tower Gardens, Mr. Jonathan A. Shaw, President
Lake Wales, FL 33853

Brookgreen Gardens, Mr. Gurdon L. Tarbox, Jr., Director
Murrels Inlet, SC 29576

Brooklyn Botanic Garden, Mr. Donald E. Moore, President
1000 Washington Ave., Brooklyn, NY 11225

Callaway Gardens, Mr. William E. Barrick, Director
U.S. Highway 27, Pine Mt., GA 31822

Canton Botanic Garden, Mr. Yu Sianglin
P.O. Box 1127, Canton, China

Cary Arboretum, Dr. Gene E. Likens, Director
Box AB, Millbrook, NY 12545

Central Park, Arthur Ross Pinetum
81st St. & Central Park West, New York, NY

Chicago Botanic Garden, Dr. Roy L. Taylor, Director
P.O. Box 400, Glencoe, Il 60022

Dawes Arboretum, Mr. Joseph B.C. White, Director
7770 Jacksontown Rd. S.E., Newark, OH 43055

Denver Botanic Gardens, Inc., Mr. Merle Moore, Director
909 York St., Denver, CO 80206

Dixon Gallery and Gardens, Mr. Paul S. Kingsley, Horticulturist
4339 Park Ave., Memphis, TN 38117

Fairchild Tropical Garden, Dr. John Popenoe, Director
10901 Old Cutler Rd., Miami, FL 33156

Filoli Center, Mr. Hadley Osborn, Director
Canada Rd., Woodside, CA 94062

Golden Gate Park, Dr. Elizabeth McClintock
1335 Union St., San Francisco, CA 94109

Holden Arboretum, Mr. C.W. Eliot Paine, Jr. Director
9500 Sperry Rd., Mentor, OH 44060

Houston Arboretum and Botanical Society, Dr. John D. Horkel, Director
4501 Woodway, Houston, TX 77024

Huntington Botanical Gardens, Mr. Myron Kimnach, Curator
1151 Oxford Rd., San Marino, CA 91108

Japan Forestry and Forest Parks, Dr. K. Doi, Director-General
P.O. Box 16, Tsukuba Norin Kenkyu, Danchi-Nai, Ibaraki, 305 Japan

Longenecker Horticultural Gardens, University of Wisconsin-Madison
Dr. Gregory D. Armstrong, Director
1207 Seminole Highway, Madison, WI 53711

Longwood Gardens, Mr. Fred Roberts, Director
Kennett Square, PA 19348

Los Angeles Department of County Arboreta and Botanic Gardens
Mr. Francis Ching, Director
301 N. Baldwin Ave., Arcadia, CA 91006

Mildred E. Mathias Botanical Garden, University of California-Los Angeles
Dr. Arthur Gibson, Director
Department of Biology, 2230 Life Sciences Bldg., UCLA, Los Angeles, CA 90024

Missouri Botanical Garden, Dr. Peter Raven, Director
P.O. Box 299, St. Louis, MO 63166

Morris Arboretum, Dr. William Klein, Director
9414 Meadowbrook Rd., Philadelphia, PA 19118

Morton Arboretum, Dr. Marion T. Hall, Director
Route 53, Lisle, IL 60532

Munchen Botanischer Garten, Dr. A. Kress
Menzinger Strasse 63, Munchen 19, D-8000, West Germany

National Arboretum, Dr. Henry M. Cathey, Director
3501 New York Ave. N.E., Washington, DC 20002

New York Botanical Garden, Dr. James M. Hester, President
Bronx, NY 10458

Old Westbury Gardens, Inc., Mr. Jethro Hurt, Director
P.O. Box 430, Old Westbury, NY 11568

Pacific Tropical Botanical Garden, Dr. William Theobald, Director
P.O. Box 340, Lawai, Kauai, HI 96765

Palmgarten, Herr Bruno Mueller
Siesmayerstrasse 67, Frankfurt am Main, D-6000, West Germany

Planting Fields Arboretum, Mr. Gordon E. Jones, Director
Planting Fields Rd., P.O. Box 58, Oyster Bay, NY 11771

Royal Botanic Gardens, Kew, Professor Arthur Bell, Director
Richmond, Surrey, TW9 3A3, England

Royal Botanical Gardens, Mr. Freek Vrugtman, Curator of Collections
P.O. Box 399, Hamilton, Ontario, Canada L8N 3H8

San Antonio Botanical Center, Mr. Eric Tschanz, Director
555 Funston Place, San Antonio, TX 78209

Shanghai Botanical Garden, Mr. Wang Da Jun
Long Wu Lu, Shanghai, China

Spring Grove Arboretum, Thomas L. Smith, Horticulturist
Cincinnati, OH 45232

Strybing Arboretum and Botanical Gardens, Mr. Walden Valen, Director
9th Ave. and Lincoln Way, San Francisco, CA 94122

University of British Columbia Botanical Garden, Acting Director Mr. Bruce Macdonald
6501 N.W. Marine Dr., Vancouver, British Columbia, Canada, V6T 1W5

University of Georgia Botanical Gardens and Campus, Dr. Roy A. Mecklenburg, Director
2450 S. Milledge Ave., Athens, GA 30602

University of Minnesota Landscape Arboretum, Dr. Francis de Vos, Director
P.O. Box 39, 3675 Arboretum Dr., Chanhassen, MN 55317

University of Washington (Washington Park) Arboretum, Dr. H.B. Tukey, Director of
    Center for Urban Horticulture
East Madison and Lake Washington Blvd. East, Seattle, WA 98195

Van Dusen Garden/Vancouver Botanic Gardens, Mr. Roy Forrester, President
5251 Oak St., Vancouver, British Columbia, Canada, V6M 4H1

Willowwood Arboretum of Rutgers University
Gladstone, NJ 07934

Winterthur Museum and Gardens
Walter O. Petroll, Head of Garden and Grounds Division
Winterthur, DE 19735

APPENDIX II-A
DIRECTORY OF NURSERY SOURCES

This Directory of nurseries is provided so readers may locate sources for the trees included. Following this Directory is the Tree Index with Nursery Source Codes (Appendix II-B). To identify sources simply locate the tree in the Tree Index, note the Nursery Codes and refer back to the Directory of Sources to obtain name and address.

Nurseries whose names are followed by (W) are wholesale growers only. Do not contact them directly, but rather furnish their name and address to your regular retail nursery center or your landscape architect. They can then obtain the trees desired.

Please note that this Directory is far from complete. It includes only those nurseries which could be readily identified by the editorial group. It is the Editor's intention to provide a complete list of Nursery Sources in the *Supplement to Plants That Merit Attention—Volume I—Trees.* To that end the Editor wishes to draw the attention of nurserymen to Appendix II-C—Invitation for Directory Listing. It is a cut-out form which nurseries growing any of the trees included in this publication are requested to complete and return to

Timber Press
P.O. Box 1631
Beaverton, OR 97075

The names, addresses, telephone numbers and trees grown will be included in the Supplement to this volume.

Source Code	Name and Address
ABC	ABC Nursery, Inc. (W) 424 E. Gardena Blvd. Gardena, CA 90248 (213) 217-9121
ALD	Aldridge Nursery, Inc. (W) Von Ormy, TX 78073 (512) 622-3491
APP	Appalachian Nurseries (W) Box 87 Waynesboro, PA 17268
ARB	Arbor Lane Gardens P.O. Box 27 Uwchland, PA 19480
BAI	Bailey Nurseries, Inc. (W) 1325 Bailey Rd. St. Paul, MN 55119 (612) 459-9744
BEK	Berkeley Horticultural Nursery 1310 McGee Avenue Berkeley, CA 94703
BER	Bernardo Beach Native Plant Farm Star Rte. 7, Box 145 Veguita, NM 87062
BET	Berthold Nursery 434 Devon Ave. Elk Grove Village, IL 60007 (312) 439-2600

Source Code	Name and Address
BLU	Blue Oak Nursery 2731 Mountain Oak Ln. Rescue, CA 95672 (916) 933-6692
BOE	Boething Treeland Nursery (W) 23475 Long Valley Rd. Woodland Hills, CA 91364 (213) 347-8822
BOM	Bomberger Bros, Inc. Box 2 Leola, PA 17540 (717) 563-1238
BOU	Bill Bounds Nursery 2815 Campbell Rd. Houston, TX 77080 (713) 462-6447
BOV	The Bovees Nursery 1737 S.W. Coronado Portland, OR 97219 (503) 244-9341
BRI	Briggs Nursery, Inc. (W) 4407 Henderson Blvd. Olympia, WA 98501 (206) 352-5405
BRO	Martin Brooks Rare Plant Nursery 235 Cherry Lane Doylestown, PA 18901 (215) 348-4309

Source Code	Name and Address
BYE	Byers Nursery (W) 6001 Moores Mill Rd. Huntsville, AL 35811 (205) 859-0690
CAA	Calaveras Nursery (W) Rte. 1, E. Hwy. 12 Valley Springs, CA 95252 (209) 772-1823
CAE	Carman's Nursery 16201 Mozart Avenue Los Gatos, CA 95030 (408) 356-0119
CAL	Carroll Gardens Box 310, 444 E. Main St. Westminster, MD 21157 (301) 848-5422
CAR	Carroll Nurseries R.D. #4 Cochranton, PA 16314 (814) 425-8123
CED	Cedar Lane Farms (W) 3790 Sandy Creek Rd. Madison, GA 30650 (404) 342-2626
CHO	Chrome Run Nursery 350 Howarth Rd. Media, PA 19063 (215) 566-1827
CHR	Christensen Nursery Co. (W) 935 Old Country Rd. Belmont, CA 94002 (415) 593-7893
CLA	Clavey's Woodstock Nursery, Inc. (W) 6223 Alden Rd. Woodstock, IL 60098 (815) 943-7778
CLY	Clayton Nursery Co. (W) Route 2, Box 2152 Nampa, ID 83651 (208) 286-7801
COA	Leonard Coates Nurseries (W) 400 Casserly Rd. Watsonville, CA. 95076 (408) 724-0651
COE	Coenosium Gardens 425 E. Fifth St. Lehighton, PA 18235 (717) 368-4201
COK	L.E. Cooke Co. (W) 26333 Rd. 140 Visalia, CA 93277 (209) 732-9146
COM	Commercial Nursery Co. (W) P.O. Box 487 Decherd, TN 37324 (615) 967-5525
CON	Conrad Pyle Nursery (W) Rose Hill Rd. West Grove, PA 91309
COR	Cornelius Nursery 2233 S. Voss Rd. Houston, TX 77042 (713) 782-8640
CRA	Cramer Nursery, Inc. (W) Centre de Jardin & Bureaux 1101, boul, Don Quichotte Ile Perrot, Quebec J7V 5V6 Canada (514) 453-6323
CUL	Cultra Nursery Co. P.O. Box 126 East Roosevelt Rd. Onarga, IL 60955 (815) 268-7211
DAU	Daubers Nurseries Rear 1705 N. George St. Box 1746 York, PA 17405 (717) 848-6088
DIL	Dilatush Nursery 780 Route 130 Robbinsville, NJ 08691 (609) 585-5387
DIX	Dixon Tree Farm and Nursery (W) R.D. #1, Box 215-1 Glenmoore, PA 19343 (215) 363-1773
DOD	Tom Dodd Nurseries, Inc. (W) P.O. Drawer 45 Semmes, AL 36574 (205) 649-1960
DUT	Dutch Mountain Nursery 7984 N. 48th St., Rte. 1 Augusta, MI 49012 (616) 731-5232
EAB	East Bay Nursery 2332 San Pablo Avenue Berkeley, CA 94702

Source Code	Name and Address
EAS	Eastville Plantation Box 337 Bogart, GA 30622 (404) 548-2530
EIS	Eisler Nurseries 219 E. Pearl St., Box 70 Butler, PA 16001 (412) 287-3703
EVE	Evergreen Nursery Co. (W) 5027 County Trunk TT Sturgeon Bay, WI 54235 (414) 743-4464
FAR	Farr Nursery and Landscape Co. P.O. Box 128 Womelsdorf, PA 19567 (215) 589-2525
FIL	Filoli Garden Shop Canada Rd. Woodside, CA 94025
FIO	Charles Fiore Nurseries (W) Box 67, 17010 W. Hwy. 22 Prairie View, IL 60069 (312) 634-3400
FOF	Forestfarm 990 Tetherath Williams, OR 97544 (503) 846-6963
FOR	Forest Hills Nurseries (W) 310 Knollwood Ave. Cranston, RI 02910 (401) 944-8282
FOS	Forest Nursery Co. (W) Rte. 2, Box 118-A McMinnville, TN 37110 (615) 473-2133
FOU	Four Fives Nursery 5555 Summer Avenue Memphis, TN 38134
GOG	Goodness Grows 156 S. Woodlawn Dr. P.O. Box 576 Crawford, GA 30630
GOH	Gem of Hawaii, Inc. 1199 Dillingham Blvd. Honolulu, HI 96817 (808) 845-4566
GOS	Gossler Farms Nursery 1200 Weaver Rd. Springfield, OR 97477 (503) 746-3922
GRA	Grandview Nursery (W) Rt. 2, Box 44 Youngsville, LA 70592
GRE	Greener 'n Ever Tree Nursery 8940 Carmel Valley Rd. Carmel, CA 93921 (408) 624-2149
GRR	Greer Gardens 1280 Goodpasture Island Rd. Eugene, OR 97041-1794 (503) 686-8366
GUR	Gurney Seed and Nursery Co. Yankton, SD 47078 (605) 665-4451
HAL	Halka Nurseries (W) R.D. 2 Sweetmans Lane Englishtown, NJ 07726 (201) 462-8450
HAN	Hansen Nurseries P.O. Box 8 Sassamansville, PA 19472 (215) 754-7911
HES	Hess's Nurseries (W) Rte. 553, Box 326 Cedarville, NJ 08311 (609) 447-4213
HET	Hester's Nursery 3029 Todville Rd. Seabrook, TX
HIL	Hillier Nurseries (Winchester) Ltd. Ampfield House Ampfield, Romsey Hants. S05 9PA England
HLL	Hill's Nursery (W) P.O. Box 134 U.S. 42, E. River Rd. Warsaw, KY 41095 (606) 567-5821
HIN	Hinsdale Nurseries, Inc. (W) 7200 S. Madison Rd. Hinsdale, IL 60521 (312) 232-1411
HIS	Hines Wholesale Nurseries (W) P.O. Box 11208 12621 Jeffrey Rd. Santa Ana, CA 92711 (714) 559-4444

Source Code	Name and Address
HOB	Charles Hobbs and Sons 9300 W. Washington St. Box 31227 Indianapolis, IN 46231 (317) 241-9253
HOL	Hollandia Nursery Co. (W) 10725 39th Ave., N.E. Seattle, WA 98125 (206) 363-6080
HON	Hoogendoorn Nurseries Inc. (W) 408 Turner Rd. Newport, RI 02840 (401) 847-3405
HOO	Hooks Nursery, Inc. P.O. Box 455 Lake Zurich, IL 60047 (312) 438-7190
HOR	Hortica Gardens Box 308 Placerville, CA 95667 (916) 622-7089
ING	Ingleside Plantation Nurseries (W) Box 1038 Oak Grove, VA 22443 (804) 224-7111
ISE	Iseli Nursery, Inc. (W) 30590 S.E. Kelso Rd. Boring, OR 97009 (503) 663-3822
JOH	Johnston's Nursery R.D. #1, Box 100 Creekside, PA 15732 (412) 465-5685
KAI	Kailua Nursery 41-820 Kakaina St. Waimanalo, HI 96795 (808) 259-9248
KEI	Keil Bros. 220-15 Horace Harding Blvd. Bayside, NY 11364 (212) 229-5042
KEL	Forrest Kelling Nursery (W) Elsberry, MO 63343 (314) 898-5571
KLE	Charles Klehm and Son Nursery 2 E. Algonquin Rd. Arlington Heights, IL 60005 (312) 437-3880

Source Code	Name and Address
KOO	Koolau Farmers 45-580 Kam Hwy. Kaneohe, HI 96744 (808) 247-3911
KRI	Michael A. & Janet L. Kristick R.D. 1, Mockingbird Rd. Wellsville, PA 17365 (717) 292-2962
LAN	Landscape Supply, Inc. 24300 Brest Rd. Taylor, MI 48108 (313) 946-7000
LAW	Lawyer Nursery (W) 950 Hwy. 200 W. Plains, MT 59859 (406) 826-3881
LIV	Live Oak Gadens P.O. Box 284 New Iberia, LA 70560 (318) 367-3485
LOU	Louisiana Nursery Rte. 7, Box 43 Opelousas, LA 70570 (318) 948-3696
LOW	Lowery Nursery 2823 Sleepy Hollow Rd. Conroe, TX 77302
LUS	Baier Lustgarten Farms and Nurseries (W) Rte. 25 Middle Island, NY 11953 (516) 924-3444
MAG	Magnolia Gardens Nursery (W) 18810 Turtle Creek Magnolia, TX 77355 (713) 356-1213
MAK	Makiki Nursery 2179 Makiki Heights Dr. Honolulu, HI 96822 (808) 941-0000
MAP	Maplewood Nursery 311 Maplewood Ln. Roseburg, OR 97470
MAR	Marshall Nurseries Arlington, NE 68002
MAX	Maxalea Nurseries, Inc. Oak Hill Rd. Baltimore, MD 21239 (301) 377-7500

Source Code	Name and Address	Source Code	Name and Address
MCG	A. McGill & Son (W) P.O. Box 70 Fairview, OR 97024 (503) 665-4156	OLI	Oliver Nurseries 1159 Bronson Rd. Fairfield, CT 06430 (203) 259-5609
MCK	McKay Nurseries Waterloo, WI 53594 (414) 478-2121	ONA	Onarga Nursery Co. (W) Onarga, IL 60955 (815) 268-7244
MCL	MacLean Nurseries 9010 Satyr Hill Rd. Baltimore, MD 21234 (301) 882-6714	ORN	Orchard Nursery 4010 Mount Diablo Blvd. Lafayette, CA 94549
MEN	Mendo-Natives Nursery (W) P.O. Box 351 Gualala, CA 95445 (707) 884-3727	PAC	Pacific Nurseries of California (W) 2099 Hillside Blvd. Colma, CA 94014 (415) 755-2330
MIT	Mitsch Nursery, Inc. (W) 6652 S. Lone Elder Rd. Aurora, OR 97002-9399 (503) 266-9652	PAF	Pacific Tree Farms (W) (formerly Nelson's Pine Patch) 4301 Lynwood Dr. Chula Vista, CA 92010 (619) 422-2400
MOL	Moller's Nursery, Inc. (W) 34519 S.E. Lusted Rd. Gresham, OR 97030 (503) 663-3515	PAN	Panfield Nurseries 322 Southdown Rd. Huntington, NY 11743 (516) 473-9170
MON	Monrovia Nursery Co. (W) Box Q, 18331 E. Foothill Blvd. Azusa, CA 91702 (213) 334-9321	PRI	Princeton Nurseries (W) P.O. Box 191 Princeton, NJ 08542 (609) 924-1776
MUS	Musser Forests Box 340 Indiana, PA 15701-0340 (412) 465-5686	RAN	Rancho Volvere Nursery & Tree Farm (W) 26734 13th Ave. Madera, CA 93637 (209) 674-5435
NAK	Nakamura Nursery 2842 Date St. Honolulu, HI 96816 (808) 737-8183	RED	Redwood Nursery 2800 El Rancho Dr. Santa Cruz, CA 95060 (408) 438-2884
NAT	Native Son Plant Nursery (W) 507 Lockard Dr. Austin, TX 78704	SAL	Salter Tree Farm Rte. 2, Box 1332 Madison, FL 32340 (904) 973-6312
NAV	Navelet's Nursery 520 20th St. Oakland, CA 94612	SAN	San Marcos Growers (W) 125 S. San Marcos Rd. P.O. Box 6827 Santa Barbara, CA 93110 (805) 964-5089
OAK	Oak Lane Gardens Nurseries, Inc. P.O. Box 57, 152 Limekiln Pike Maple Glen, PA 19002 (215) 646-2839	SAR	Saratoga Horticultural Foundation (W) P.O. Box 308, 20605 Verde Vista Ln. Saratoga, CA 95070 (408) 867-3214
OKI	OKI Nursery Co. (W) P.O. Box 7118 Sacramento, CA 95826 (916) 383-5665		

Source Code	Name and Address	Source Code	Name and Address
SCA	Schaffer's Nursery, Inc. 2319 Hwy. 395 Fallbrook, CA 92028 (619) 728-7090	SNI	Snipes Farm and Nursery U.S. Rte. 1 Morrisville, PA 19067 (215) 295-1138
SCH	J. Frank Schmidt & Son Co. (W) 9500 S.W. 327th Ave. Boring, OR 97009 (503) 663-4128	STG	Styer's Garden Center Box 37, Rte. 1 Concordville, PA 19331 (215) 459-4040
SCR	Schroeder's Nursery (W) 23379 W. Rte. 60 Grayslake, IL 60030 (312) 546-9444	SWE	The Sweetbriar P.O. Box 25 Woodinville, WA 98072 (206) 821-2222
SCW	Schwarz Nursery (W) 21 W020 Army Trail Rd. Addison, IL 60101 (312) 627-4940	SYN	Synnestvedt Nursery Co. Burr Oak Div. Rte. 1, Box 310 Round Lake, IL 60073 (312) 546-4700
SHA	Shadow Nursery Rte. 1, Box 37A Winchester, TN 37398 (615) 967-6059	TRI	Triangle Nursery (W) Rte. 2 McMinnville, TN 37110 (615) 668-8022
SHE	Shemin Nurseries, Inc. (W) 4N755 Lombard Rd. P.O. Box 857 Addison, IL 60101 (312) 773-8090	TUR	Matt Tures Sons Nursery (W) 9810 Dundee Rd. Huntley, IL 60142 (312) 669-5024
SHR	Sherman Nursery Co. (W) Charles City, IA 50616 (515) 228-1124	VAL	Valley Nursery Box 4845 Helena, MT 59601 (406) 442-8460
SHO	The Shop in the Sierras Box 1 Midpines, CA 95345 (209) 966-3867	VIE	Martin Viette Nurseries Northern Blvd. East Norwich, NY 11732 (516) 922-5530
SHP	Sharon's Plants Ltd. 41-614 Waikupanaha St. Waimanalo, HI 96795 (808) 259-7137	VIW	Viewcrest Nurseries, Inc. (W) 12713 N.E. 184th St. Battle Ground, WA 98604 (206) 687-5167
SIE	The Siebenthaler Co. 3001 Catalpa Dr. Dayton, OH 45405 (513) 293-1691	WAI	Waipahu Garden Shop 94-378 Pupupani St. Waipahu, HI 96797 (808) 677-0311
SMI	Smith Nursery Co. P.O. Box 515 Charles City, IA 50616 (515) 228-3239	WAR	Warren County Nursery, Inc. (W) Rte 2 McMinnville, TN 37110 (615) 668-8941
SMT	Smithfield Gardens Rt. 17 Crittenden, VA 23433 (804) 238-2511	WAT	Watkin's Nursery 1500 Midlothian Pike Midlothian, VA 23113 (804) 794-5016

Source Code	Name and Address
WAU	Waynesboro Nurseries, Inc. (W) P.O. Box 987 Waynesboro, VA 22980 (703) 942-4141
WAY	Wayside Gardens Hodges, SC 29695 (803) 374-3387
WEH	Western Hills Nursery 16250 Coleman Valley Rd. Occidental, CA 95465
WES	Weston Nurseries E. Main St. Rte. 135, Box 186 Hopkinton, MA 01748 (617) 435-3414
WFF	White Flower Farm Route 63 Litchfield, CT 06759
WIG	Wight Nurseries (W) Box 390 Cairo, GA 31728 (912) 377-3033
WII	Dave Wilson Nursery (W) 4306 Santa Fe Avenue Hughson, CA 95326 (209) 833-4405
WIL	Wilson Nurseries, Inc. (W) Rte. 1, Box 25 Hampshire, IL 60140-9704 (312) 683-3700
WIN	Winsel-Gibbs Nursery (W) 31479 W. Pacific Coast Hwy. Malibu, CA 90265 (213) 457-7672
WIT	Winterthur Museum and Gardens Winterthur, DE 19735 (302) 656-8591
WOD	Woodlanders, Inc. 1128 Colleton Ave. Aiken, SC 29801 (803) 648-7522

APPENDIX II-B
TREE INDEX WITH NURSERY SOURCE CODES

Abies concolor, CONCOLOR FIR
BEK, BLU, CAR, CHR, CLA, COA, EAB, EVE, FAR, FIO, FOF, FOR, GRE, GRR, HES, HIL, HOO, ISE, JOH, KEI, KLE, LAN, LAW, LUS, MAR, MAX, MCK, MUS, NAV, ORN, PAN, RAN, TUR, VAL, VIE, VIW, WES, WFF, WIL

Abies koreana, KOREAN FIR
HIL, VIE, WES, WFF, WEH

Abies nordmanniana, NORDMANN FIR
BEK, CAL, DAU, MAX

Acer buergerianum, TRIDENT MAPLE
FOU, GOS, GRR, HOR, MAP, MON, OLI, SHA, SMI, SWE, WEH

Acer campestre, HEDGE MAPLE
BER, BOV, CAR, CLA, DUT, EIS, FAR, FIO, FOR, GRR, HAN, HES, HIL, HIN, KEI, KLE, LAN, LAW, LUS, MAP, MAR, MCL, MOL, OAK, OLI, ONA, PAN, PRI, SCH, SCR, SHA, SHE, SNI, WIL

Acer davidii, CHINESE STRIPED BARK MAPLE
BOV, GOS, GRR, LUS, MAP, VIE

Acer ginnala, AMUR MAPLE
BAI, BEK, BER, BET, BOV, CAL, CAR, CLA, CLY, COM, CRA, CUL, DIX, EIS, EVE, FAR, FIO, FOF, FOR, FOS, GUR, HOO, HOR, HOV, ING, KEI, KLE, LAN, LAW, MAP, MAR, MCG, MCL, MOL, OAK, ONA, PAN, PRI, SCH, SCR, SCW, SHA, SHE, SIE, SMI, SMT, SNI, STG, SYN, TUR, VAL, VIE, VIW, WAT, WES, WIL

Acer griseum, PAPERBARK MAPLE
APP, BEK, BOV, CAL, DIX, EAB, FOR, FOU, GOS, GRR, HAN, HOL, HON, ISE, KEI, LAN, MAP, MAX, OLI, ONA, PRI, SMT, SNI, SWE, VIE, WEH

Acer miyabei, MIYABE MAPLE

Acer nikoense, NIKKO MAPLE
HIL, KRI

Acer triflorum, THREE-FLOWERED MAPLE
GOS, MAX

Aesculus carnea 'Briotii', RUBY HORSECHESTNUT
BEK, BOM, BRO, CAR, EAB, HAN, HIL, OAK, MON, NAV, PRI, SNI

Aesculus flava, YELLOW BUCKEYE
FIO, HOO, MAR, TUR

Alectryon excelsus

Alnus glutinosa, EUROPEAN ALDER
BEK, BER, BET, CAR, CLA, FIO, HES, HOO, KLE, OKI, MON, SCR, SCW, SHE, SMI, SYN, TUR, WEH, WIL

Amelanchier x grandiflora, APPLE SERVICEBERRY
BAI, BER, GOG, HLL, KEL, KLE, LUS, PAN, SYN, TUR, VIE

Arbutus unedo, STRAWBERRY TREE
BEK, EAB, HOL, MON, NAV, ORN, WEH, WOD

Asimina triloba, PAWPAW
DUT, EAS, FOF, FOS, FOU, GUR, HET, LOU, LOW, SAL

Bauhinia forficata
BOE, GRA, LOU, LOW, NAV

Betula nigra, RIVER BIRCH
ALD, BAI, BEK, BER, BET, BOU, BYE, CAR, CED, CLA, CLY, CUL, COM, DOD, DUT, EIS, EVE, FAR, FIO, FOF, FOS, HES, HIS, HOB, HIN, HOO, KEL, KLE, LAN, LAW, LIV, LOU, LUS, MAG, MAR, MAX, MCG, MCK, MOL, ONA, PAN, SAL, SCH, SCR, SCW, SHA, SHR, SIE, SMI, SYN, TRI, TUR, WAR, WAT, WAU, WAY, WES, WIL

Betula platyphylla japonica 'Whitespire', WHITESPIRE, JAPANESE WHITE BIRCH
EVE, SCR

Calocedrus decurrens, INCENSE CEDAR
BEK, BLU, BOV, BRI, CAL, CHR, COA, COE, EAB, FOF, GRE, HIS, LAW, LUS, NAV, OKI, OLI, ORN, PAC, PAF, RAN, RED, SAR, SHO, WAT, WAY

Carpinus betulus, EUROPEAN HORNBEAM
BER, BOM, BRO, DIX, EIS, FAR, FOR, KEI, HAN, LAN, LUS, OAK, ONA, PAN, PRI, SCH, SIE, SMT, SNI, SCR, VIE, WAY, WES, WIL

Carpinus caroliniana, AMERICAN HORNBEAM
DUT, FIO, FOF, HES, HOB, HOO, LOW, MAX, PRI, SAL, SCR, SCW, SMI, SNI, WAR, WIL, WOD

Carya ovata, SHAGBARK HICKORY
EAS, FIO, GUR, JOH, LAW, LOW, MAR, MUS, SMI, WAU

Cedrus atlantica 'Glauca', BLUE ATLAS CEDAR
ABC, BOM, BRI, BRO, CHR, HIL, HIS, HON, ISE, MIT, OAK, OKI, PRI, SNI, STG, WES, WIN

Cedrus deodara, DEODAR CEDAR
ABC, APP, BEK, BRO, BOU, BYE, CED, CHR, COK, GRR, HES, HIL, HIS, ISE, LAW, LOU, MAX, MIT, MON, NAV, OAK, OKI, PRI, RAN, SNI, STG, VIE, VIW, WAT, WAU, WES, WIN

Cercidiphyllum japonicum, KATSURA TREE
BER, BET, BOM, BOV, CAR, CLA, COM, DAU, DIX, DUT, EIS, FAR, FIO, FOR, FOU, GOS, GRR, HAN, HIL, HOO, HOR, KEI, KLE, LAN, LAW, LAU, LUS, MAX, MOL, OAK, PAN, PRI, SCW, SMI, SYN, TUR, VIE, VIW, WAT, WAY, WEH, WES

Cercis canadensis f. alba, WHITE REDBUD
BER, BET, FIO, HIL, HOO, LAN, LOW, ORN, VIE

Chaemaecyparis nootkatensis 'Pendula', ALASKA CYPRESS
BRI, BRO, CHO, DIX, GRR, HES, HIL, ISE, KEI, OLI, PAN, SNI, VIE, WEH, WES

Chilopsis linearis, DESERT WILLOW
ALD, BER, LOW, NAT

Chionanthus retusus, CHINESE FRINGE TREE
HIL, SAL, WEH

Chionanthus virginicus, AMERICAN FRINGE TREE
BYE, CAL, CAR, CED, COM, DAU, DUT, EIS, FIO, FOF, FOR, FOU, HET, HOB, HOO, ING, KLE, LAN, LOU, LUS, MAX, OAK, PRI, SAL, SMI, SNI, TUR, VIE, WAT, WAY, WEH, WES, WOD

Cladrastis lutea, AMERICAN YELLOWWOOD
CED, CUL, DAU, DUT, EIS, FIO, FOF, FOR, FOU, HIL, HOO, KEI, KLE, LUS, MAR, OLI, PRI, SHA, SHE, SIE, SMI, TUR, VIE, WAY, WES, WOD

Cornus alternifolia, PAGODA DOGWOOD
BAI, CAL, CAR, CLA, CUL, EIS, EVE, FIO, GRR, HOB, HOO, KLE, LAN, LUS, MCK, ONA, SCR, SCW, SHE, SIE, SMI, WAY, WIL

Cornus kousa, KOUSA DOGWOOD
ARB, BOM, CAL, CAR, CED, COM, CUL, DAU, DIX, DUT, EAB, EIS, FAR, FIO, FOF, FOR, FOS, FOU, GRR, HIL, HOB, HOL, HON, ING, KEI, KEL, LAN, LUS, MAX, MOL, OLI, ORN, PAN, PRI, SAL, SHA, SHE, SMT, SWE, TUR, VIE, VIW, WAT, WAY, WES, WIL, WIT

Cornus nuttallii, PACIFIC DOGWOOD
BEK, BLU, BOV, CAA, CHR, COA, FOF, GRR, HIL, HOL, MEN, ORN, RED, SHA, SHO, VIW, WEH

Cornus officinalis, JAPANESE CORNEL DOGWOOD
BAI, CAR, KEL

Corylus colurna, TURKISH FILBERT
FIO, FOU, HOB, KLE, LAW, MAX, SYN

Cotinus obovatus, AMERICAN SMOKE TREE
EAB, HIL, SHA, SMT

Crataegus viridis 'Winter King', GREEN HAWTHORN
BER, BET, CAR, COM, CUL, EIS, FIO, HLL, HOB, HOO, KEL, KLE, LUS, MCG, MCK, MOL, SCH, SCR, SCW, SIE, SNI, SYN, TUR, WES

Crescentia cujete, CALABASH TREE
SHP

x Cupressocyparis leylandii
ABC, BRI, CAL, EIS, FOF, FOU, GOG, GRR, HIL, HOL, ING, ISE, KEI, MAX, MIT, MON, NAV, OKI, ORN, PAN, SCA, SNI, VIE, WAY, WAT, WEH, WIG, WIN

Cydonia sinensis, CHINESE QUINCE TREE
FOU, MAX, NAV, ORN

Davidia involucrata, DOVE TREE
APP, BEK, BOV, CAL, DAU, GOS, GRR, HIL, LOU, NAV, WIT

Diospyros virginiana, AMERICAN PERSIMMON
ALD, BYE, COM, EAS, FOF, FOS, GUR, HIL, KEL, LOU, SAL, SHA, TRI, WAR, WAU, WES

Eucommia ulmoides, HARDY RUBBER TREE
FOF, FOU, PRI, SHA, SIE, WES

Evodia danielli, BEBE TREE
HIL, WOD

Fagus sylvatica 'Asplenifolia', FERN LEAVED BEECH
BRO, CAR, COE, EAB, EIS, FIO, FOR, GRR, HES, LUS, NAV, OAK, ORN, SIE, SMT, VIE, WEH, WES

Firmiana simplex, CHINESE PARASOL TREE
GRA, LIV, LOU

Franklinia alatamaha, FRANKLIN TREE
BEK, BRO, CAL, EIS, DIX, FOF, FOR, GOG, GOS, GRA, HIL, HOB, KEI, LOU, LUS, MAX, MON, PAN, PRI, SMG, VIE, WAT, WAY, WIT, WES, WOD

Fraxinus oxycarpa 'Raywood', RAYWOOD ASH
BEK, HIS, MON, NAV, OKI, ORN, SAR

Fraxinus quadrangulata, BLUE ASH
BET, FIO, HOO, SCH, TUR

Fraxinus texensis, TEXAS WHITE ASH
BOU, COR, HET, LOW

Geijera parviflora, AUSTRALIAN WILLOW
EAB, HIS, NAV, OKI, ORN

Gordonia lasianthus, LOBLOLLY BAY
DOD, GOG, LOU, LOW, MAG, MON, WEH, WOD

Guaiacum officinale, LIGNUM VITAE
NAK, SHP

Gymnocladus dioicus, KENTUCKY COFFEE TREE
BAI, BER, BET, CAR, COM, CRA, DUT, EIS, FIO, HIL, HIN, HOB, HOO, KEL, KLE, LAW, LUS, MAR, ONA, PRI, SMI, SNI, SYN, TRI, TUR, VAL, WAR, WAT, WES, WIL

Halesia monticola 'Rosea', MOUNTAIN SILVER BELL
BOV, COM, HIL, MAX

Hoheria populnea, LACEBARK
BEK, CAE, FIL, WEH

Hovenia dulcis, JAPANESE RAISIN TREE
PRI

Idesia polycarpa, IIGIRI TREE
FOF, HIL, WOD

Ilex x altaclerensis 'James G. Esson'
MCL, WES

Ilex x aquipernyi 'San Jose'
MAX, MCL, MON, PAN, VIE, WES

Ilex opaca 'Miss Helen'
MAX, MCL

Ilex pedunculosa, LONG STALK HOLLY
APP, BRO, CAR, FOU, LOU, MCL, PAN, VIE, WES

Kalopanax pictus, CASTOR-ARALIA
FOF, OAK

Koelreuteria bipinnata, CHINESE FLAME TREE
ABC, ALD, BEK, BOU, BYE, CED, COR, LIV, LOU

Koelreuteria paniculata, GOLDEN RAINTREE
ABC, ALD, ARB, BEK, BOU, BYE, CAR, CHR, CLY, COM, COR, DAU, DIX, EAB, EAS, FIO, FOR, FOU, HES, HOB, HOO, ING, KEI, KEL, LOU, LUS, MAR, MAX, MON, NAV, OAK, OKI, ONA, ORN, PRI, SNI, VIE, WAT, WAY, WES

Laburnum x watereri 'Vossii', GOLDEN CHAIN TREE
BEK, CAL, DAU, EAB, EIS, FIO, FOR, HIL, KEI, LUS, MCG, MOL, OKI, PAN, WAT, WAY, WEH, WES

Lagerstroemia indica 'Alba', WHITE CRAPE MYRTLE
ABC, ALD, BOU, BYE, COR, DOD, GRR, HET, HIS, LIV, LOW, MAX, OKI, SHA, WAT

Larix decidua, EUROPEAN LARCH
BEK, CAL, CAR, CLA, EIS, EVE, FIO, FOR, GRR, HIL, HOO, JOH, KEI, KLE, LUS, MUS, PAN, PRI, SMI, WES

Larix kaempferi, JAPANESE LARCH
BET, CLA, EVE, FIO, FOF, GRR, HIL, HOB, MUS, TUR, VIE, WES

Luma apiculata
BEK, FIL, WEH

Maackia amurensis, AMUR MAACKIA
HIL, WES

Magnolia acuminata, CUCUMBER TREE
EIS, HIL, KEI, LOU, VIE, WOD

Magnolia heptapeta, YULAN MAGNOLIA
BEK, DAU, GOS, GRR, LOU, HOL, MAG

Magnolia x loebneri 'Merrill'
CAL, CAR, EAB, EIS, FOR, FOU, GOS, HIL, HIN, HON, HOO, KLE, LOU, LUS, MON, OLI, ONA, ORN, PAN, SCW, SMT, SYN, TUR, WAT, WAY, WES

Magnolia virginiana, SWEET BAY
BRO, CAR, CED, CLA, COM, EIS, FAR, FIO, FOR, FOU, GOS, GRR, HAN, ING, LOU, LOW, KLE, LUS, MAG, MAX, PAN, PRI, SAL, SMT, SNI, VIE, WAY, WES, WOD

Malus 'Adams', ADAMS CRAB APPLE
CLA, MCG, SCH, WES

Malus 'Donald Wyman', DONALD WYMAN CRAB APPLE
SCH, WES

Malus hupehensis (theifera), TEA CRAB APPLE
FAR, FIO, FOR, FOU, HAN, HIL, HOO, LUS, MOL, PRI, SIE, SYN, TUR, WES

Malus 'Mary Potter', MARY POTTER CRAB APPLE
KLE, MAR, SCH, WAY, WES

Malus 'Professor Sprenger', PROFESSOR SPRENGER CRAB APPLE
SCH

Metasequoia glyptostroboides, DAWN REDWOOD
APP, BEK, BOV, BYE, CAR, CED, DAU, DOD, EAB, EIS, FIO, FOF, FOR, FOS, FOU, GOG, GRR, GUR, HIL, HOB, HOL, HON, ING, KEI, KLE, LOU, MAX, MON, NAV, ORN, OKI, OLI, ONA, PAN, PRI, SNI, SCR, VIE, WAY, WEH, WOD

Metrosideros excelsus, NEW ZEALAND CHRISTMAS TREE
HIL, HIS, NAV, SMT, WEH

Michelia doltsopa
GOS, HIL, LOU, MON, NAV, WEH

Nothofagus antarctica, NIRRE
GOS, HIL, SWE

Nyssa sylvatica, SOUR GUM
BEK, BOV, CAR, CED, COM, FIO, FOF, FOU, GOS, GRR, HAL, HES, HOB, ING, KEI, KEL, LAN, LOU, LUS, MAX, MON, MUS, NAV, OAK, OKI, ORN, PRI, SAL, SIE, TRI, VIE, WAR, WAT, WAU, WEH, WES

Olmediella betschleriana, COSTA RICA HOLLY

Ostrya virginiana, IRONWOOD
BER, CED, CLA, CUL, DUT, FIO, FOF, HES, HIL, HOB, HOO, ING, KLE, LUS, PRI, SCR, SIE, SMI, SMT, SYN, WAR, WAU, WOD

Oxydendrum arboreum, SOURWOOD
APP, ARB, BEK, BYE, CAR, CED, DIX, DOD, EAB, FIO, FOF, FOS, FOU, GOS, GRR, HOO, ING, KEI, KLE, LAN, LOU, LUS, MAX, MON, OLI, PAN, PRI, SMI, STG, TRI, VIE, WAR, WAT, WAY, WEH, WES, WOD

Parkinsonia aculeata, JERUSALEM THORN
ALD, HET, HIS, LOU, NAT, NAV

Parrotia persica, PERSIAN PARROTIA
BOV, DAU, FOU, GOS, HIL, HOL, WEH

Phellodendron amurense, CHINESE CORK TREE
BAI, BER, BET, CAR, COM, CRA, DUT, EIS, FIO, FOF, FOR, FOU, HAL, HIL, HIN, HOO, KEI, KEL, LUS, MAR, ONA, PRI, SCW, SIE, SMI, SYN, TUR, VAL, WES

Picea omorika, SERBIAN SPRUCE
ARB, BRI, CAL, CAR, DAU, DIX, EIS, EVE, FAR, FIO, FOF, FOR, GRR, HES, HIL, HOL, HOO, ISE, JOH, KEI, LUS, MAX, MUS, OLI, PAN, PRI, VIE, WAT, WEH

Picea orientalis, ORIENTAL SPRUCE
APP, ARB, BRO, CAL, DAU, DIX, FOF, FOR, FOU, HIL, HON, PAN, VIE, WEH

Pinus bungeana, LACEBARK PINE
ARB, BRO, CAL, CHO, DAU, DIX, FOF, FOU, HES, HON, HOO, MAR, MAX, OLI, PAN, PRI, SNI, TUR, VIE, WAY, WES

Pinus cembra, SWISS STONE PINE
ARB, BRO, CAL, CHO, DAU, DIX, FIO, FOR, FOU, HES, HIL, HON, HOO, KEI, LAW, LUS, MUS, OAK, OLI, PAN, PRI, SHA, SNI, STG, TUR, VAL, VIE, WES

Pinus flexilis, LIMBER PINE
BER, BET, CAL, EVE, FOU, HES, HIL, ISE, KEI, KLE, LAW, MAX, OAK, OLI, PAF, PAN, RED, SCR, SHA, SHO, SIE, SNI, SYN, VAL, VIE, WES

Pinus koraiensis, KOREAN PINE
FOF, FOU, HES, KEI, OLI, PAN, VIE, WES

Pinus parviflora 'Glauca', JAPANESE WHITE PINE
BOU, BRO, CHO, DAU, DIX, FOU, GRR, HES, HIL, HON, ISE, KEI, NAV, OLI, PAN, SMT, VIE, WEH, WES

Pinus wallichiana, HIMALAYAN WHITE PINE
CAL, COE, DAU, FOF, FOU, GRR, HES, VIW

Pithecellobium flexicaule, TEXAS EBONY
BOU, LOW, NAV

Prunus maackii, AMUR CHOKE CHERRY
FOF, LAW, SCR, SCW, SMI, VAL, WAY, WES

Prunus 'Okame', OKAME CHERRY
CON, WAY

Prunus sargentii, SARGENT CHERRY
EIS, FIO, FOR, FOU, HES, MAX, PAN, PRI, SIE, TUR, VIE, WES

Prunus subhirtella 'Autumnalis', DOUBLE-FLOWERED HIGAN CHERRY
BEK, COM, EAB, EIS, FOR, GRR, HIL, MOL, ORN, PRI, SHA, SCH, SMT, VIE, WAY, WES

Pseudolarix kaempferi, GOLDEN LARCH
EAB, WEH, WES

Ptelea trifoliata, HOP TREE
FIO, VIE

Pterostyrax hispida, EPAULETTE TREE
WIT

Pyrus ussuriensis, USSURIAN PEAR
LAW

Quercus acutissima, SAWTOOTH OAK
BER, BET, BOU, CAR, CED, COM, FIO, FOS, FOU, HAN, HES, HOO, HOR, ING, KEI, LOU, LUS, MAR, MAX, MUS, PRI, SMI, TRI, VIE, WAR, WAT

Quercus bicolor, SWAMP WHITE OAK
BAI, BER, BOU, FIO, HAL, HIL, KEL, KLE, MAR, MAX, MOL, OAK, SCH, SIE, SMI, WAR

Quercus imbricaria, SHINGLE OAK
BOU, EIS, FIO, HAN, HOB, KLE, LUS, MUS, OAK, PRI

Quercus macrocarpa, BUR OAK
ALD, BER, BET, BOU, EIS, EVE, FIO, HIL, HOO, KEL, KLE, LAW, LUS, MAR, MOL, MON, MUS, NAT, OAK, PRI, SHR, SIE, SMI, SNI, VAL, WES

Quercus robur, ENGLISH OAK
BER, BET, BOU, CED, CHR, COE, COM, CRA, DAU, EIS, FAR, FIO, FOU, HAL, HES, HIL, HOB, KEI, KEL, KLE, LUS, MAR, MUS, PRI, SMT, SCW, SMI, TUR, WES

Quercus shumardii, SHUMARD OAK
BOU, CED, COR, DOD, EIS, HES, HIL, JOH, KEL, LIV, LOU, LUS, MAG, SAL, SCH, SIE, SNI, WAT, WES

Roystonea regia, ROYAL PALM
KAI, KOO, MAK, SHP, WAI

Sapindus drummondii, WESTERN SOAPBERRY
ALD, NAT

Sapium sebiferum, CHINESE TALLOW TREE
ALD, BOU

Sciadopitys verticillata, JAPANESE UMBRELLA TREE
APP, BEK, BRO, CAL, CHO, DAU, DIL, EAB, FIO, FOF, FOR, GRR, ISE, KEI, LUS, MAX, OAK, OLI, ORN, PAN, SMT, VIE, WAT, WAY, WEH, WES, WFF

Sophora japonica 'Regent', JAPANESE PAGODA TREE
BEK, CAL, CLA, DIX, HOO, ING, KEI, MAX, PAN, PRI, SCH, SMT, SNI, STG, VIE, WAT, WAY, WES

Sophora secundiflora, MESCAL BEAN
COR, LOU, LOW, MON, NAT

Sorbus alnifolia, KOREAN MOUNTAIN ASH
DUT, FOF, HIL, LAW, MAX, PRI, VIE, WAY, WES

Stewartia koreana, KOREAN STEWARTIA
BEK, EIS, GOS, GRR, HIL, MAX, PRI

Stewartia monadelpha, TALL STEWARTIA
BEK, GOS, GRR, LOU, SWE

Stewartia pseudocamellia, JAPANESE STEWARTIA
BEK, BOV, BRO, DIX, FOR, GOS, GRR, HIL, HOB, LUS, MAX, OAK, OLI, PAN, PRI, WAY, WIT

Styrax japonica, JAPANESE SNOWBELL
ARB, BEK, BOV, CAL, CED, DIX, EIS, FOF, FOR, FOU, GOG, GOS, GRR, GUR, HIL, HOL, HOR, ING, KEI, LOU, LUS, MAX, OAK, OLI, PAN, PRI, SMT, SNI, SWE, WAY, WEH, WES

Styrax obassia, FRAGRANT SNOWBELL
BEK, CAL, FOF, FOU, GOS, LOU

Symplocos paniculata, SAPPHIREBERRY
HIL

Syringa reticulata, JAPANESE TREE LILAC
BAI, BER, CAR, CLY, CUL, EIS, EVE, FIO, FOF, HOB, HOO, KLE, LAW, LUS, MAR, MAX, PRI, SCW, SMI, SYN, TUR, VAL, WES

Tabebuia chrysotricha, GOLDEN TRUMPET TREE
MON, SAN

Tamarindus indica, TAMARIND TREE
GOH, KOO, NAV, SMT

Taxodium distichum, COMMON BALD CYPRESS
ALD, ARB, BET, BOU, CAL, CLA, COM, COR, DAU, DIL, DIX, DOD, EAS, FOF, FIO, FOS, FOU, GOG, GRR, HAL, HES, HOB, HOO, ING, KEI, KEL, KLE, LIV, LOU, LOW, LUS, MAG, MAR, MAX, MCL, NAT, PRI, SAL, SHE, SMI, SMT, SNI, SYN, TRI, WAR, WAY, WEH, WOD

Thuja plicata, WESTERN RED CEDAR
BOV, BRI, CHR, DIX, FOF, FOR, HIL, ISE, LAW, MAX, MIT, WES

Tilia tomentosa, SILVER LINDEN
EIS, FIO, FOF, HIL, LUS, MAX, PRI, SNI, VIE

Torreya nucifera, JAPANESE TORREYA
HIL

Trochodendron aralioides, WHEEL TREE
BOV

Ulmus japonica, JAPANESE ELM
MAX, VIE

Ulmus parvifolia, CHINESE ELM
ABC, ARB, BOU, CHR, DIX, EAB, FOF, HIS, KEI, LAW, LIV, LOU, MON, MUS, OKI, SCA, SMT, STG, TRI, WAR, WAT, WAU, WES, WIN

Xanthoceras sorbifolium, SHRUB YELLOWHORN
HIL, WEH

Zelkova serrata 'Village Green', JAPANESE ZELKOVA
GOG, HAN, ING, MAX, MOL, PRI, SCH, SIE, SMT, VIE, WES

APPENDIX II-C
INVITATION FOR DIRECTORY LISTING

Nurseries growing trees included in this volume or growing other unusual but garden-worthy trees are requested to complete this form and return to:

Plants That Merit Attention
c/o Timber Press
P.O. Box 1631
Beaverton, OR 97075

Names and addresses with list of trees grown will be included in the *Supplement to Plants That Merit Attention—Volume 1 Trees.*

Name of Nursery _____

Street Address _____

City, State, ZIP _____

Contact person_____ Telephone_____

Check one: _____Wholesale only _____ Wholesale/Retail _____ Retail
_____ Catalog

List of unusual but garden-worthy trees grown. Please list alphabetically by botanic name followed by common name. If this form has an insufficient number of lines, front and back, to complete list kindly attach this form to your catalog or price list.

_____

_____

_____

_____

_____

_____

_____

_____

_____

_____

_____

_____

APPENDIX III
TREES GROUPED BY SITE AND
HABIT CHARACTERISTICS

TREES FOR USDA HARDINESS ZONES, WITH HARDINESS RANGE

ZONE 2
  Larix decidua 2-6

ZONE 3
  Abies concolor 3-7
  Acer ginnala 3 8
  Asimina triloba 3-8
  Carpinus caroliniana 3-9
  Cornus alternifolia 3-8

  Maackia amurensis 3-7
  Phellodendron amurense 3-7
  Pinus cembra 3 7
  Prunus maackii 3-6
  Quercus macrocarpa 3-8

ZONE 4
  Abies nordmanniana 4-7
  Aesculus flava 4-8
  Alnus glutinosa 4-7
  Amelanchier x grandiflora 4-7
  Betula platyphylla japonica 'Whitespire'
    4-7
  Carya ovata 4-9
  Cercis canadensis f. alba 4-9
  Cladrastis lutea 4-8
  Fraxinus quadrangulata 4-7
  Gymnocladus dioicus 4-8
  Magnolia acuminata 4-9
  Magnolia x loebneri 'Merrill' 4-8
  Malus hupehensis 4-8

  Nyssa sylvatica 4-9
  Ostrya virginiana 4-9
  Picea omorika 4-7
  Pinus koraiensis 4-7
  P. parviflora 'Glauca' 4-7
  Prunus sargentii 4-7
  Ptelea trifoliata 4-9
  Pyrus ussuriensis 4-7
  Quercus bicolor 4-8
  Sorbus alnifolia 4-7
  Syringa reticulata 4-7
  Taxodium distichum 4-9
  Tilia tomentosa 4-7
  Ulmus japonica 4-6

ZONE 5
  Abies koreana 5-7 (?)
  Acer buergerianum 5-8, 9
  Acer campestre 5-9
  Acer davidii 5-7
  Acer griseum 5-7
  Acer miyabei 5-7
  Acer nikoense 5-7
  Acer triflorum 5-8
  Aesculus x carnea 'Briotii' 5-8
  Betula nigra 5-9
  Carpinus betulus 5-7
  Cercidiphyllum japonicum 5-8
  Chamaecyparis nootkatensis 'Pendula'
    5-8
  Chionanthus virginicus 5-9
  Cornus kousa 5-8
  C. officinalis 5-8
  Corylus colurna 5-7
  Cotinus obovatus 5-8
  Crataegus viridis 'Winter King' 5-7
  Diospyros virginiana 5-9
  Eucommia ulmoides 5-7
  Evodia danielii 5-8

  Fagus sylvatica 'Asplenifolia' 5-7
  Franklinia alatamaha 5-8
  Fraxinus oxycarpa 'Raywood' 5-8
  Halesia monticola 'Rosea' 5-9
  Hovenia dulcis 5-8
  Ilex opaca 'Miss Helen' 5-7
  Ilex pedunculosa 5-8
  Kalopanax pictus 5-7
  Koelreuteria paniculata 5-9
  Larix kaempferi 5-7
  Magnolia heptapeta 5 7
  Magnolia virginiana 5-9
  Malus 'Adams' 5-8
  Malus 'Donald Wyman' 5-8
  Malus 'Mary Potter' 5-8
  Malus 'Professor Sprenger' 5-7
  Metasequoia glyptostroboides 5-8
  Oxydendrum arboreum 5-8
  Parrotia persica 5-8
  Picea orientalis 5-7
  Pinus bungeana 5-8
  Pinus flexilis 5-7
  Pinus wallichiana 5-7

Prunus subhirtella 5-8
Pseudolarix kaempferi 5-7
Pterostyrax hispida 5-7
Quercus imbricaria 5-8
Quercus robur 'Fastigiata' 5-8
Quercus shumardii 5-8
Sciadopitys verticillata 5-8
Sophora japonica 'Regent' 5-8
Stewartia pseudocamellia 5-8

Styrax japonica 5-8
Styrax obassia 5-8
Symplocos paniculata 5–8
Thuja plicata 5-7
Torreya nucifera 5-8
Ulmus parviflora 5-9
Xanthoceras sorbifolium 5-7
Zelkova serrata 'Village Green' 5-8

ZONE 6

Calocedrus decurrens 6-10
Cedrus atlantica 'Glauca' 6-9
Chionanthus retusus 6-8
Cornus nuttallii 6-8
x Cupressocyparis leylandii 6-10
Cydonia sinensis 6-8
Davidia involucrata 6-8

Ilex x altaclerensis 'James G. Esson' 6-9
Ilex x aquipernyi 'San Jose' 6-8
Koelreuteria bipinnata 6-9
Laburnum x watereri 'Vossii' 6-7
Quercus acutissima 6-9
Sapindus drummondii 6-9
Stewartia koreana 6-7
Stewartia monadelpha 6-7

ZONE 7

Cedrus deodara 7-9
Firmiana simplex 7-9
Fraxinus texensis 7-9

Idesia polycarpa 7-9
Lagerstroemia indica 'Alba' 7-9
Gordonia lasianthus 7-9

ZONE 8

Arbutus unedo 8-9
Chilopsis linearis 8-10
Hoheria populnea 8-9
Luma apiculata 8-10

Michelia doltsopa 8-10
Nothofagus antarctica 8-9
Sapium sebiferum 8-10
Sophora secundiflora 8-10
Trochodendron aralioides 8-9

ZONE 9

Bauhinia forficata 9-10
Geijera parviflora 9-10
Metrosideros excelsus 9-10

Parkinsonia aculeata 9-10
Pithecellobium flexicaule 9

ZONE 10

Alectryon excelsus 10
Crescentia cujete 10
Guaiacum officinale 10

Roystonea regia 10
Tabebuia chrysotricha 10
Tamarindus officinale 10

DECIDUOUS TREES

Acer buergerianum 5-8, 9
Acer campestre 5-9
Acer davidii 5-7
Acer ginnala 3-8
Acer griseum 5-7
Acer miyabei 5-7
Acer nikoense 5-7
Acer triflorum 5-8
Aesculus x carnea 'Briotii' 5-8
Alnus glutinosa 4-7
Amelanchier x grandiflora 4-7
Asimina triloba 3-8
Bauhinia forficata (also evergreen) 9-10
Betula nigra 5-9
Betula platyphylla japonica 'Whitespire' 4-7
Carpinus betulus 5-7
Carpinus caroliniana 5-7
Carya ovata 4-9
Cercidiphyllum japonicum 5-8
Cercis canadensis f. alba 5-9
Chilopsis linearis 8-10
Chionanthus retusus 6-8
Chionanthus virginicus 5-9
Cladrastis lutea 4-8
Cornus alternifolia 3-8
Cornus kousa 5-8
Cornus nuttalli 6-8
Cornus officinalis 5-8
Corylus colurna 5-7
Cotinus obovatus 5-8
Crataegus viridis 'Winter King' 5-7
Cydonia sinensis 6-8
Davidia involucrata 6-8
Diospyros virginiana 5-9
Eucommia ulmoides 5-7
Evodia daniellii 5-8
Fagus sylvatica 'Asplenifolia' 5-7
Firmiana simplex 7-9
Franklinia alatamaha 5-8
Fraxinus oxycarpa 'Raywood' 5-8
Fraxinus quadrangulata 4-7
Gymnocladus dioicus 4-8
Hovenia dulcis 5-8
Idesia polycarpa 7-9
Kalapanax pictus 5-7
Koelreuteria bipinnata 6-9
Koelreuteria paniculata 5-9

Laburnum x watereri 'Vossii' 6-7
Lagerstroemia indica 'Alba' 7-9
Maackia amurensis 3-7
Magnolia acuminata 4-9
Magnolia heptapeta 5-7
Magnolia x loebneri 'Merrill' 4-8
Magnolia virginiana 5-9
Malus 'Adams' 5-8
Malus 'Donald Wyman' 5-8
Malus hupehensis 4-8
Malus 'Mary Potter' 5-8
Malus 'Professor Sprenger' 5-7
Nothofagus antarctica 8-9
Nyssa sylvatica 4-9
Oxydendrum arboreum 5-8
Parkinsonia aculeata 9-10
Parrotia persica 5-8
Phellodendron amurense 3-7
Prunus maackii 3-6
Prunus sargentii 4-7
Prunus subhirtella 5-8
Ptelea trifoliata 4-9
Pterostyrax hispida 5-7
Pyrus ussuriensis 4-7
Quercus acutissima 4-7
Quercus bicolor 4-8
Quercus imbricaria 5-8
Quercus macrocarpa 3-8
Quercus robur 'Fastigiata' 5-8
Quercus shumardii 5-8
Sapindus drummondii 6-9
Sapium sebiferum 8-10
Sophora japonica 'Regent' 5-8
Sorbus alnifolia 4-7
Stewartia pseudocamellia 5-8
Stewartia koreana 6-7
Stewartia monadelpha 6-7
Styrax japonica 5-8
Styrax obassia 5-8
Symplocos paniculata 5-8
Syringa reticulata 4-7
Tilia tomentosa 4-7
Ulmus japonica 4-6
Ulmus parviflora 5-9
Xanthoceras sorbifolium 5-7
Zelkova serrata 'Village Green' 5-8

CONIFERS

EVERGREEN

Abies concolor 3-7
Abies koreana 5-7 (?)
Calocedrus decurrens 6-10
Cedrus atlantica 'Glauca' 6-9
Cedrus deodara 7-9
Chamaecyparis nootkatensis 'Pendula' 5-8
x Cupressocyparis leylandii 6-10
Picea omorika 4-7
Picea orientalis 5-7

Pinus bungeana 5-8
Pinus cembra 3-7
Pinus flexilis 5-7
Pinus koraiensis 4-7
Pinus parviflora 'Glauca' 4-7
Pinus wallichiana 5-7
Sciadopitys verticillata 5-8
Thuja plicata 5-7
Torreya nucifera 5-8

DECIDUOUS

Larix decidua 2-6
Larix kaempferi 5-7
Metasequoia glyptostroboides 5-8

Pseudolarix kaempferi 5-7
Taxodium distichum 4-9

BROADLEAVED EVERGREENS

Alectryon excelsus 10
Arbutus unedo 8-9
Bauhinia forficata 9-10
Crescentia cujete 10
Geijera parviflora 9-10
Gordonia lasianthus 7-9
Guaiacum officinale 10
Hoheria populnea 8-9
Ilex x altaclrensis 'James G. Esson' 6-9
Ilex x aquipernyi 'San Jose' 6-8

Ilex opaca 'Miss Helen' 5-7
Ilex pedunculosa 5-8
Luma apiculata 8-10
Metrosideros excelsus 9-10
Michelia doltsopa 8-10
Pithecellobium flexicaule 9
Roystonea regia 10
Sophora secundiflora 8-10
Tabebuia chrysotricha 10
Tamarindus indica 10

LIGHT REQUIREMENTS

Almost all trees grow best in full sun. Listed here are those that tolerate, and some that prefer, high or partial shade.

Acer ginnala 3-8
Acer griseum 5-7
Acer miyabei 5-7
Acer triflorum 5-8
Aesculus x carnea 'Briotii' 5-8
Alectryon excelsus 10
Alnus glutinosa 4-7
Amelanchier x grandiflora 4-7
Arbutus unedo 8-9
Asimina triloba 3-8 (deep shade)
Carpinus caroliniana 3-9
Cedrus atlantica 'Glauca' 6-9
Cercidiphyllum japonicum 5-8
Cercis canadensis f. alba 4-9
Chamaecyparis nootkatensis 'Pendula' 5-8
Chionanthus retusus 6-8
Cornus alternifolia 3-8
Cornus kousa 5-8
Cornus nuttalli 6-8
Cornus officinalis 5-8
Cotinus obovatus 5-8

Cydonia sinensis 6-8
Davidia involucrata 6-8
Diospyros virginiana 5-9
Geijera parviflora 9-10
Gordonia lasianthus 7-9
Guaiacum officinale 10
Halesia monticola 'Rosea' 5-9
Hoheria populnea 8-9
Hovenia dulcis 5-8
Ilex x altaclerensis 'James G. Esson' 6-9
Ilex x aquapernyi 'San Jose' 6-8
Ilex opaca 'Miss Helen' 5-7
Ilex pedunculosa 5-8
Koelreuteria bipinnata 6-9
Koelreuteria paniculata 5-9
Larix decidua 2-6
Magnolia acuminata 4-9
Magnolia heptapeta 5-7
Magnolia x loebneri 'Merrill' 4-8
Magnolia virginiana 5-9
Malus hupehensis 4-8

Michelia doltsopa 8-10
Nothofagus antarctica 8-9
Nyssa sylvatica 4-9
Ostrya virginiana 4-9
Oxydendrum arboreum 5-8
Parkinsonia aculeata 9-10
Picea orientalis 5-7
Pinus flexilis 5-7
Pinus koraiensis 4-7
Pinus wallichiana 5-7
Prunus subhirtella 5-8
Ptelea trifoliata 4-9
Pyrus ussuriensis 4-7
Quercus acutissima 6-9
Quercus bicolor 4-8

Sapindus drummondii 6-9
Sciadopitys verticillata 5-8
Sophora japonica 'Regent' 5-8
Sophora secundifolia 8-10
Styrax japonica 5-8
Styrax obassia 5-8
Tamarindus indica 10
Taxodium distichum 4-9 (high shade)
Thuja plicata 5-7
Torreya nucifera 5-8 (deep shade)
Trochodendron aralioides 8-9
Ulmus japonica 4-6
Ulmus parviflora 5-9
Zelkova serrata 'Village Green' 5-8

SOIL MOISTURE

MOIST TO WET CONDITIONS
Abies concolor 3-7
Acer ginnala 3-8
Acer miyabei 5-7
Aesculus x carnea 'Briotii' 5-8
Aesculus flava 4-8
Alnus glutinosa 4-7
Asimina triloba 3-8
Betula nigra 5-9 (semi-aquatic)
Carpinus caroliniana 5-7
Cercidiphyllum japonicum 5-8
Cercis canadensis f. alba 4-9
Chamaecyparis nootkatensis 'Pendula'
  5-8
Cornus alternifolia 3-8

Cornus nuttallii 6-8
Franklinia alatamaha 5-8
Gordonia lasianthus 7-9
Kalopanax pictus 5-7
Larix decidua 2-6
Larix kaempferi 5-7
Magnolia virginiana 5-9
Michelia doltsopa 8-10
Nyssa sylvatica 4-9
Ostrya virginiana 4-9
Quercus bicolor 4-8
Taxodium distichum 4-9
Torreya nucifera 5-8
Trochodendron aralioides 8-9

ARID CONDITIONS
Abies concolor 3-7 (when established)
Abies nordmanniana 4-7
Acer campestre 5-9
Alectryon excelsus 10
Betula platyphylla japonica 'Whitespire'
  4-7
Cedrus atlantica 'Glauca' 6-9
Chilopsis linearis 8-10
Cotinus obovatus 5-8
Fraxinus oxycarpa 'Raywood' 5-8

Fraxinus quadrangulata 4-7
Geijera parviflora 9-10
Gymnocladus dioicus 4-8
Ilex pedunculosa 5-8
Koelreuteria paniculata 5-9
Nothafagus antarctica 8-9
Pithecellobium flexicaule 9
Sapindus drummondii 6-9
Sophora japonica 'Regent'

SEACOAST PLANTING
Abies koreana 5-7 (?)
Alectryon excelsus 10
Calocedrus decurrens 6-10
Guaiacum officinale 10

Metrosideros excelsus 9-10
Nothofagus antarctica 8-9
Parkinsonia aculeata 9-10

RESISTANCE TO PESTS AND DISEASES

Abies concolor 3-7
Abies koreana 5-7 (?)
Abies nordmanniana 4-7
Acer buergerianum 5-8, 9
Acer campestre 5-9
Acer davidii 5-7
Acer ginnala 3-8
Acer griseum 5-7
Acer miyabei 5-7
Acer nikoense 5-7
Aesculus x carnea 'Briotii' 5-8
Aesculus flava 4-8
Alectryon excelsus 10
Arbutus unedo 8-9
Asimina triloba 3-8
Bauhinia forficata 9-10
Betula platyphylla japonica 4-7
Carpinus betulus 5-7
Carpinus caroliniana 3-9
Cercidiphyllum japonicum 5-8
Chamaecyparis nootkatensis 'Pendula'
   5-8
Chilopsis linearis 8-10
Chionanthus retusus 6-8
Chionanthus virginicus 5-9
Cladrastis lutea 4-8
Cornus kousa 5-8
Cornus officinalis 5-8
Corylus colurna 5-7
x Cupressocyparis leylandii 6-10
Davidia involucrata 6-8
Diospyros virginiana 5-9
Eucommia ulmoides 5-7
Evodia danielii 5-8
Firmiana simplex 7-9
Fraxinus oxycarpa 'Raywood' 5-8
Fraxinus texensis 7-9
Geijera parviflora 9-10
Gordonia lasianthus 7-9
Guaiacum officinale 10
Gymnocladus dioicus 4-8
Halesia monticola 'Rosea' 5-9
Hoheria populnea 8-9
Hovenia dulcis 5-8
Ilex x altaclerensis 'James C. Esson' 6-9
Ilex aquipernyi 'San Jose' 6-8
Ilex pedunculosa 5-8
Kalopanax pictus 5-7
Koelreuteria bipinnata 6-9
Luma apiculata 8-10
Maackia amurensis 3-7

Magnolia acuminata 4-9
Magnolia heptapeta 5-7
Magnolia x loebneri 'Merrill' 4-8
Magnolia virginiana 5-9
Malus 'Adams' 5-8
Malus 'Donald Wyman' 5-8
Malus hupehensis 4-8 (fair)
Malus 'Mary Potter' 5-8
Malus 'Professor Sprenger' 5-7
Metasequoia glyptostroboides 5-8
Metrosideros excelsus 9-10
Michelia doltsopa 8-10
Nothofagus antarctica 8-9
Nyssa sylvatica 5-8
Ostrya virginiana 4-9
Oxydendrum arboreum 5-8
Parkinsonia aculeata 9-10
Parrotia persica 5-8
Phellodendron amurense 3-7
Pinus cembra 3-7
Pinus koraiensis 4-7
Pinus parviflora 'Glauca' 4-7
Pinus wallichiana 5-7
Pithecellobium flexicaule 9
Prunus sargentii 4-7
Pseudolarix kaempferi 5-7
Ptelea trifoliata 4-9
Pterostyrax hispida 5-7
Pyrus ussuriensis 4-7
Quercus acutissima 6-9
Quercus imbricaria 5-8
Quercus robur 'Fastigiata' 5-8
Quercus shumardii 5-8
Roystonea regia 10
Sapindus drummondii 6-9
Sapium sebiflorum 8-10
Sophora secundiflora 8-10
Stewartia koreana 6-7
Stewartia monadelpha 6-7
Stewartia pseudocamellia 5-8
Styrax japonica 5-8
Styrax obassia 5-8
Symplocos paniculata 5-8
Syringa reticulata 4-7
Tabebuia chrysotricha 10
Tamarindus indica 10
Torreya nucifera 5-8
Trochodendron aralioides 8-9
Ulmus japonica 4-6
Ulmus parviflora 5-9
Zelkova serrata 'Village Green' 5-8

CONSPICUOUS BLOOM

WHITE

Acer ginnala 3-8
Acer nikoense 5-7
Amelanchier x grandiflora 4-7
Arbutus unedo 8-9
Bauhinia forficata 9-10
Cercis canadensis f. alba 4-9
Chionanthus retusus 6-8
Chionanthus virginicus 5-9
Cladrastis lutea 4-8
Cornus alternifolia 3-8
Cornus kousa 5 8
Crataegus viridis 'winter king' 5-7
Davidia involucrata 6-8
Evodia danielii 5-8
Franklinia alatamaha 5-8
Gordonia lasianthus 7-9
Hoheria populnea 8-9
Hovenia dulcis 5-8
Lagerstroemia indica 'Alba' 7-9
Luma apiculata 8-10
Maackia amurensis 3-7

Magnolia heptapeta 5-7
Magnolia x loebneri 'Merrill' 4-8
Magnolia virginiana 5-9
Malus hupehensis 4-8
Malus 'Mary Potter' 5-8
Malus 'Professor Sprenger' 5-7
Oxydendrum arboreum 5-8
Pithecellobium flexicaule 9
Pterostryrax hispida 5-7
Pyrus ussuriensis 4-7
Sorbus alnifolia 4-7
Stewartia koreana 6-7
Stewartia monadelpha 6-7
Stewartia pseudocamellia 5-8
Styrax japonica 5-8
Styrax obassia 5-8
Symplocos paniculata 5-8
Syringa reticulata 4-7
Xanthoceras sorbifolium 5-7

BLUE TO VIOLET

Asimina triloba 3-8
Chilopsis linearis 8-10

Guaiacum officinale 10
Sophora secundiflora 8-10

YELLOW TO ORANGE

Acer miyabei 5-7
Acer nikoense 5-7
Acer triflorum 5-8
Aesculus flava 4-8
Cornus officinalis 5-8
Firmiana simplex 7-9
Koelreuteria bipinnata 6-9
Koelreuteria paniculata 5-9
Laburnum x watereri 'Vossii' 6-7

Magnolia acuminata 4-9
Michelia doltsopa 8-10
Parkinsonia aculeata 9-10
Ptelea trifoliata 4-9
Sapindus drummondii 6-9
Sapium sebiferum 8-10
Sophora japonica 'Regent' 5-8
Tabebuia chrysotricha 10
Tamarindus indica 10

PINK TO RED

Aesculus x carnea 'Briotii' 5-8
Cydonia sinensis 6-8
Halesia monticola 'Rosea' 5-9
Malus 'Adams' 5-8
Malus 'Donald Wyman' 5-8

Metrosideros excelsus 9-10
Parrotia persica 5-8
Prunus sargentii 4-7
Prunus subhirtella 5-8

GREEN

Cotinus obovatus 5-8
Trochodendron aralioides 8-9

TOLERANCE OF ENVIRONMENTAL STRESS

Acer buergerianum 5-8, 9
Acer campestre 5-9
Acer ginnala 3-8
Alectryon excelsus
Carpinus betulus 5-7 (somewhat)
Chilopsis linearis 8-10
Chionanthus retusus 6-8
Chionanthus virginicus 5-9
Corylus colurna 5-7
Cotinus obovatus 5-8
Crataegus viridis 'winter king' 5-7
Diospyros virginiana 5-9
Evodia danielii 5-8 (some air pollution)
Fraxinus quadrangulata 4-7
Fraxinus texensis 7-9
Guaiacum officinale 10 (salt spray)
Gymnocladus dioicus 4-8
Halesia monticola 'Rosea' 5-9
Ilex x altaclerensis 'James G. Esson' 6-9 (moderate)
Ilex x aquipernyi 'San Jose' 6-8
Ilex opaca 'Miss Helen' 5-7
Ilex pedunculosa 5-8

Koelreuteria bipinnata 6-9
Koelreuteria paniculata 5-9
Maackia amurensis 3-7
Malus 'Adams' 5-8 (fair)
Malus 'Donald Wyman' 5-8 (fair)
Malus 'Mary Potter' 5-8 ("believed tolerant")
Malus 'Professor Sprenger' 5-7 (highly tolerant)
Nothofagus antarctica 8-9
Phellodendron amurense 3-7
Pinus wallichiana 5-7
Prunus sargentii 4-7
Ptelea trifoliata 4-9
Pterostyrax hispida 5-7
Quercus macrocarpa 3-8
Sapindus drummondii 6-9
Sophora japonica 'Regent' 5-8
Tilia tomentosa 4-7
Ulmus japonica 4-6
Ulmus parviflora 5-9
Zelkova serrata 'Village Green' 5-8

FRAGRANCE

Acer ginnala 3-8
Cydonia sinensis 6-8
Diospyros virginiana 5-9
Franklinia alatamaha 5-8
Gordonia lasianthus 7-9
Gymnocladus dioicus 4-8 (female)
Hovenia dulcis 5-8
Koelreuteria bipinnata 6-9
Koelreuteria paniculata 5-9
Magnolia acuminata 4-9
Magnolia heptapeta 5-7
Magnolia x loebneri 'Merrill' 4-8
Magnolia virginiana 5-9

Malus hupehensis 4-8
Michelia doltsopa 8-10
Parkinsonia aculeata 9-10
Pithecellobium flexicaule 9
Ptelea trifoliata 4-9
Pterostyrax hispida 5-7
Sophora secundiflora 8-10
Styrax japonica 5-8
Styrax obassia 5-8
Symplocos paniculata 5-8
Syringa reticulata 4-7
Tilia tomentosa 4-7

CONSPICUOUS AUTUMN FOLIAGE

Acer buergerianum 5-8, 9
Acer davidii 5-7
Acer ginnala 3-8
Acer griseum 5-7
Acer nikoense 5-7
Acer triflorum 5-8
Carpinus caroliniana 3-9
Cercidiphyllum japonicum 5-8
Cladrastis lutea 4-8
Cotinus obovatus 5-8
Cornus alternifolia 3-8
Cornus kousa 5-8
Cornus nuttallii 6-8

Crataegus viridis 'winter king' 5-7
Fagus sylvatica 'Asplenifolia' 5-7
Firmiana simplex 7-9
Franklinia alatamaha 5-8
Fraxinus oxycarpa 'Raywood' 5-8
Gordonia lasianthus 7-9
Larix kaempferi 5-7
Malus hupehensis 4-8
Metasequoia glyptostroboides 5-8
Nothofagus antarctica 8-9
Nyssa sylvatica 4-9
Oxydendrum arboreum 5-8
Parrotia persica 5-8

Phellodendron amurense 3-7
Prunus sargentii 4-7
Pseudolarix kaempferi 5-7
Pterostyrax hispida 5-7
Pyrus ussuriensis 4-7
Quercus shumardii 5-8
Sorbus alnifolia 4-7
Stewartia koreana 6-7
Stewartia monadelpha 6-7
Stewartia pseudocamellia 5-8